T0330629

ROUTLEDGE LIBRARY EDITIONS: SOVIET ECONOMICS

Volume 19

SOVIET GEOGRAPHY

SOVIET GEOGRAPHY

The New Industrial and Economic Distributions of the U.S.S.R.

N. MIKHAYLOV

Routledge
Taylor & Francis Group

LONDON AND NEW YORK

First published in 1935 by Methuen & Co. Ltd.

This edition first published in 2023
by Routledge
4 Park Square, Milton Park, Abingdon, Oxon OX14 4RN

and by Routledge
605 Third Avenue, New York, NY 10158

Routledge is an imprint of the Taylor & Francis Group, an informa business

© 1935

British Library Cataloguing in Publication Data
A catalogue record for this book is available from the British Library

ISBN: 978-1-032-48466-2 (Set)
ISBN: 978-1-032-48899-8 (Volume 19) (hbk)
ISBN: 978-1-032-48901-8 (Volume 19) (pbk)
ISBN: 978-1-003-39132-6 (Volume 19) (ebk)

DOI: 10.4324/9781003391326

Publisher's Note
The publisher has gone to great lengths to ensure the quality of this reprint but points out that some imperfections in the original copies may be apparent.

Disclaimer
The publisher has made every effort to trace copyright holders and would welcome correspondence from those they have been unable to trace.

SOVIET GEOGRAPHY

The New Industrial and Economic Distributions of the U.S.S.R.

by

N. MIKHAYLOV

With a Foreword by

THE RT. HON.
SIR HALFORD J. MACKINDER

WITH 38 MAPS

METHUEN & CO. LTD. LONDON
36 Essex Street W.C.

First published in 1935

PRINTED IN GREAT BRITAIN

FOREWORD

MESSRS. METHUEN have asked me for a few words of introduction to this book, written for them by a geographer in
Russia who has had access to official sources of information
which are closed to foreigners. They believe that it presents
such a comprehensive account of the economic development
of the U.S.S.R. as is at the present time unobtainable else-
where.

Undoubtedly it is a remarkable book, well worthy of the
attention of many readers. Not unfairly it may be described
as a political pamphlet of the indirect order, a vivid geographical description charged with political electricity.
It is written in clear and virile English, oratorical rather
than literary, by a born and trained geographer, with vision
and a power of terse imagery. Its short sentences, each with
definite, unqualified meaning, succeed one another like shots
from a machine gun. Altogether it affords a noteworthy
insight into the dynamic mentality of those who, with com-
mand of a working population of 160 millions, claim to be
re-making the geography, physical as well as human, of one
seventh of the land on this globe.

That our author does not discriminate nicely between
fact and prophecy was to be expected; to a revolutionary
plans may appear more important than achievement.
Geography is a study of the present, but the present is the
past flowing into the future. There is no such thing as a
static present; your description of the present depends on
whether your face is turned to the future or the past. Only
the future will tell whether these 'engineers' both of society
and environment have underrated the momentum of human
values from the past. In that difference of outlook is
the great rift between Soviet Russia and the Western
democracies.

Meanwhile we have brought to us in this book, from behind a screen which is in itself one of the major, although, let us hope, temporary features of human geography, a first sketch of the new map of Scythia. Whatever our reserves of scepticism, it will be at our peril that we neglect to take account of it.

H. J. MACKINDER

November 1st, 1935

CONTENTS

TABLES

MAPS

INTRODUCTION

THE pilot was flying over a foreign land. A map, drawn up only three or four years before, lay on his plane-table. But the pilot had lost his way. Settlements and factories, railways and motor-roads, none of which were marked on the map were rising unexpectedly before his eyes. The pilot had lost his bearings; for the map on his plane-table was a map of the U.S.S.R.—the Union of Soviet Socialist Republics—a country whose contours have been transformed.

The face of the country has changed within a few years. It is still changing at an unprecedented rate. Text-books on geography can hardly keep pace with real life. Maps very soon become out of date.

Industry is being distributed anew. Industrial centres of world-wide importance have sprung up in the deserts of yesterday. Agriculture has penetrated into territories in which it never existed before and where it was considered impossible. Old agricultural crops have been cultivated in new and different ways and new ones are being introduced. The country is cut across by new railways and motor-roads. Human masses are moving. They are changing their place of abode. Scores of towns have been built. Hundreds of square kilometres of new lands—an area no less than that of the largest States in Europe—have been explored for the first time and put on the map. Knowledge of the underground world of the country has been so enriched that it may well be considered newly discovered.

The mighty process of harnessing the natural forces has begun. The water systems of different regions are being altered. The drainage of marshes is increasing the area of cultivable land. New artificial water sources are being brought into existence for the irrigation and watering of arid regions. Deserts are rendered habitable, watersheds are cut by canals, river-beds are deepened. Poor soil is enriched. In some places forests are removed; in others forests are planted. The migration of old species of animals and the acclimatization of new species have begun.

The process of correcting and utilizing the manifold powers of nature in the U.S.S.R. is varied, diverse, and fruitful.

Every known mineral on the face of the earth, every soil from the tundra to red earth, eternal ice in the North Land and three harvests in Colchis; the Caspian Sea which lies 26 metres lower than the ocean, and Stalin Peak in the Pamirs towering 7½ kilometres above sea-level; table-like plains and mountains resembling rigid flames; climatic zones ranging from polar to sub-tropical, extreme cold in Yakutia-Siberia (where the minimum air temperature is −70° C.), and equatorial heat in Turkmenia, in Central Asia (the maximum soil temperature is +70° C.); places where not a drop of rain falls the whole summer (the desert Kara-Kum), and places where there is sometimes a quarter of a metre of rainfall in one day (Western Georgia in Transcaucasia); impassable forests and boundless steppes; beasts from the polar bear to the tiger: plants from the lichen to the lotus. This, all this, constitutes the U.S.S.R.

The transformation of the physical features is taking place on a huge scale over vast areas. With an area of 21,267,714 square kilometres, the Soviet Union possesses the largest continous territory in the world—nearly three U.S.A., ninety Englands, seven hundred Belgiums. The distance from its western to its eastern frontier is not much shorter than that from the Pole to the Equator. There is a ten hours' difference in time. It covers a seventh part of the earth's surface, has 168 million inhabitants,[1] 185 nationalities. . . .

A Colossus is moving. The era of great discoveries has long since passed, but is not the transformation of old Russia into the U.S.S.R. the discovery of a new continent?

Every economic order forms its own peculiar geography. One of the distinguishing features of each social era is its outline on the map, which, like a sensitive record, catches and reflects changes of scenery, the birth of towns, the fate of States.

The map is a social document. It fixes time with its

[1] January 1st 1934.

symbolism, alternation of colours, and peculiarity of design. The lines on the map are the handwriting of History.

The economic map speaks not only of towns and roads, of cornfields and mines; it speaks of men as well. It speaks of the activities of men, of their laws, of the relations between man and man.

The map rouses either indignation or enthusiasm. It marks growth and declines. Now it unmasks, now it extols.

The map can be read like a book. The map of former

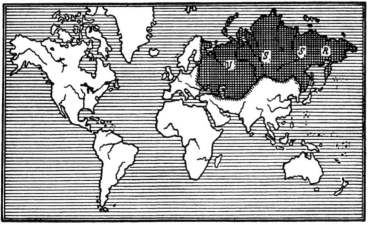

1. THE U.S.S.R. AND THE WORLD

Russia tells of the poverty of a rural country, of the oppression of its peoples, of the feebly developed industry, of foreign dependence, of rich, but lost opportunities. The map of the U.S.S.R. tells of its economic transformation, of the union of nations, of new principles of life, of the wonderful achievements in economics and culture.

Geography has changed. This means that history has taken a new course.

In November 1917 the proletarian revolution, organized and led by the Communist Party under the guidance of Lenin, emerged victorious in Russia. The Union of Soviet Socialist Republics grew out of the ruins of the Russia that belonged to the *bourgeois* and landlord, a backward, agricultural, and weak country standing at a low level of culture.

A State organization of a new type was created—the dictatorship of the proletariat, which was the embodiment of a union between the workers and peasants under the leadership of the working class.

The basis of Soviet society is socialist property. To-day the principle of socialist property is triumphant in every branch of national economy in the U.S.S.R. Industry and transport, with a few exceptions of no importance, are in the hands of the State. Agriculture has also, for the most part, become socialized. Credit, banks, the soil, the mineral wealth of the earth, and foreign trade all belong to the Soviet power. Trade is controlled by the State and by socialist co-operation.

Economic activities in the U.S.S.R. are regulated by a single and general State plan. All enterprises, whether industrial, agricultural, transport, or commercial, are given a planned task for the fulfilment of which they are responsible. The plan penetrates into every sphere of national economic life. The possibility of crises has been eliminated. The development of production is not subject to the principle of competition and the securing of capitalist profits, but to the principle of planned guidance and systematic raising of the material and cultural level of the masses.

After passing through the difficult period of civil war, economic blockade, and the economic ruin consequent upon this, the U.S.S.R. had by 1926 restored its ruined national economy and then devoted itself entirely to reconstruction and the accomplishment of its grandiose plans of construction.

The First Five Year Plan of development of Soviet national economy was completed in 1932, a year before its appointed limit.

During this period a powerful industrial system was built up—the basis of the reorganization of the whole economy.

The agriculture of petty individual farms became a collective and mechanized industry conducted on a larger scale than anywhere else in the world. Unemployment disappeared. The country cast away the cloak of backwardness and medievalism. Capitalist elements actively opposing socialist construction have been vanquished in a strenuous struggle. The foundations of the socialist society have been laid.

In 1937 the Second Five Year Plan will be completed. The plan of the first three years is already fulfilled. The welfare of the people must be increased twofold or threefold. The technical reconstruction of national economy will be completed. Soviet democracy is developing. The main political problem of the Second Five Year Plan—the abolition of class differences within the U.S.S.R.—is being solved. But already the socialist order reigns supreme and is the leading force in the whole of the national economy.

THE PROPORTION OF SOCIALIZED ECONOMY TO THE NATIONAL INCOME (in per cents)[1]

1913	—
1928	44·0
1932	93·0
1934	96·0
1937	100·0

The U.S.S.R. is developing rapidly and is maintaining a struggle for peace. The Communist Party and its leader Stalin—the best pupil and successor of the late Lenin—are leading the U.S.S.R. towards Communism.

The country is changing, its geography is changing.

Each new fact that changes the map of the U.S.S.R. has a profound economic and political significance. In this book the author deals with the main changes in the distribution of the productive forces of the country and discusses their inner significance. It is a description of the work of remaking the map of one seventh part of the world. It is not intended to give a full description of the national economy of the U.S.S.R. or of its geography. Its aim is to depict the changes in the economy of the country.

The geographic changes are dealt with in connexion with

[1] The figures given here and in the following table for 1934 are preliminary; for 1937 are according to the plan.

the different branches of national economy. The reader should not expect to find in the book a detailed description of economic regions.

The regional changes could well be the subject of a companion volume. But another topic that would repay analysis is the people of the Soviet Union, who by their well-calculated and energetic action, based on the principles of planned economy, are decisively re-fashioning both their country and themselves.

SOVIET GEOGRAPHY

Chapter 1

THE COUNTRY

LOOK at the map (*No. 2 (a) and (b)*). Before you lies a country which occupies the east of Europe and the north of Asia. With the map in your hand read the following short geographical survey; you will find it easier to read the ensuing chapters.

In the middle of the European part of the U.S.S.R. lie the Moscow Region and the town of Moscow—the capital of the Union of Soviet Socialist Republics and of the Russian Socialist Federal Soviet Republic. The ancient Kremlin, surrounded by the many-storied buildings of the new era, stands here. Congresses of the Soviets and of the Communist Party meet in the Kremlin. Stalin lives and works in Moscow.

To the north-west of the Moscow Region lies the Kalinin Region, while bordering on this is the Leningrad Region: moraines of ancient Scandinavian glaciers, damp meadows along the rivers, forests uprooted to make way for wheat-fields, the moist breath of the Atlantic. On the coast of the Gulf of Finland stands Leningrad, a city of straight avenues and stone-built canals, a great machine-building centre and a most important port.

The Karelian Autonomous Republic lies to the north of Leningrad, side by side with Finland. Here are powerful timber mills, erected in the region of pine-covered rocks; canals with up-to-date sluices utilizing the numerous lakes and rivers; concrete hydro-electric stations drawing on the power of the forest waterfalls.

In the north the continent penetrates beyond the Arctic Circle and terminates in the Kola Peninsula, which cuts into the Arctic Ocean. Rounded mountains with patches of snow stretch under the gloomy sky. Dotted here and there amidst the stunted tangled fir trees are the rare settlements of the Saami-Lapps, the inhabitants of the north, and new Arctic centres of the mining industry. Amidst the marshes and stones lie the ploughlands and kitchen-gardens of agricultural enterprises—the pioneers of polar agriculture. A railway, which is in process of electrification, crosses the deer-paths. In a deep Arctic fiord, warmed by a branch of the Gulf Stream, lies the port of Murmansk, which never freezes.

To the north-east of the Moscow Region lie the Ivanov Region, and the Gorky (former Nijni-Novgorod), Kirov (former Viatka), and Northern Areas. The taiga, the dense coniferous forest of the north, borders on this side of Moscow. As it approaches the south it alternates more and more frequently with ploughlands, and makes way for growing industrial towns. Towards the north the domination of the forest becomes more and more complete. Impassable thickets, the elemental power of the conifers—but amidst these dense forests there can be seen new timber combines, the first oil derricks, and the first coal-mines. The summer is short here, whilst the winter is long and severe.

To the west of the Moscow Region—between it and Poland —lie the Western Region and the White Russian Soviet Socialist Republic: towns and villages and new peat-fuel electric power stations amidst drained marshes and uprooted copses. The more one moves to the west the milder is the climate, and the coniferous forests give way to glades of wide-leaved trees: maples and oaks, hornbeams and limes.

To the south of the Moscow Region the forest zone is superseded by the forest steppe. The almost treeless expanses of the Kursk and Voronezh Regions and of the Kuibishev (former Central Volga) and Saratov Areas stretch for hundreds of kilometres: a slightly undulating black soil plain, an extensive agricultural region in which towns with new industries are dotted here and there. Before the Revolution these regions were remarkable for their strong survivals of serfdom, the particular poverty of their peasantry, and the barbarous three-field system which exhausted the soil. Now a large-scale and mechanized socialist agricultural industry has been created here with scientifically organized crop-rotation, resulting in the growing well-being of its collectivized peasantry.

2a. EUROPEAN PART
ADMINISTRATIVE TERRITORIAL DIVISIONS (*see Appendix, p. 221*)

1. Mariinsk Autonomous Province
2. Chuvash A.S.S.R.
3. Adighe Autonomous Province
4. Cherkess Autonomous Province
5. Karachai Autonomous Province
6. Abkhazian A.S.S.R.
7. Kabardin-Balkar Autonomous Province

8. Autonomous Province of Northern Osetia
9. Chechen-Ingush Autonomous Province
10. South Osetian Autonomous Province
11. Ajar A.S.S.R.
12. Nakhichevansk A.S.S.R.
13. Karabai Mountain Autonomous Province

3

The last copses disappear as one goes farther south. The boundless flat steppe commences: to the west, bordering on Rumania and Poland, lies the Ukrainian S.S.R.; to the east, towards the Volga, lie the Azov-Black Sea, and Stalingrad Areas. The white huts of the villages are surrounded by gardens. Proprietary boundaries on the fields have been ploughed up. New crops have been introduced into the crop-rotation.

Industrial patches lie amidst the agricultural tractor-ploughed expanses; the Donetz basin, clad in the smoke of factory chimneys and strewn with coal; a group of new works around the gigantic hydro-electric station on the Dnieper; Kharkov, Rostov-on-Don, Stalingrad—growing centres of machine-building; Kiev, standing aloft on the high banks of the Dnieper; the capital of the Ukraine which is being rapidly covered with new buildings and enterprises and is one of the most ancient towns in the country.

In the south the Crimean Peninsula takes the continent to the Black Sea. The south coast of the Crimean Autonomous Soviet Socialist Republic, protected from the north by a ridge of mountains, is a 'Mediterranean' region of cypresses, grapes, and health-resorts.

The plains of the North Caucasian Area give place to mountains in the south. The snow-capped wall of the Caucasian mountains, chief of which is the two-headed Elbrus, the highest peak in Europe, stretches from the Black Sea to the Caspian Sea. A forest of fir trees covers the sides of the mountain valleys, which are traversed by blue torrents. Shining glaciers descend into the ravines. The mountain dwellers of the Caucasus live in the labyrinth of valleys and in high mountain villages. Electric power stations, roads, new villages, and even new towns are springing up in the mountain folds.

The difficult passes of the Caucasus and the narrow strips of the Black Sea and Caspian coasts lead to the extreme south, to the Transcaucasian Federative Republic, the mountain land of Georgians, Armenians, and Turks.

Through the leaves of the palm trees on the Black Sea coast one can see the eternal snow of the mountain summits.

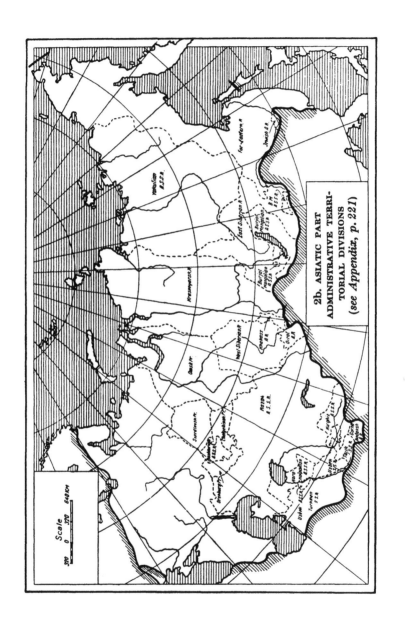

2b. ASIATIC PART ADMINISTRATIVE TERRI-
TORIAL DIVISIONS
(see Appendix, p. 221)

Scale
300   0   370   640 KM

Barren rock alternates with soil bearing sub-tropical flora. Waterless sun-parched expanses lie near marshes which never dry up because they are exposed to daily torrents of rain. Irrigation canals are constructed in the dry lands and marshes are drained. Shepherds' huts stand side by side with new hydro-electric stations, chemical works, and mechanized agricultural enterprises.

Tiflis, the capital of Soviet Georgia, is situated in the centre of the Transcaucasus. On the coast of the Caspian Sea lies the petroleum town of Baku, the capital of Soviet Azerbaijan. To the south of Erivan, the capital of Soviet Armenia, rises Ararat like a frontier landmark. Turkey lies beyond.

The European and Asiatic parts of the U.S.S.R. are divided by the wooded Urals, in which region lie the Sverdlovsk, Chelyabinsk, and Orenburg Regions and the Bashkirian Autonomous Soviet Socialist Republic.

The Ural range is ancient. It has been denuded by time. The richest deposits of useful minerals are revealing themselves on the earth's surface: iron, copper, gold, platinum, and precious stones. Industry was started here long ago, but in the modern Urals, side by side with the old partly hand-worked mines which have almost become museum relics, there stand new blast-furnaces which are the largest in Europe, and new machine-building works. The whole of the Ural Region is covered with scaffolding.

Asia lies beyond the Urals. The immense West Siberian lowlands, crossed by the Ob and its tributary the Irtish, lie here. They contain the Omsk Region and the West Siberian Area. In the north there is nothing but fallen timber, marshes, burnt forests, and the taiga. Farther south, along the Trans-Siberian Railway, there is a belt of forest steppe —black soil ploughlands and birch woods. To the south of this lies the steppe. In the south-east, at the foot-hills of the Altai mountains, a new industrial region has sprung up. This is the Kuznetzk district: large-scale coal-mining, up-to-date metallurgy, and chemical works in the depths of Siberia.

In the south, the Urals and the West Siberian lowlands

border on Kazakstan, the extensive Cossack[1] Republic, whose nomad inhabitants are gradually becoming settled.

Boundless expanses. Not a tree to be seen. Few rivers. Agriculture which endeavours to combat droughts. Herds on the steppe pastures. Enterprises equipped with the most modern technique extracting coal, copper, and oil. Newly constructed railways.

To the south of Kazakstan lies Central Asia—five socialist republics, whose names speak of the nationalities which inhabit them: the Uzbek, Turkmen, Tajik, Kirghiz, and Kara-Kalpak Republics.

This is the extreme south of the U.S.S.R. Here the country borders on Persia, Afghanistan, and West China. India begins 15 kilometres from the frontier of Central Asia.

Before the Revolution, Central Asia was a land of semi-slave and colonial labour. Now it has become a land of equal nationalities, socialist agriculture, and newly created industry.

A yellow plain, poor in humidity, lies under the blue dome of the sky. Rare but animated oases stand amidst the immense deserts. Cotton-fields traversed by irrigation channels; clay villages marked by majestic pyramidal poplars; new blocks of industrial buildings side by side with the ruined mosques of Timur's day. Intense heat.

There are mountains in the south of Central Asia—the Pamirs and Tien-Shan. A world of ice and rock beyond the clouds, crossed by camel-tracks and motor-roads.

To the east of the West Siberian lowlands rise mountain ranges. From the Yenisei, whose abundant waters cross the whole land from south to north, to the coast of the Pacific Ocean there extends a land which is gathered in folds and furrowed by powerful upheavals. The taiga stretches here, and here, too, are mechanized mines, hunting grounds, air routes.

This is the territory of the Krasnoyarsk, East Siberian and Far Eastern Areas, and the Yakut Autonomous

---

[1] A Turkic people. The same name was borne by a Russian estate group before the Revolution which owned land and performed military service on its own horses and with its own equipment.

Soviet Socialist Republic, equal in area to the whole of Europe. A land of grandiose dimensions: great rivers, the world centre of water-power; almost untouched, boundless forests, vast mineral resources—gold, coal, and non-ferrous metals, and the deepest lake in the world—Baikal, a true sea in the mountains.

The south of the eastern half of the U.S.S.R. is the most highly developed: it is the part which lies by the Trans-Siberian Railway. There are ploughlands here, a comparatively dense population, and industrial towns.

The Far Eastern Area takes the U.S.S.R. to the shores of the Pacific Ocean. The land is densely populated in the southern plains along the beds of the Amur and Ussuri. Rice and wild grapes grow in this region of Pacific Ocean monsoons. The tiger lives here. In the Far East there are new factories, new roads, new towns. The country is rapidly becoming industrialized.

Opposite the continent lies the island of Sakhalin, whose northern part belongs to the U.S.S.R. Coal and oil are extracted here.

To the north of Sakhalin is the peninsula of Kamchatka— a mountainous and forest region rich in oil, fur, and fish. The highest active volcanoes in the world are to be found here.

An extensive coastline faces the polar basin—forestless tundra inhabited by the rare peoples of the north, deer-breeders and fishermen.

There are islands in the Arctic Ocean. There are scientific stations and wireless poles on these islands. The polar night lasts for many months here. The islands are covered with snow. Ice-fields extend on all sides. These are the Arctic regions. The boundaries of the Soviet part of the Arctic regions meet at the North Pole.

Chapter 2

A NEW DIVISION

Dots, lines, circles, and points are being generously added to the map by the growing country. The new contents of the map cannot but alter the framework itself of the administrative and territorial network. The new contents must be fitted into a new frame.

The regional system of Tsarist Russia was archaic. Since the days of Catherine II the police division of the land into governments (*gubernias*), based solely on the necessity of administering the collecting of taxes and the recruiting of soldiers, had remained unchanged. Economically compact districts were often separated by boundary-lines. The boundary sometimes traversed even towns. For instance, one part of the industrial town, Orekhovo-Zuevo belonged to the Moscow government, and the other to the Vladimir government.

The lands of the national minorities were purposely divided by boundaries in order to facilitate the Russification of the subjugated nationalities and to weaken their resistance to autocracy.

The old administrative and territorial divisions—evidences of arbitrary lawlessness and the Tsarist police régime— could not remain unchanged after the State was built up on a new basis. The Revolution soon put new boundary-lines on the map, conceived on national and economic principles.

It was Lenin who formulated the principle: 'We want a voluntary union of nations, such as would permit of no violation of one nation by another.'

Self-determination and even State separation became the right of the liberated nations. Under the protection of the Soviet power, nations grew and consolidated themselves, and new States were created.

The map became bright with the colours of the republics

of the Soviet Union. Of these there are seven: the Russian Republic, the Ukrainian, the White Russian, the Transcaucasian, the Uzbek, the Turkmen, and the Tajik. All seven have equal rights. The power of the Federal Union of Soviet Socialist Republics extends to representation in international affairs, alteration of external frontiers, the establishment of the principles and general plan of national economy, and the like. Beyond these limits, which are laid down by agreement, the republics of the Soviet Union govern themselves independently. Each republic is free to withdraw from the U.S.S.R.

Some of the republics belonging to the U.S.S.R. are themselves federations. The map is covered with the hitherto unknown names of twenty-one autonomous republics[1] and fifteen autonomous areas. (*See fig. 3 and Appendix, p. 221.*)

Dissecting the map are the complicated frontier lines of the smaller subdivisions: 9 national districts and 240 national regions. In addition to this there are over 5,300 national village soviets. The Far Eastern Area, for instance, inhabited by many nationalities, has a complicated administrative and territorial structure, which ensures the carrying out of Lenin's national policy and aids the economic and cultural growth of the different nationalities. It consists of the Jewish Autonomous Area—the new region of Jewish settlement; the Koriak and Choukot National Districts, inhabited by the small nationalities of the north; the Ukrainian National Regions; the Chinese National Village Soviets.

The Soviet Central Asiatic Republics may be taken as a striking illustration of the policy of national demarcation.

In the nineteenth century Russia conquered Central Asia. The Tsarist army seized a colony which yielded revenue of something like one hundred million roubles a year.

Eight million natives were kept in subjugation by the army and the police. Administrative boundaries were brought to the aid of the administrative apparatus.

The Tsarist legislator sketched the internal boundaries on his map, purposely dividing national and economic units

[1] Including the three main Transcaucasian republics.

in order to make them more easy to govern. He cut up the living body of the country. He cast a net, woven out of frontier lines, over Central Asia, which was inhabited by several nationalities.

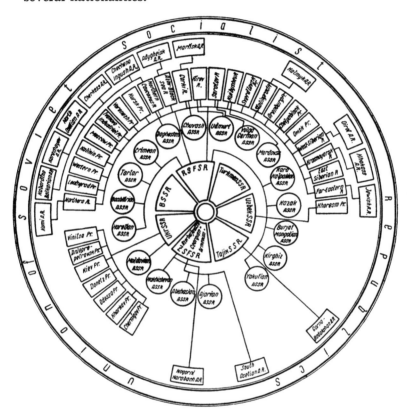

3. DIAGRAM ILLUSTRATING THE ADMINISTRATIVE TERRITORIAL DIVISION OF THE U.S.S.R.

AR = Autonomous region. ASSR = Autonomous Soviet Socialist Republic. Pr. = Province. R = Region. SSR = Soviet Socialist Republic. SFSR = Soviet Federated Socialist Republics. RSFSR = Russian Soviet Federated Socialist Republics. BSSR = White Russian Soviet Socialist Republic. UKrSSR = Ukrainian Soviet Socialist Republic. ZSFSR = Transcaucasian Soviet Federated Socialist Republics.

The frontier line divided the Kirghizes, some of whom found themselves in the Turkestan province, others in the Steppe province—both under the rule of different governor-generals.

The Bukhara Protectorate and the vassal State of Khiva
cut into Russian Turkestan: they were playthings of geography, retaining their formal independence, and inhabited
by the same peoples as the neighbouring Russian possessions.

The boundary between Bukhara and the Turkestan
province in the Kizil-Kum desert was laid down in such a
way as to provide the route taken by the Russian troops
when they were attacking Khiva with a sufficient quantity
of wells.

The boundary cut right through the Zeravshan valley,
and, traversing the only irrigation system, gave the upper
parts of the Zeravshan to Russia and the lower parts to
Bukhara. Russia took possession of the water, i.e. the
power.

The Uzbeks, who lived on the banks of the Zeravshan,
were artificially separated; whilst in Khiva the boundary
united the Uzbeks and the Turkmens.

Nationalities were divided and purposely joined to each
other. Thus enmity and oppression between different
nationalities were created.

When soviets were established in Central Asia the old
frontiers were at first retained.

On the territory of the Turkestan province there came
into being the Turkestan Soviet Socialist Republic which
entered the U.S.S.R. (through the R.S.F.S.R.), while the
Bukhara and Khorezma Soviet National Republics, which
did not enter the U.S.S.R., were formed on the territory
of Bukhara and Khiva (Khorezma).

In 1924, when the Civil War in Central Asia came to an
end and peaceful construction began, the peoples of the
Turkestan, Bukhara, and Khorezma Republics declared
their will to form new States on their territory which should
be organized as national units and should enter the Soviet
Union. (See Map No. 4.)

National demarcation was effected. The following
national States are marked now on the map of Central
Asia: the Uzbek Republic, which was formerly torn into
three parts; the Turkmen Republic, formerly broken up
into three States; the Tajik Republic, once divided between

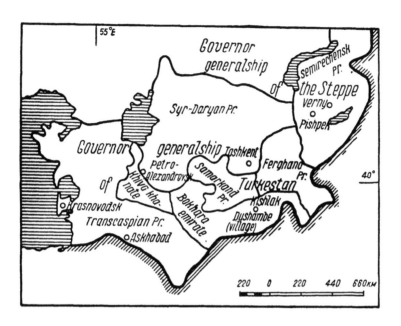

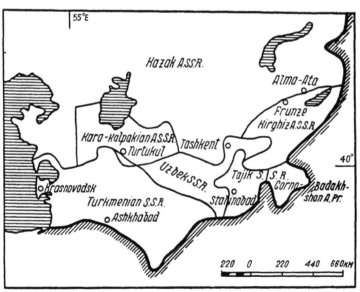

4. OLD (ABOVE) AND NEW (BELOW) ADMINISTRATIVE TERRITORIAL
DIVISIONS OF CENTRAL ASIA

Bukhara and Russia; the Kirghiz Republic, divided before
the Revolution between two governor-generalships; the
Kara-Kalpak Republic, whose territory formerly belonged
partly to Khiva and partly to Russia. New frontier lines
marked national territories.

History has placed the different nationalities where they
are in haphazard formation, and therefore the boundary-
lines of the Soviet Republics are often undulating and
sometimes broken. In the Fergan valley the frontier lines
of the Uzbek, Tajik, and Kirghiz Republics form a fantastic design. The Khorezma region of the Uzbek Republic
is inhabited by a mass of Uzbeks living amongst Turkmens
and geographically quite separate from Uzbekistan proper.

But care was taken in laying down the frontiers in
accordance with the national principle not to clash in any
way with the economic divisions. Regions that were
economic units were not broken up. Each irrigation
system, for instance, was included as a rule in one State.
The national principle was completed and corrected by the
economic principle.

National self-determination and entry into the U.S.S.R.
ensured the powerful economic development of the Soviet
States which had been created on the territory of Tsarist
Russia—the prison of peoples. National culture developed
within the new national frontiers; the population rallied
round their soviets and united with them; enmity between
the nationalities disappeared.

The only official language in Tsarist Russia was the
Russian language—the language of an imperialist nation.
In the national units of the U.S.S.R. business, education,
and other activities are carried on in the local language.

Backward nationalities have passed straight over to
socialism, escaping the capitalist stage of development.

Tsarist Russia not only deprived the 'aliens' of national
unity and language; it deprived them of their name as well.
The Kazaks were called Kirghizes; the Kirghizes, Kara-
Kirghizes; the Nentsi-Samoyeds, the Uzbeks-Sarts. But
even these names could not be found on the map of Tsarist
Russia. Lands were not supposed to be named after the

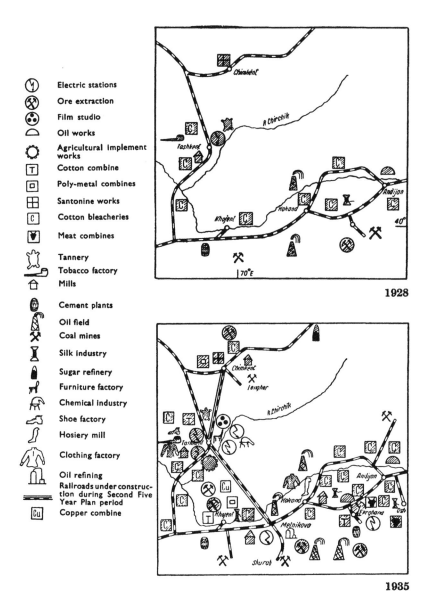

Electric stations

Ore extraction

Film studio

Oil works

Agricultural implement works

Cotton combine

Poly-metal combines

Santonine works

Cotton bleacheries

Meat combines

Tannery

Tobacco factory

Mills

Cement plants

Oil field

Coal mines

Silk industry

Sugar refinery

Furniture factory

Chemical industry

Shoe factory

Hosiery mill

Clothing factory

Oil refining

Railroads under construction during Second Five Year Plan period

Copper combine

1928

1935

5. THE INDUSTRIALIZATION OF THE DISTRICT ADJACENT TO TASHKENT, CENTRAL ASIA. 1928 AND 1935

Large enterprises shown. Shaded figures working enterprises. Unshaded figures enterprises under construction during Second Five Year Plan period.

nationalities which inhabited them. Not only have the correct national names been restored, but these have been included in the geographical nomenclature.

The large republics of the U.S.S.R. are divided into areas (or regions) so as to represent the best combination of productive powers within the general system of Soviet national economy, each specializing in a definite field.

The administrative map of the U.S.S.R. continues to alter with the development of the country. Some maps are still to be seen in which Uzbekistan and Tajikistan are coloured alike. But already more than five years have passed since Tajikistan has grown, on the basis of the national right to self-determination and in accordance with the will of the toiling masses, from an autonomous republic included in Uzbekistan, into a republic entering directly into the U.S.S.R. It is only on a few of the newest maps that Kara-Kalpakia is shown as an autonomous republic. Until quite recently it was an autonomous area. Maps have just been published showing the Jewish Autonomous Area, formed only a few months ago out of a national region. The economic and cultural growth of the peoples gradually leads them from the lowest to the highest forms of organization.

The interior boundaries of the U.S.S.R. do not become rigid and immovable for years and years; they do not turn into shackles that hinder the rapid development of the country. The introduction of new economic contents into different areas, the rapid growth of new works and new branches of industry, the necessity of administrative separation, cause some of these areas to be broken up into smaller regions. Thus, for example, according to a Government decree the Lower Volga Area has been divided into two areas, the Saratovsky and Stalingradsky Areas, the Central Black Earth Region into two regions, the Voronezhsky and Kursky Regions, etc.

Formerly the barren coast of the Kara-Bougaz Bay in Central Asia was included partly in the Turkmen and partly in the Kazak Republics. At the present time the richest deposits in the world of Glauber's salt (sulphate of natrium) are being exploited in Kara-Bougaz. The industrial

development of the desert has begun and its administrative boundary has been altered. Kara-Bougaz, whose
growth chiefly depends on its connexion with the economy
of Turkmenia, has been wholly included in the territory of
that republic.

National self-determination and economic importance,
each supplementing the other, are the basis of the regional
division of the U.S.S.R. The new administrative and
territorial network on the map is no longer a prison network.

The new administrative divisions reflect, and at the same
time stimulate, the economic and cultural growth of the
peoples.

Chapter 3

THE DISCOVERY OF NEW NATURE

Russia of the olden days knew itself very superficially. The industrial development of the country—and consequently the mapping of the details of its geography—proceeded slowly and unevenly.

The railways and waterways carried away the wealth of the huge State from within, sending it to the industrial centre. Sea-routes licked the country from without, exporting its raw materials right out of Russia. The science of geography was, in the main, a private business man's liability item, and therefore the distant regions of the country, which were far both from the centre and from the frontier, for a long time remained unknown to anybody. Their exploration would have cost too much; there was no guarantee that the money laid out would be returned the next day in the form of a reliable and profitable income.

The geographer pulled up short at the chaos of mountains and the desert expanses. In the schools in Tsarist times 'commercial' geography was taught instead of 'economic' geography.

However, some distant regions were investigated even then. Scientists in army uniforms—Przhevalsky, young Kropotkin, and others—penetrated into unexplored regions under cover of bayonets, but the field of their often extremely valuable scientific work was insignificant compared with the territory of Russia which awaited exploration. The empire, through the work of its officer-geographers, only explored the frontier regions, and even then it preferred to study the frontier regions of other countries rather than its own. The significance of their work is expressed by the monument which stands over Przhevalsky's grave on the bank of the Issik-Koul in Kirghizia: a bronze eagle spreading its wings over the map of Asia. . . .

Many of the lands which did not lie near trade routes and military zones remained unexplored. Ugly white spaces lay like gigantic, unseeing eyes on the map of blind Russia: the north, distant Siberia, the depths of the Pamirs, of the Kara-Kum desert, and of Tien-Shan.

The economic development of the U.S.S.R. accompanies its cultural development. The country gets to know itself scientifically: it studies the grounds of socialist construction. The science of geography helps the spreading of a new life, of new social relations, over the whole of the territory of the Soviet Union to its farthermost ravines.

Year after year scientific expeditions depart for the icy expanses of the Soviet Arctic regions, for the forests of Siberia, for the Pamir mountains—to fight for new and undiscovered lands, and to explore them. There is a revival of the heroic times of the great explorers, but it is no longer caravels that carry the Soviet scientists to the unknown, but powerful ice-breakers, motor-cars, aeroplanes, and aerosledges. It is only in the wildest jungles that they go on horseback or even on foot. Soviet expeditions are not enterprises undertaken by determined individuals. They are complex organizations which methodically realize a single plan of investigation of the country.

Geographers explore unknown regions. Topographers draw maps of new lands. Geologists seek for industrial raw material. Every year—from spring till autumn—white tents and bonfires show the presence of expeditions in the farthermost regions of the U.S.S.R.

Within the short period of five years or so hundreds of thousands of square kilometres of land were visited and investigated for the first time. Uncharted regions on the map have to a large extent been filled in. Areas which, as far as men were concerned, did not exist have been drawn into the circle of science and economics.

There still remain regions in Siberia which are difficult of access and where no man has yet set foot, and the Arctic regions promise new discoveries. But soon the last geographic secrets of the country will be revealed, the last 'white spaces' on its map deciphered.

The north-eastern corner of Siberia is remote and inaccessible. The mountains, covered by the impenetrable taiga, bar the way to a tremendous unexplored region. No explorer was ever there, nor did one ever aspire to go there. Science did not know what lay within the stone arc of the Verkhoyansky, Kolimsky, and Anadirsky ranges. Pre-revolutionary geography was satisfied with putting in on the map blue lines for the supposed rivers, and brown lines for the probable mountains, in accordance with the results of the chance questioning of natives. This concocted drawing was included, to the shame of pre-revolutionary Russian science, in atlases of the world and was taught in schools.

In 1926 a Soviet expedition, headed by Professor Obrouchev, was the first to penetrate into this mysterious region. It resulted in astounding discoveries. There was discovered what is probably the last great mountain system in the world—over 1,000 kilometres long, 300 kilometres wide, and up to 3,000 metres high. The mountains did not at all stretch in radii within a great arc or between the sources of rivers, as the maps showed, but ran parallel to the great arc and the rivers cut through them. (*See Map No. 6.*)

The map of a huge country was re-drawn. The new mountains were named the Chersky Range in honour of the revolutionary who was exiled by the Tsarist Government to Siberia and became an explorer there.

In 1913 the ships of a hydrographic expedition came to the shores of an unknown land to the north of Cape Chelius-khin in the Arctic Ocean. (*See Map No. 7.*)

The Russian flag was hoisted on the shore at the foot of the grim mountains covered with autumn snow. But the approaching polar winter caused the expedition to depart hastily.

Since that time a winding line, 250 miles long, which represented the portion of coastline seen in 1913, was traced on the maps of the polar basin. A timid dotted line of conjectures marked some sort of contour. Perhaps there were single small islands, perhaps there was an archipelago, perhaps a large stretch of land. The Tsarist Government

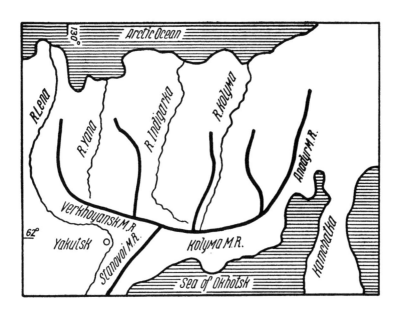

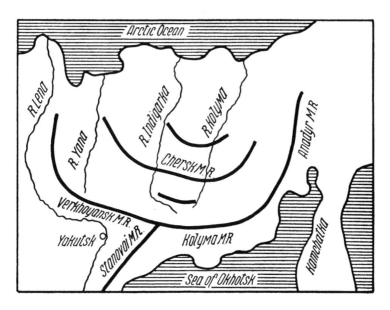

6. THE MOUNTAIN CHAINS OF YAKUTIA
Maps drawn before (above) and after (below) the expedition of 1926.

21

did not explore this new territory, though the discovery was called Nicolas II Land.

In 1930 a Soviet expedition reached the Northern Land in the ice-breaker *Sedov*. Four people remained here—Oushakov, Ourvantsev, Khodov, and Zhouravliev. During the two years they lived here the expedition went over 3,000 kilometres in dog-drawn sledges and surveyed the land under the most severe polar conditions. The geography of a new archipelago, over 36,000 square kilometres in area—larger than the area of Holland!—was studied. Tin ore was discovered. New geographical names were inserted in the map: October Revolution Island, Bolshevik Island, Komsomolets Island, Pioneer Island, Stalin Bay, Straits of the Red Army, Rosa Luxembourg Cape, etc.

For a long time there had been a dotted line on the maps of the Kara Sea which marked the hypothetical Wiese Island—an island that was discovered by Professor Wiese in his study at home, and which he foretold on the grounds of certain scientific facts. The *Sedov* expedition in 1930 proved that Wiese Island does indeed exist.

The Kara Sea, difficult of passage, has been crossed in many different directions by Soviet ice-breakers. A new archipelago was discovered not far from Northern Land—the Sergius Kamenev Islands. To the north of them was discovered Schmidt Island, to the south Voronin Island, Samoilovich Island, Issachenko Island, and Kirov Island. Fifteen new islands have been discovered in the region of Novaya Zemlya.

No country in the world makes such intense efforts to explore the Arctic regions as the U.S.S.R. The Arctic Ocean is crossed by different expeditions every year. The network of meteorological and wireless stations, already wide, is being extended. Before the Revolution there were five polar stations: now there are nearly forty. The Soviet Arctic regions are now in constant wireless communication. Year after year successive groups of scientists spend the winter in the most remote spots. The staff of scientists wintering in the Arctic regions consisted in 1934 of nearly five hundred persons.

An unremitting search is being made for useful minerals on the coasts and islands of the Arctic Ocean. Asbestos has been found in Novaya Zemlya. Vaigach Island has acquired fame for its non-ferrous metals. Coal-beds have been discovered on Franz-Josef Land. Oil and mica have been discovered on the Taimir Peninsula. The industrial exploitation of minerals has been started in many places.

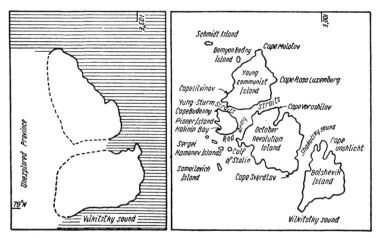

7. NORTHERN LAND MAPS DRAWN BEFORE AND AFTER THE
EXPEDITION OF 1930-2

Meteorological observations in the Arctic regions are a key to the study of the weather of the whole of the U.S.S.R.

One of the main scientific tasks carried on in the Soviet Arctic region at the present time is the plotting of the North Passage from the Atlantic Ocean to the Pacific Ocean. (*See Map No. 8.*)

For centuries seamen and scientists had dreamt of this passage. Only three men overcame it—Nordenskjold, Vilkitsky, and Amundsen—but each of them was obliged to spend the winter on the way. A winter spent on the way, however, deprives the North Passage of all practical significance. Soviet polar explorers have undertaken the task of connecting the west and east of the country by a sea-route which can be covered in one voyage.

In 1932 the expedition headed by Professor Schmidt in the ice-breaker *Sibiriakov* passed, for the first time in history, from the Atlantic Ocean to the Pacific Ocean without spending the winter on the way.

In 1933 Schmidt, on the steamer *Cheliuskhin*, repeated the expedition. He went the whole way and came out into the Bering Strait, but heavy ice-floes carried the ship back to the Chukot Sea. The *Cheliuskhin* was crushed by the ice. Soviet airmen, under the most unfavourable flying conditions, heroically saved the crew from the ice-floes.

In 1934 the ice-breaker *Litke* sailed the North Passage from the Pacific Ocean to the Atlantic.

The main task now is to equip the passage with a sufficient number of ports, fuel bases, lighthouses, and so on. The practical exploitation of the Northern Sea passage is to begin in the summer of 1935.

The problem of studying and developing the Soviet Arctic regions will be an organic part of the economic plan of the U.S.S.R.

Up till recent times there has been no complete geographical map of the sand desert of Kara-Kum, which, together with the adjoining desert of Kizil-Kum, is the largest sand desert in the world. The map was covered with 'white spaces'.

In 1933 the automobile expedition Moscow–Kara-Kum–Moscow crossed the least investigated north-western region of the desert, where it meets the clay-and-stone plateau of Oust-Ourt, whose boundaries were marked on the maps by a hypothetical line. The expedition defined this line more accurately, removing the boundary to another place. In 1934 a composite expedition of the Soviet Union Academy of Sciences was working in Kara-Kum. It filled in many of the blanks on the maps.

Winds are born and glaciers melt in the mountains of Central Asia. Water and wind rush down into the valleys, and in the valleys cotton grows. But the cotton is in the power of water and the weather. To grow cotton one must

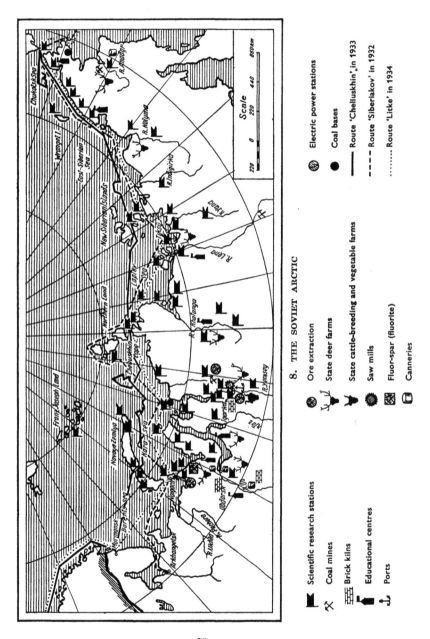

8. THE SOVIET ARCTIC

Scientific research stations

Coal mines

Brick kilns

Educational centres

Ports

Ore extraction

State deer farms

State cattle-breeding and vegetable farms

Saw mills

Fluor-spar (fluorite)

Canneries

Electric power stations

Coal bases

———— Route 'Chelluskhin' in 1933

– – – Route 'Siberiakov' in 1932

.... Route 'Litke' in 1934

Scale

220   0   220   440   660 km

25

know the laws determining weather-changes in the mountains and the forces determining the water-supply in the mountain rivers which feed the irrigation channels. But in the depths of mountainous Asia there are unexplored lands—lands where man has never yet set foot.

Soviet Kirghizia and the Sinkiang province of China are divided by Tien-Shan ('The Celestial Mountains'), a mass of gigantic snow-covered mountain ranges. Just on the Chinese frontier there rises Khan-Tengri out of the knot of glaciers and mountain chains: this is the highest peak of Tien-Shan, 7,000 metres above sea-level. Khan-Tengri towers above the icy land like a shining white tooth. The regions at the foot of Khan-Tengri have not been explored; its glaciers have not been studied.

In 1902–3 the German scientist Merzbacher did much towards the study of the Khan-Tengri range, which he compared in grandeur to the Himalayas; but even after Merzbacher hundreds of square kilometres of the most inaccessible glaciers and ravines were still represented by a 'white space' on the maps of the region.

Now Soviet expeditions depart for the Khan-Tengri range year after year.

In 1930 Soukhodolsky penetrated for the first time into the 'white space' of North Inilchek glaciers at the foot of Khan-Tengri, passing, by way of the steep rocks surrounding it, round a glacier lake, the largest in the U.S.S.R., which barred the way to the unexplored region. The same year an expedition consisting of Goussev, Zinaida Kossenko, Mikhailov, and Rizhov penetrated into the 'white space' through the perpendicular ice cliffs of the newly discovered mountain pass, 'The Proletarian Press'. In 1932 a Ukrainian expedition completed the geographical and geological investigation of North Inilchek. An area of 400 square kilometres has been added to the map of the Kirghiz Autonomous Republic. The glacier of North Inilchek, where hitherto no man has ever been, has been studied, as also many central regions of the country.

In 1931 a Ukrainian group—Pogrebetsky, Sauberer, and Turin—climbed to the peak of Khan-Tengri, that awesome and seemingly inaccessible mountain. One of the largest glaciers in the world—South Inilchek—was traversed by an expedition on horseback, a unique feat in the history of mountain expeditions.

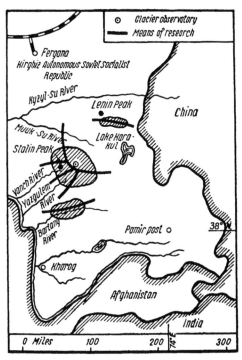

9. PRINCIPAL UNEXPLORED REGIONS OF THE PAMIRS, FIRST VISITED AND EXPLORED BY SOVIET EXPEDITIONS

In 1932 to 1934 the glacier regions to the south of Khan-Tengri, which hitherto were quite unknown, were explored.

A vast unexplored region lay in the depths of the Pamirs —'The Roof of the World'—at the point where their eastern cup-shaped valleys above the clouds pass into the deep and narrow gorges in the west. According to legend, beyond the icy passes there lived a mysterious tribe which killed everybody from the outside world who fell into its hands. By 1928 expeditions had traced a firm contour round the 'white space'. In 1928 a planned storming of the unexplored regions of the Pamirs was begun. It lasted for several years. At the present time the geographical investigation of the 'white space' in the Pamirs is nearing completion. (*See Map No. 9.*)

The complicated knot of snow ranges has been disentangled. The gigantic glacier Fedchenko has been explored. The location of the highest mountain in the U.S.S.R.—Stalin Peak (7,495 metres)—has been determined. Abolakov and Gorbounov made the ascent of this mountain in 1933.

The scientific conquest of the Pamirs has been secured by the construction of a glacier observatory on the Fedchenko glacier at a height of 4,300 metres. And now a group of scientific observers live the whole year round on the former 'white space'.

Automatic meteorological apparatus has been placed on Stalin Peak at heights of 5,600 metres and 6,850 metres.

The Tajik-Pamir Composite Expedition, which has been working for a number of years already, has discovered some valuable minerals. A new region of tin ores has been discovered. The wealth of optic fluorite discovered will be invaluable to Soviet optic science. The beds of fluor-spar can satisfy all the requirements of the country. Gold, asbestos, mica, radium, bismuth, arsenic, beryl, and other minerals have been discovered.

The fact that the most important metals in Central Asia are distributed there in zones has been established. One can thus prognosticate the existence of new strata with accuracy.

Thus the earth's riddles are being solved, 'white spaces' are filled in. The new social order enriches the geographical map. (*See Map No. 10.*)

But what is an 'unexplored region'? Is it simply a land which no man has ever visited? No: in Tsarist Russia these were not the only unexplored regions.

This rich country was poor in the knowledge of its wealth. The hammer-blows of the Soviet geologist at times revealed considerable stores of wealth even in the most thickly populated and, as it seemed, long 'investigated' regions. People

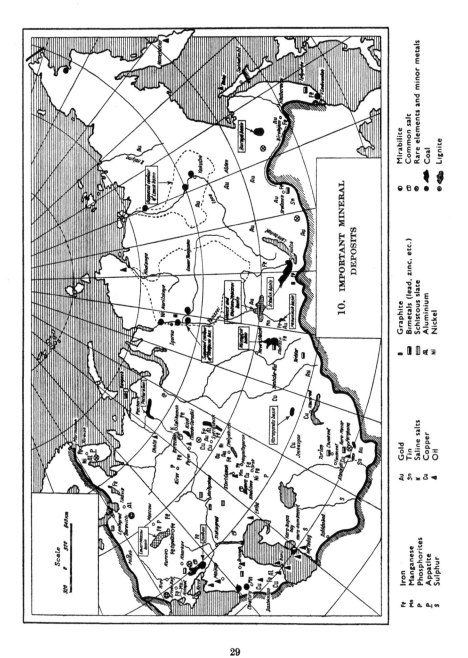

10. IMPORTANT MINERAL DEPOSITS

Fe Iron   Au Gold   ░ Graphite   ◐ Mirabilite
Mn Manganese   Sn Tin   ▯ Bimetals (lead, zinc, etc.)   ◑ Common salt
P Phosphorites   к Saline salts   ▭ Schistous slate   ⊗ Rare elements and minor metals
P₁ Appatite   Cu Copper   ◭ Aluminium   ♠ Coal
S Sulphur   ▲ Oil   Ni Nickel   ● Lignite

29

lived on the land, often without knowing what was concealed in its depths.

The concentration of all the mineral wealth of the earth and all the explorative work in the hands of the State has ensured great activity and fruitful results in geological investigation. Rich new strata and new kinds of mineral resources have been discovered. A revolution has taken place in the former estimate of the mineral resources of the country. The geological map has been made anew.

The investigated resources of coal in the U.S.S.R. have increased from 220 to 1,263 milliard tons, i.e. five times.[1]

The Kuznetzk coal-field, which lies in Western Siberia, was presumed to have 13 milliard tons of coal before the War; it is now known to have 400. A tremendous coal region has been discovered and investigated: one of the largest in the world.

Kuznetzk coal could cover the U.S.S.R.—that huge country—with a layer 2 centimetres thick. If the consumption of coal remained constant, the resources of the Kuznetzk coal-field would suffice for the whole world for about 300 years. The thickness of the coal seams in the Kuznetzk basin exceeds 16 metres. In quality the Kuznetzk coals are on a level with the best coal in the world. There are different kinds of Kuznetzk coal; it is a high quality calorific fuel, suitable for coke production, as well as a raw material for the production of liquid fuel, and is thus the basis of a future chemical industry.

The rich Karaganda coal region in the steppes of Kazakstan has been explored, and preliminary calculations give an estimate of 20 billion tons. Investigation continues. Karaganda is becoming the third most important coal-field in the U.S.S.R.

There was talk about Pechora coal (in the northern area) a hundred years ago. But the taiga, tundra, frost, and barrenness of the region were obstacles in the way of the scientific exploitation of the area. Soviet geologists were the

---

[1] The increase of investigated geological resources of useful minerals is given for the period starting with the last pre-War year 1913, up to the beginning of 1934.

first to begin the systematic exploration on the banks of arctic Pechora. In 1923 Professor Chernov discovered huge outcrops of coal there. The geological investigation of this extremely difficult region is still in progress. The resources so far discovered amount to 60 billion tons.

The great Tunguz coal-field has been discovered in the Yenisei regions of Siberia. Little investigation has so far been made, but enough to give every reason to expect that it will rival the Kuznetzk coal-field in the wealth of its resources.

The old coal regions have been evaluated anew. The investigated resources of the Donetz basin in the Ukraine, the most important coal region in the country which was explored, as it seemed, long ago, have increased from 55 to 71 billion tons. Exploration, which still continues, will further increase this figure. The known resources of the Moscow coal-field have been multiplied by 5·5, those of the Ural by 46. New coal regions in Central Asia have been investigated. The resources of the Far East have been greatly increased. In the upper part of the River Bourei there has been discovered a new coal-bearing region with huge resources of coke-forming coals.

Investigated petroleum resources in the U.S.S.R. amount to 3 milliard tons. Pre-revolutionary Russia had known resources of 0·9 milliard tons of oil, according to approximate calculations.

Soviet geology is endeavouring to render more even the distribution of petroleum. The problem is to find it in the eastern regions, those which are developing industrially but are lacking in petroleum resources. A heroic front of explorative work has been spread over a huge area. Heavy boring machines are scattered about the dense roadless taiga. The eternally frozen soil of the shores of the Arctic Ocean is being bored. Derricks are being constructed in the waterless deserts.

And these efforts have been rewarded. A chain of new petroleum strata has revealed itself along the entire western slope of the Urals—from north to south.

It is true that oil was formerly known to be present on

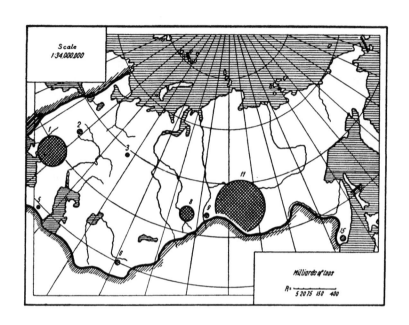

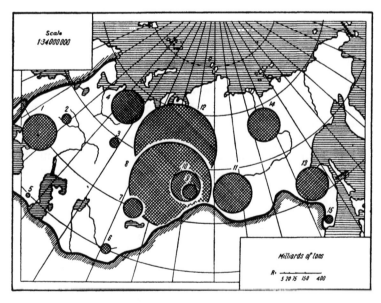

11. COAL DEPOSITS AS ESTIMATED IN 1913 AND 1934

(*see table opposite*)

32

the banks of the Oukhta, in the Pechora basin and in the Arctic taiga, but the competition of the old rich regions before the Revolution rendered it of no interest.   Soviet expeditions

IMPORTANT COAL DEPOSITS

	In millions of tons	
	1913	1934 (Jan. 1)
1. DON BASIN . . . . . . (Ukrainian S.S.R. and Azov-Black Sea Region)	55,000	71,088
2. MOSCOW BASIN . . . . . (Moscow Province)	1,080	5,930
3. URAL . . . . (Sverdlovsk and Chelyabinsk Provinces)	109	5,038
4. PECHORA BASIN . . . . . (Northern Region)	—	60,000
5. TRANSCAUCASUS.	95	189
6. CENTRAL ASIA	157	5,263
7. KARAGANDA BASIN . . . . (Kazak A.S.S.R.)	—	19,999
8. KUZNETZK BASIN . . . . (West Siberian Region)	13,000	400,000
9. MINUSINSK BASIN . . . . (Krasnoyarsk Region)	160	14,005
10. KANSK BASIN . . . . . (Krasnoyarsk Region)	—	40,000
11. IRKUTSK BASIN . . . . . (East Siberian Region)	150,000	74,848
12. TUNGUZ BASIN . . . . . (Krasnoyarsk Region)	—	400,000
13. BUREINSK BASIN . . . . (Far Eastern Territory)	—	60,000
14. YAKUTIA	—	60,000
15. MARITIME PROVINCE . . . (Far Eastern Region)	1,225	3,775

have prepared an extensive oil-bearing area on the Oukhta for exploitation.

To the south of Pechora petroleum has been discovered in the neighbourhood of Cherdin.

3

To the south of Cherdin petroleum has been found near the Choussov Gorodki. The first fountain gushed out unexpectedly; the bore was seeking the limits of Solikam potassium, and the pit-hole revealed petroleum. Intensive boring is proceeding here at the present time.

Petroleum has also been found in the neighbourhood of Perm.

A hundred years ago barge-haulers on the White River at Sterlitamak in Bashkiria used, during their halts, to throw handfuls of earth on their bonfires to make them burn brighter. Who would have thought that these poor people who pulled their barges by ropes were on the edge of a great discovery? Last century some enthusiast, who was made the laughing-stock of official science, helplessly tried, at his own risk and on his own responsibility, to bore holes here; but, finding no oil, he was ruined.

Industrial prospecting at Sterlitamak was organized for the first time by Soviet geologists under the direction of Blokhin, the assistant of Professor Goubkin. Since 1932 one pit-hole after another is yielding petroleum. An extremely rich oil-bearing region has been discovered. Prospecting continues.

The oil chain stretches still farther to the south of Sterlitamak. Through Kairovka and Jouss, which show signs of oil, it reaches Emba.

This region was known as an oil-bearing region in the past. But the area bored was insignificant. Now the region has been extended beyond recognition. The oil-bearing area from the Caspian Sea has reached the southern foot-hills of the Urals; it stretches for hundreds of kilometres. There are several hundred favourable geological structures here, of which two hundred show signs of petroleum. In many places industrial oil has been obtained. The region promises to be one of the largest in the world. Exploration has only just begun, but even now the resources at Emba are reckoned at 639 million tons. This figure will be further increased.

And thus the petroleum belt stretches along the Urals. But what is remarkable is the fact that the bed which yields oil on the western slope of the Urals—the upper stratum of carbon covered by Perm deposits—stretches from the east to the west, occupying the whole area from the Urals to the Volga. All this huge territory promises petroleum. This scientific conjecture is being justified: the pit-holes along the Volga have given liquid oil which in chemical composition resembles the Bashkirian oil. A new petroleum country is coming into being.

Still farther south, in Turkmenia, vast petroleum resources in the region of the mountain Neftedag have been discovered. Gigantic fountains, ejecting on some days 10,000 tons of oil, gushed out here.

Signs of petroleum have been found in a number of districts in Siberia, including the banks of the river Khatanga in the extreme north. Prospecting is in progress there in arctic conditions. Khatanga oil, together with the Pechora, Tunguz, and Yakut coal, will become the fuel base of the Northern Sea Passage.

The investigated petroleum resources of Sakhalin in the Far East have been increased to a very great extent: in some parts of the island there are whole lakes of oil. Oil has also been discovered in Kamchatka.

The most important oil region of Russia—Baku in the Transcaucasus—had not been charted geologically right up to the Revolution. During the last few years the oil wealth of Baku has been more fully investigated. New deep strata have been discovered in the old regions; rich new regions have been found near the old regions. In Baku, where oil has been extracted for over sixty years already, powerful fountains are gushing out to this day—a sign of the fantastic wealth of the earth's entrails. According to data given by Professor Goubkin, Baku possesses 1,325 million tons of petroleum. Industrial oil has been found in many places in Transcaucasia, outside of Baku.

The resources of the second most important oil region of the U.S.S.R.—Grozny in the North Caucasus—have also greatly increased. Here 138 million tons of oil are hidden under the earth. Large quantities of petroleum have been found in the North Caucasus in several regions besides Grozny.

Estimates of resources of investigated iron ores and ferrous quartzites in the U.S.S.R. have increased from 2 to 260 milliard tons, i.e. 130 times.

Long before the Revolution it was noticed that the magnetic needle showed signs of disturbance at Kursk. The earth exercised a powerful magnetic attraction. The maximum magnetic power of the Kursk steppes exceeded, by nearly four times, the power of the northern magnetic pole. The physicist Leist endeavoured by boring to reach the metal foretold by him, but the pit-holes of the solitary scientist did not uncover the secret. His means and energy were exhausted, while official Russian science declared the iron of Kursk to be a fantasy.

The Civil War had not yet terminated when Lenin sent the Soviet scientists Goubkin, Lazarev, and Arkhangelsky to Kursk. At that time the military front crossed the Kursk steppes. The field of scientific work was the field of battle. Geological investigation started under fire. In 1922 iron ore was discovered at a depth of 160 metres, and in such quantities that the world's resources of iron may be said to have doubled.

The total potential yield of this stratum has been calculated at 200 milliard tons of iron ore and quartzites containing, on the average, 30 to 40 per cent of iron. In some regions the ores are much richer—as much as 65 per cent. The Kursk magnetic anomaly, which possesses as much iron as all the iron-ore regions in the world taken together, will become the most important basis of the metallurgical industry of the U.S.S.R.

In 1928 in the southern foot-hills of the Urals in the eastern part of the Orenburg Region—the Khalilov stratum of iron ores was discovered near the town of Orsk. The discovery is remarkable for the fact that the ore contains chromium and nickel. Its resources are estimated at 400 million tons.

The metallurgical industry of Western Siberia has grown up on the basis of the rich coke-forming coals of Kuznetzk. But the ore is brought here 2,000 kilometres from the Urals. Geologists were therefore faced with the task of easing the geographical disunion between the coal and the ore. The needs of industry stimulated them to search for more convenient sources, with excellent results. New beds of iron ore have been found in Western Siberia, as well as in mountainous Shoria, a region adjacent to the metallurgical works, of which one is working and the other is in course of construction. Their needs will be partly met by local ore, though the combination of Kuznetzk coal with Ural ore continues to be of great importance.

In the Kola fiord—the most northerly boundary of the European part of the U.S.S.R.—ships cannot sail according to the compass: it points to the coast, and not to the pole. Before the Revolution officials went no further than declaring the presence here of 2 million tons of ferrous quartzites.

During the First Five Year Plan the estimate of investigated resources of iron ore in the Kola peninsula increased from 2 to over 400 million tons. The ore lies on the coast of the Kola fiord and near the Lake of Imandra. Leningrad, the foremost centre of Soviet machine-building, which at present imports metal from the Ukraine and the Urals—now has the means for the development of its own metallurgical industry.

Science in old Russia considered the eastern part of the country poor in iron; but the results of prospecting within the last few years have refuted this opinion.

The increase of available resources of iron ore in the U.S.S.R. is not only a result of new discoveries. Old, long-known, and exploited mines have been estimated anew. For instance, the resources of iron ore in the Urals, rich as they are—the Magnet mountain alone contains about 500 million tons of ore—are now known to be several times greater than before.

The principal industrial iron-ore region in Russia—Krivoi Rog in the Ukraine—presents an entirely new aspect. Its rich ores are now known to be more than five times its estimated former yield. The resources of its less rich ores —the ferriferous quartzites in Krivoi Rog—amount to the huge total of 21 billion tons. And this is not all. It was found that Krivoi Rog was only part of a great iron-ore field stretching eastwards to the Don coal-field, and promising considerable increase to the total resources of iron.

The investigated resources of manganese in the U.S.S.R. have increased fourfold, from 168 to 665 million tons. The knowledge of its distribution has been changed out of recognition.

The creation of a metallurgical centre in the new eastern regions was accompanied by the discovery of new strata of manganese ore in the east in Bashkiria, Kazakstan, and Western Siberia.

The investigated copper resources in the U.S.S.R. have increased since 1913 from 628 to about 17,000.

In 1928 the geologist Roussakov discovered the Kounrad copper-bed on the northern shore of the Lake of Balkhash in Kazakstan, in the clay and stone semi-desert; this is one of the largest copper-beds, and its resources exceed those of all the beds known to old Russia. Exploration has increased the estimate of the resources of Kounrad to 2 million tons of copper.

Equally rich beds of copper ores have been discovered and investigated in Jezkasgan and Boshche-Koul (Kazakstan), and in Almalik (Central Asia). The copper resources of the Urals and of Transcaucasia have also been explored and found to be larger than was thought.

The known lead and zinc resources have been extended eightfold. The estimated resources of the old regions— North Caucasus, Altai, and others—have increased. Hitherto little-known regions—Kara-Mazar in Central Asia, Tourlan in Kazakstan, and others—have become prominent. Zinc and lead have been found in the Donetz coal-field.

Newly investigated beds of bauxite and nickel already serve as bases of the recently created aluminium and nickel industries.

Immense strata of apatite and nepheline have been discovered in the Khibin mountain in the Kola Peninsula: a place which lies far to the north of the Arctic Circle and used to be marked by a 'white space' on the old Russian maps.

About 2 milliard tons of all the resources of apatite lie

in the Khibin mountains: these contain the richest apatite strata in the world. Apatite contains as much as 40 per cent phosphates. It is used for the manufacture of super-phosphates, but it has more than twenty other uses besides.

Nepheline, the second constituent of the Khibin ores, has also about twenty different uses, of which the most important are the manufacture of aluminium, glass, fertilizers, and tannin. The resources of nepheline are practically inexhaustible. In addition to apatite and nepheline, innumerable kinds of rare minerals have been found in the Khibin mountains, forty of which are already being used in industry.

The credit of the discoveries of all these Khibin riches is due to the scientific expeditions which have been working under the direction of Professor Fersman the Academician—a great geo-chemist who combines erudition with energy. Fersman travels untiringly over the huge Soviet area—from the Kola Peninsula to the Kara-Kum desert, from the Urals to Baikal, and the catalogue of his journeys is a catalogue of valuable geological discoveries.

Near the town of Solikamsk in the Northern Urals 16 milliard tons of potassium salts have been discovered—a quantity which is several times greater than the total amount of all the known world resources of this very rare mineral. Rich beds of potassium salts have been investigated in Central Asia.

New and rich gold deposits have been discovered in Siberia, Kazakstan, and other regions.

Only the largest new mineral regions have been enumerated. Mention might have been made of new regions of antimony, mercury, tin, vanadium, wolfram, molybdenum, sulphur, and radium. . . .

But by no means have all the mineral resources of the country been investigated, although prospecting is proceeding at a high rate. Only a small proportion of the territory of the U.S.S.R. has been thoroughly investigated. By the beginning of the First Five Year Plan only 11·5 per cent of the territory of the country had been explored. By the beginning of the Second Five Year Plan this figure had been increased to 25 per cent, i.e. within the four years of the

Plan more had been accomplished in cartographic survey than during the whole preceding period.

Geological work in the U.S.S.R. is conducted by a large State economic organization, 'The Chief Geologo-Hydro-Geodesic Administration', which covers a whole network of geological investigation institutions and directs an immense scientific productive process. In 1933 there were working in the C.G.H.G.A. nearly 6,000 engineers and technicians and 100,000 workers. Besides the C.G.H.G.A. a large number of State economic organs—e.g. the coal-mining industry, the oil industry, etc.—are prospecting. Thousands of engineers, technicians, and workers are employed in this work.

All the prospecting organizations are working in accordance with a plan agreed upon beforehand and strictly subordinated to the tasks of economic practice.

Geophysical methods of exploration, almost unknown in old Russia, have been introduced into geological work—magnetometry, gravimetry, seismometry, radiometry. Not only is the geological stratification of the mineral studied, but its technological properties as well. Far-reaching geochemical ideas are being worked out which establish the laws of distribution of minerals. Many valuable discoveries were foreshadowed theoretically: for example, Pamir tin, the non-ferrous metals of the Northern Urals, and others.

The Academy of Sciences, the highest scientific institution in the U.S.S.R., and one of the most important scientific institutions in the whole world, is conducting investigation work on a tremendous scale.

In many places—in the Urals, in Tajikistan, in the Far East—branches of the Academy of Sciences have been formed. Every year the Academy sends expeditions all over the country. The total number of these expeditions during the seventeen years following the Revolution exceeds one thousand.

This expeditionary work of the Academy of Sciences is directed by one of its special organs, 'The Council for the Study of Natural Resources'.

At the head of the 'Council for the Study of Natural

Resources' and of the 'Chief Geologo-Hydro-Geodesic Administration' stands Goubkin, a former school teacher whose scientific work has made him world-famous. He is one of the highest authorities on the minerals of the earth, and his name is bound up with the enriching of the land with a number of discoveries of new and vast strata of petroleum, iron ores, and so on.

The expeditionary work of the Academy of Sciences, carried on according to plan and subjected to the needs of socialist construction, is extremely wide, comprising the study of the 'white spaces', geological work, the investigation of seas, rivers, soils, etc. The expeditionary activities of the Academy are bound up with the raising of the standard of culture of the backward peoples of the U.S.S.R., with the struggle for the settlement of nomads, with medical work in remote regions, and so on. There is scarcely a branch of economy and culture in which the expeditionary work of the Academy of Sciences is not reflected.

The country is indebted to the Academy for very valuable discoveries.

Central Asia, considered a poor region in useful minerals, has been transformed by the expeditions of the Academy of Sciences into an extremely wealthy region of non-ferrous metals and chemical raw material. The iodine, bromine, and salt industry of the Crimea is based entirely on the discoveries of the Academy of Sciences. The industrial utilization of sapropelites, a source of power and of raw materials for chemical industry new to the country, in the Leningrad and Ivanov regions and in White Russia is linked up with the activities of the Academy of Sciences. The extremely valuable minerals of the Kola Peninsula, the sulphates of the Kouloundin lakes in Siberia, the salt resources of the new lakes in the lower Volga—all these and a great deal more became known and were investigated as a result of the expeditions of the Academy of Sciences. During the summer of 1934 the expeditions of the Academy explored new beds of uranium ores in the Pamirs and in the Kola Peninsula, manganese in the Kuznetzk region and in Western Siberia, siderite in the Urals, mica in Kamchatka.

The united forces of the scientific and economic institutions of the U.S.S.R. have led to the discovery of a new underground world in the country. The U.S.S.R. has already taken first place among all countries as regards resources of iron, manganese, gold, petroleum, phosphorus, potassium, and peat; and second place as regards coal (total amount of calories).

THE U.S.S.R. RESERVES OF POWER AND MINERALS AS COMPARED WITH WORLD RESERVES

Iron with Quartz	52·0	per cent
Oil	32·1	,,
Coal	15·0	,,
Copper	14·4	,,
Zinc	14·8	,,
Manganese	73·4	,,
Potassium salts	83·0	,,
Phosphorites and Apatite	62·0	,,
Peat	72·7	,,
Lead	8·7	,,
Nickel	9·0	,,
Hydro Resources	35·7	,,

Stalin, speaking in 1931 at a conference of economists, was fully justified in saying: 'As far as natural resources are concerned we are completely provided for.'

Chapter 4

THE NEW DISTRIBUTION OF INDUSTRY

I. THE PRINCIPLES OF THE CHANGES

INDUSTRY in Tsarist Russia was unevenly distributed over the country; this was its distinguishing feature. Factories and works were massed together at one end and at the other end there were none at all.

Fully half the output of Russian industry was concentrated in the area of the present Moscow, Leningrad, Ivanov Region, and western part of the Gorky Area.[1] The overwhelming portion of the metal and chemical industries and the whole of the textile industry were concentrated in this centre.

But this is by no means the natural physical centre. It is an edge of the country, an out-of-the-way district, merely the beginning of the land; a plain worn down by an ancient glacier, the upper course of the Russian rivers, its soil is clayey; there is nothing remarkable about it except that it is the geographical meeting-place of navigable rivers which was utilized by trade.

But on the economic map of Tsarist Russia this region appears as an island in the ocean, a peak on a plain, a centre indeed. The empire was centred here. It was here that industrial capital originated and developed. From here radiated the tentacles of Tsarist conquest, holding the huge land of agriculture and raw material subject to the industrial centre.

Almost one-third of the industrial output originated in the bases of this centre area—the Ukraine and the Urals. The Ukraine was a source of coal and metal for the centre, without having any developed metal industry of its own. The backward Ural region furnished the centre with metal, but itself scarcely worked up any metals.

The remainder was spread over the rest of the country.

[1] Here, as everywhere in the following pages, the figures do not take into account those territories of Tsarist Russia which do not enter the U.S.S.R.

The map of most of the regions of Siberia, the North, and Central Asia was a blank sheet traversed by mountain chains and river-beds.

The path of Russia's development was obstructed by contradictions. Feudal survivals hampered the growth of monopolist capital. The limited home market was soon satiated and the manufacturer demanded an outlet for his goods. If not within, then without—and Tsarist Russia made a rush for the untouched expanses of Asia. The centre started the colonization of the outlying districts and the extension of its markets. It was thus that the explosion of the contradictions which were suffocating old Russia was postponed.

The manufacturer of the centre widened the circle of his customers—he dressed the inhabitant of Asia in Moscow cotton. The sale of manufactured articles pursued a cruel but victorious course. There was little resistance and the handicraft industry of the east was ruined. A simple arithmetic decided its fate. Aniline dyes ate away the fine art of carpet-making; the mechanical weaving-loom spelt the death-sentence of the hand-frames. Russian manufactured goods were introduced into the patriarchal life of the national borderlands, but they included neither reapers nor automatic hunting guns. The goods were of a primitive kind: coarse teacups and flowered cottons.

The competition of manufactured goods coming from the centre was supported by administrative persecution. The centre thrust on to the borderlands a compulsory specialization in raw materials. Manufacture in the outlying regions was not developed. Trade with 'non-Russians' enriched the metropolis, which tried to secure for itself a monopoly of the trade. Russian Asia remained on the whole a continent without factories. In Central Asia cotton-purifying works did exist, but only in order to increase the net weight of the cotton and to facilitate its export to the centre. The only textile mill in the Russian outlying districts was situated in Transcaucasia (Baku), but it worked solely for the Persian market, whilst Transcaucasia itself, which produced its own cotton, was supplied with fabrics by the centre.

Centres of extractive industry on the map of the Border-
land were few and far between; there were the oil industry
in Transcaucasia, lead-mines in the Altai mountains, the
gold-fields in Siberia. These constituted a strange exception,
rare outposts in a remote and uncivilized land. Central Asia
provided over 2 per cent of the output of Russian industry,
Western Siberia and Kazakstan, 0·5 per cent—and this from
a third of Asia—the largest continent in the world! How
could this be called an outlying district when it was thirty
times as large as the central area? But it was indeed an
outlying district: not outlying on the physical, but on the
economic and social map of pre-Revolution Russia. It was
not an outlying district as far as territory was concerned,
but a pool of historical stagnation.

The centre denoted factories, towns, and money. It was
an industrial patch which grew into a metropolis.

In the outlying districts raw materials, wide spaces,
poverty; these were colonies which differed from other
colonies in the world only by the fact that they were physi-
cally linked to the centre.

The economic features of the country were distorted.
Russia was a preposterous mixture of social orders—from
monopolist capital in Baku, for instance, to nomad Turkic
huts outside the town. The distribution of industry was
characterized by an inequality which can be explained but
not justified.

The distribution of industry did not correspond to the
distribution of its raw materials. The economic map did
not tally with the map of natural resources. There were no
coal strata or oil cupolas or veins of ore at the base of the
industry concentrated in the centre. Under Leningrad there
was a swamp; under Moscow there was clay. True, there
was a natural base near at hand: combustible shale in the
Leningrad Region and ores and brown coal in the Moscow
Region. These resources lay within the limits of the centre,
but the centre cared nothing at all for them: it was not they
that fed industry. The fuel which the centre burned was
not its own. It was obtained in the outlying districts and
was brought from afar: the coal from Ukraine, the oil from

the Transcaucasus, the timber from the north. Raw
materials, except flax, also came from other parts. They
were brought from the outlying districts (unless bought
abroad): cast iron from the Ukraine, cotton from Central
Asia, wool from Kirghizia.

The wealthy manufacturer added new industries to old,
though there might be no connexion between them. In some
flax-and-hemp-producing Rzhev on the upper Volga there
would suddenly spring up a silk-spinning works, 4,000 kilometres away from the silkworms. A copper-working factory
(the Kolchouginsky) grew up in the Ivanov Region, having
no copper ores and importing copper from the distant
Urals.

Manufacture was separated from the raw material. Cheap
raw material was brought from the outlying district to the
centre, where it was worked up into finished articles and
then taken back to the outlying districts. Thus the centre
consolidated its dominion. Social labour was wasted, but
the colony bore the expense. The Uzbek, the producer of
cotton, was not paid a fair price and he also paid exorbitant
sums for the finished fabric. And meanwhile the centre did
not cease to grow.

But even within the centre industry was distributed
unevenly and irrationally. The factories, repeating each
other, clung close to the capital and the large towns, making
them even larger. Thus it was with Leningrad (formerly
St. Petersburg) and Moscow. The high price of land in the
town forced industry to the barriers; separated industries
which were technologically connected; placed a stifling ring
of factories round the town.

The hands of the ruined handicraftsmen were cheaper than
electricity. Capital penetrated into the village to the handicraft centres, and scattered hundreds of toy village factories
over the Moscow and Ivanov Regions. Feudal survivals
hampered the relinquishment of the land by the peasant,
and if the peasant did not go to the factory, the factory
went to the peasant.

The Leningrad Region owed its 'central position' to
Leningrad alone—a port connecting Russia with the West

—the only industrial town amidst scattered villages and swamps.   In Leningrad were concentrated 100 per cent of the electro-technical industry of the Leningrad Region, 100 per cent of the tobacco industry, 99 per cent of the printing trade, 99 per cent of the boot and shoe industry, 99 per cent of the sewing industry, 90 per cent of the food industry, 90 per cent of the textile industry.

But in that very industrial centre, within a stone's throw of the towns, patriarchy and savagery still prevailed.

The dependence of Russia on foreign capital contributed to the circumstance that every third manufacturing enterprise was situated on the western frontier, including Poland, and the ports of the Baltic States, which are not now part of the U.S.S.R.

The natural resources of the outlying districts were exploited irrationally and greedily.   They were plundered by imperialists who chose the best pieces of land and exploited them.   Oil was pumped blindly out of the upper layers and richest wells.   Only ores that were easily accessible were extracted.   The best kinds of trees in the forests were sought out and felled.

Water flooded the oil strata, mines were exhausted and abandoned, forests along the rivers and railways were destroyed.   And around lay regions unknown to anybody, undiscovered lands, unrevealed treasures.

Extractive industrial enterprises in the outlying districts were isolated outposts in surroundings which were entirely indifferent to them.   Baku, the town of petroleum, of large-scale monopolist capital, was more closely connected with Moscow and London than with nomad Azerbaijan, which lay around.   With the exception of a certain amount of unskilled labour everything was brought to Baku—the money, pipes, and lime.   All the oil extracted was carried away from Baku.

The distant, multi-national outlying districts of old Russia!   Thousands of miles of steppe, thousands of miles of forest, thousands of miles of mountains.   A chain of military fortifications, sparsely scattered trading centres in a conquered country of nomad tents, forest huts, mountain mud-huts. Away off from the industrial centre, from ocean to ocean there extended an illiterate continent, the land of 'foreigners' and beggars, of hunters and shepherds, who, it is true, no longer lived in the Stone Age, but were still shackled by hunger, oppression, and the most primitive patriarchal and feudal organization of life. In the Yakut nomad settlements a family consumed on the average 160 kilogrammes of pine and larch sap-wood a year. Tribes died out to the sounds of the priest's timbrel and the policeman's cries.

'To the north of Vologda, to the south-east of Rostov-on-Don and of Saratov, to the south of Orenburg and of Omsk, and to the north of Tomsk extend huge, boundless expanses which could contain a large number of great cultured States. And on all these expanses a patriarchal régime of semi-savagery and real savagery prevails. And what of all the outlying peasant regions in the rest of Russia, where hundreds of miles of country roads, or rather roadless country, separate the village from the railway, from material connexion with culture, with capitalism, with large-scale industry, with the large towns? Does not the same patriarchal régime of sloth and semi-savagery predominate in all these places?'

Thus wrote Lenin.[1]

In comparison with the great industrial countries, the industries of Tsarist Russia were feebly developed and had a low productivity of labour. Heavy industry existed, but light industry—the cotton industry in particular—predominated in the industrial structure. Foreign capital played a highly important role in it.

Nevertheless the absolute magnitude of Russian industry was considerable. The concentration of production and capital attained a high level in Tsarist Russia. The ranks of the industrial proletariat in the country were filling up.

At the end of the period of restoration the Communist Party proclaimed the policy of socialist industrialization. The U.S.S.R. fought for economic independence.

[1] Lenin: *The Food-Tax* (1921).

As a result of the active pursuance of the policy of industrialization under Stalin's leadership, the U.S.S.R., from being an agricultural country, has become an industrial and economically independent country. In order to reach this goal the Communist Party had to overcome great difficulties, not the least of which was the introduction into the country of forms of technique which she had never known before, the mastery of new industries, the creation, during the process of development, of native skilled industrial workers, resistance on the part of class enemies, and so on.

The industry of the U.S.S.R., which belongs to the socialist State, works according to plan, and knows nothing of crises. It has developed rapidly and powerfully, and has become a large-scale and technically advanced industry.

The increase in industrial output for 1937 alone—the last year of the Second Five Year Plan—will exceed the total annual output of industry in Tsarist Russia.

With regard to industrial output in 1928, i.e. at the beginning of the First Five Year Plan, the U.S.S.R. occupied the fifth place in the world. By the end of the First Five Year Plan it took third place, and by the end of the Second Five Year Plan it is due to assume second place (on the 1929 figures of production in other countries). The reconstruction of the national economy will have been completed and new technique mastered.

TOTAL OUTPUT OF FACTORY INDUSTRY
AT 1926–7 PRICES[1]
(in billions of roubles)

1913	10·3
1920	1·4
1928	15·8
1932	36·8
1934	47·6
1937	83·6

Lenin said that old Russia was 'four times worse than England, five times worse than Germany, ten times worse

[1] Excluding timber and fishing. Census industry.

4

than America'. But now the face of the country has changed.
By the end of the Second Five Year Plan the U.S.S.R. will
possess the most powerful industrial apparatus in Europe.

THE SHARE OF LARGE-SCALE INDUSTRY
IN THE TOTAL OUTPUT OF INDUSTRY
AND AGRICULTURE

1913	.	.	.	. 40·6 per cent
1920	.	.	.	. 54·5 ,,
1932	.	.	.	. 70·7 ,,
1934	.	.	.	. 73·1 ,,

At the same time as old enterprises were being reconstructed, a gigantic construction of new enterprises was in
progress in the U.S.S.R. The choice of each site of construction was made on a general State plan. At the XVIth
Congress of the Communist Party (1930) Stalin placed the
problem of the rational geographical distribution of industry
foremost amongst the economic problems under considera-
tion. Together with changes in industrial methods came
changes in the distribution of industry itself. The problem
stated by Lenin was being solved to create

'a rational distribution of industry in Russia from the
point of view of proximity to raw material and the
minimum waste of labour in the graduated process from
the working-up of raw materials to all the following stages
of manufacturing the unfinished goods and even to the
production of the finished article'.

A rational 'lay-out' of industry from the point of view of
the national economy as a whole was thus created. New
works were so placed that the territorial separation between
the raw material and its utilization in manufacture was
minimized. The path taken by the product was shortened
and social labour was economized; its intensivity grew.
Industry penetrated for the first time into backward regions
whose natural wealth was explored anew—indeed, newly
discovered.

Planned socialist production and distribution excluded competition from the centre. In the place of the old prohibitive laws there grew up the policy of industrial and cultural development of the national outlying districts.

All the peoples inhabiting the U.S.S.R. have equal rights. Equality *de jure* of all the nationalities was established in the very first days of the October Revolution. But in order to destroy inequality *de facto* it is necessary to destroy the economic backwardness of the population of the former colonies of Russia.

'In addition to the schools and language' (said Stalin at the XIIth Congress of the Communist Party in 1923) 'the Russian proletariat must do everything to ensure that centres of industry are set up in the outlying districts in the culturally backward republics—which are backward not because of any fault of their own, but because they were formerly looked upon as sources of raw material. This task must be achieved.'

Therefore the national regions—Central Asia, Transcaucasia, and others—are being industrialized at a rapid rate. Large-scale enterprises with model technical equipment, revolutionizing the patriarchal system, are built there. Hunters and shepherds are becoming industrial workers. The map bears witness to this fact. (*See Map No. 12, pp. 52-3.*)

Bashkirians are building a motor-works. Uzbek women have cast aside the veils from their faces, and are working in new textile combines. Turkmens are becoming chemical workers. Kirghizians are producing their own cloth and sugar. From the nomad saddle to the complex machine, from the tambourine of the priest to polytechnic education.

New vistas have been opened up with the development of the extractive industry in the outlying districts, where formerly the raw material was taken to the centre or exported abroad—now the outlying districts themselves demand coal, oil, manganese, and metal ores.

Mining enterprises are no longer isolated spots in alien surroundings. They combine with the other economic

1928

Nukha

Stepanokert

R. Koro

Banja

R. Terter

Lake Sevan

N

Bori

Tiflis

Altaverdy

Erivan

Leninakan

Borzhom

Chiaturi

Hutais

Legend:

Ferrous metal-lurgical plant

Extraction of minerals

Electric power stations

Film studios

Margarine works

Timber combines

Cotton seed oil works

Woollen Industry

Copper plant

Ferro-manganese plant

Cotton mill

Aluminium works (experimental)

Meat combinat

Carbide factory

Tobacco factories

Tanneries

Silk Industry

Clothing factory

(continued below)

52

1935

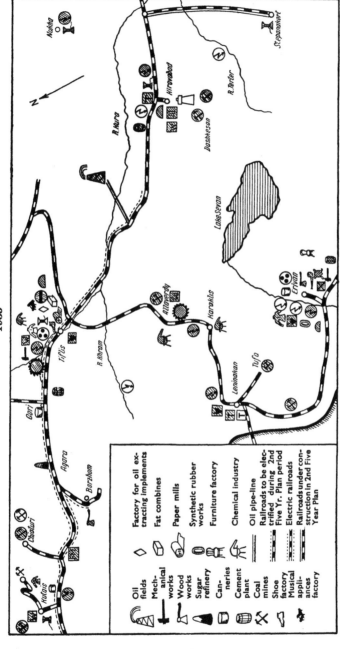

Legend (key):

	Oil fields
	Mechanical works
	Wood works
	Sugar refinery
	Canneries
	Cement plant
	Coal mines
	Shoe factory
	Musical appliances factory
	Factory for oil extracting implements
	Fat combines
	Paper mills
	Synthetic rubber works
	Furniture factory
	Chemical industry
	Oil pipe-line
	Railroads to be electrified during 2nd Five Yr. Plan period
	Electric railroads
	Railroads under construction in 2nd Five Year Plan

Place names: Nukha, Kirovabad, R. Kura, Dashkesan, R. Terter, Stepanakert, Lake Sevan, Borzhom, Agara, Gori, R. Khram, Tiflis, Karaklis, Alaverdy, Leninakan, Tufa, Erivan

12. INDUSTRIALIZATION IN TRANSCAUCASUS (CENTRAL PART) IN 1928 AND 1935

Large enterprises indicated. Shaded figures functioning enterprises. Unshaded figures enterprises under construction in Second Five Year Plan.

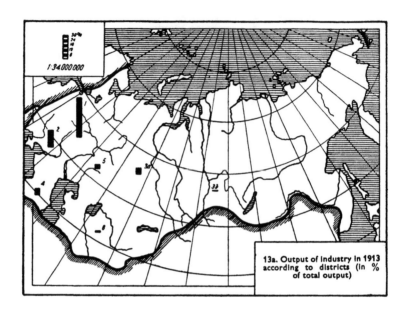

13a. Output of industry in 1913 according to districts (in % of total output)

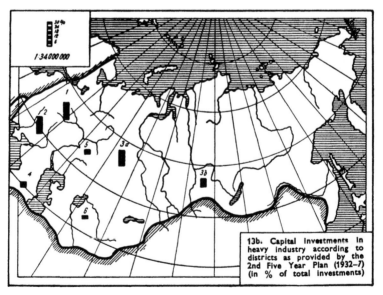

13b. Capital investments in heavy industry according to districts as provided by the 2nd Five Year Plan (1932–7) (in % of total investments)

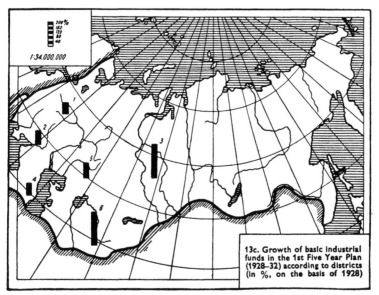

13c. Growth of basic industrial funds in the 1st Five Year Plan (1928–32) according to districts (in %, on the basis of 1928)

13abc. THE TENDENCY TOWARDS MORE EVEN DISTRIBUTION OF INDUSTRY (*see table on p. 57*)

undertakings of the region in which they are situated and become part of it.

The industrial centre is no longer an island on the map of the U.S.S.R. And it is not surrounded by a desert. It is true that it is still larger than the newly created industrial regions, and it is continuing to grow; but they are growing faster than the centre. During the First Five Year Plan the industrial funds of the centre increased by 87 per cent, while those of Central Asia increased by 277 per cent, of West Siberia and Kazakstan by 283 per cent. The difference in the rate of growth destroys the difference of levels.

Industry is moving to the east. There, amidst extraordinarily difficult conditions due to remoteness and general lack of development, new powerful industrial combines are coming into being. The most important of them is the Ural-Kuznetzk Combine, based on the combination of the iron ore of the Urals and the coal of the Kuznetzk coal-field in Siberia. The Soviet Far East is rapidly becoming industrialized. During the Second Five Year Plan nearly half of

all the capital investments directed towards new construction
in heavy industry will be allocated to the eastern regions—
the agricultural and raw-material colonies of yesterday. In
the U.S.S.R. there are no longer any purely agricultural
regions. The formerly backward village is rising to the level
of the advanced city. The distribution of industry is being
smoothed out. (*See Map No. 13.*)

It is not only the economic aspect of the centre which
has changed—from a textile region to a machine-building,
electro-technical, and chemical region. Its geography has
changed as well. An area which formerly subsisted entirely
on what was brought to it began to find its own fuel and
raw material. Coal from the Moscow coal-field is now burning together with the Ukraine coal in the furnaces of Moscow.
The swamps of the centre produce peat; the rivers provide
hydro-electric power. Metallurgy in the centre is becoming
a solid and powerful industry. The outline of the natural
map is revealing itself on the economic map of the centre.
New minerals are brought to light in mines, pits, and quarries.

The transformation of the industrial geography of the
centre was not a simple matter. The region had to be pros-
pected for minerals. In order not to burn imported oil in
the furnaces, it was necessary to find a method of burning
the local low-calorific coal. In order to do without expensive
and distant Ukrainian coke, the centre is learning to use
peat for the smelting of ores.

The senseless accumulation of works and factories ceased
after the Revolution. The absence of private ownership of
land does not hinder the choice of rational sites. New
factories do not interfere with each other. They are laid
out according to a plan which combines calculation with
hygiene.

In the large towns—in Moscow and Leningrad—new
factories have not been built since 1932. They move
to the 'provinces', i.e. the rural areas, so as to raise the
industrial and cultural level of the latter. For example, the
First Five Year Plan gave birth to a new group of industries
outside the city boundaries of Leningrad. The Volkhov and
Svir electric power stations, the Siass cellulose and paper

combine, the Zvanka aluminium combine and many others have been constructed in the Leningrad Region, which was formerly mainly an agricultural district. Factories are no longer clinging to the frontiers. Their technical level is not measured by their closeness to the frontier as before.

CHANGES IN INDUSTRIAL CONCENTRATION TENDING TOWARDS A MORE EQUALIZED TERRITORIAL DISTRIBUTION

Regions	Basic Industrial Funds in per cents of total		The Growth of the Basic Industrial Funds during the First Five Year Plan (1928–32) in per cents, Based on 1928 Figures	Capital Investments in Heavy Industry according to Second Five Year Plan (1932–7) in per cents of Total
	1928	1932		
1. Central Region . . .	47·5	41·2	86·5	16·7
2. Ukrainian S.S.R. . .	22·0	21·8	113·3	16·4
3. Regions included in the Ural-Kuznetzk Combine —incl.	6·1	10·9	283·3	22·7
(a) Ural Region . .	—	—	—	14·8
(b) West Siberian Region and Kazakstan .	—	—	—	8·0
4. Transcaucasian S.F.S.R. .	6·4	6·1	105·6	4·5
5. The Volga Region . .	4·6	4·7	123·8	3·8
6. Central Asia . . .	0·9	1·6	277·2	2·7
Other Regions . . .	12·5	13·7	137·4	10·4
U.S.S.R. . .	100·0	100·0	125·2	100·0

The role of the centre in the economic development of the country and in the re-making of its geography is still of the utmost importance. New centres of industrialization in the eastern and other backward regions are being created on the basis of the development of the old industrial centre. The development of light industry in Transcaucasia began by the centre taking one of its textile mills to pieces and transplanting it in the region which in Tsarist Russia had been a mere colony. Industrial problems of the outlying districts are studied in the scientific institutes of the centre. The centre sends complex machines to the outlying districts. Engineers who have studied in the centre are sent to work

THE PLACE OF THE U.S.S.R. AMONGST THE INDUSTRIAL POWERS OF THE WORLD[1]

Industries	1913	1928	1932[2]	1937[2]	
	In the World	In the World	In the World	In the World	In Europe
Total industrial production	—	5	3	3	1
Electrical power . .	15	10	7	2	1
Coal	6	6	4	4	3
Peat	—	—	1	1	1
Petroleum	2	3	2	2	1
Pig iron	5	6	5	2	1
Steel	5	5	5	2	1
General Engineering . .	4	4	2	2	1
Agricultural Engineering .	—	4	2	2	1
Tractors	—	4	2	2	1
Combines	—	—	2	2	1
Motor-cars	—	12	7	5	3
Lorries	—	11	6	2	1
Copper	7	9	9	3	1
Aluminium	—	—	11	2	1
Cement	—	8	7	2	1
Superphosphate . . .	—	18	9	2	1
Footwear	—	5	3	2	1
Soap	6	5	5	2	1

in the new factories of the outlying districts. The centre, with its science and technique, its specialists and experience, is helping the former colonies of Tsarist Russia to grow quicker than it is growing itself.

The formation of the new geography of the U.S.S.R. differs from the movement of industry in many other

[1] The capitalist world, according to *Annuaire Statistique de la Société des Nations*, 1932.
[2] 1932 and 1937 according to production of capitalist countries for 1929.

countries by the fact, amongst others, that while new regions in the U.S.S.R. grow up the old ones do not fall into decay, but continue to grow, though at a slower rate.

The changes in the distribution of industry bring in their train changes in other branches of economic life. A country is in course of creation with an even and harmonious development, ridding itself of the agelong disparity between town and village, and capable of defending its frontiers.

II. FUEL

The coal industry of Tsarist Russia was practically confined to the Donetz coal-field (in the Ukraine), which was large but not mechanized. The windlasses of the Donetz pits bore nearly the whole of old Russia's requirements in coal. The right bank of the North Donetz—a small tributary of the Don—provided 87 per cent of the total output of coal in the country, although it possesses only 55 per cent of its coal resources. There was thus the constant risk of dependence on this one source.

The coal-field of the centre—the Moscow coal-field—could not develop because of the competitive pressure of Donetz coal supported by the low railway charges granted to Donetz coal. The coal-fields of the east were dead because of the absence of any industry in the east. For the most part they were simply unknown. Only here and there, along the railway tracks, coal was extracted for feeding locomotive engines.

In the monopolistic Donetz basin itself, the coal-mining methods were irrational, conflicting with the natural formation of the coal basin. The Donetz basin is made up of a complex of strata with different kinds of coal, including some that are suitable for use in blast-furnaces, and others that are suitable for fuelling.

But no one thought of the morrow. Huge quantities of coal which might have been turned into good coke were mined and consumed in furnaces only because it was easier to extract them and more advantageous to sell them.

The U.S.S.R. have reconstructed the coal industry and trebled the total output.

COAL PRODUCTION
(millions of tons)

1913	29·1
1920	8·6
1927–8	35·5
1932	64·4
1934	93·5
1937	152·5

With the creation of new industries in the east the distribution of coal-requirements has changed: the east must have its own fuel. The Donetz basin has lost its monopoly. The map shows the rise of new coal centres. Coal-mining moved to the east.

The output of the Kuznetzk coal-field, whose resources are nearly six times greater than those of the Donbas, was insignificant before the Revolution—774,000 tons, about 26 per cent of the coal output in Russia. All of it went into the tenders of the Siberian Railway. Few knew that in the distant foot-hills of the Altai mountains in Siberia was hidden one of the richest coal-fields in the world—32 per cent of the coal resources of Russia.

Soviet Kuzbas developed rapidly. Its output in 1934 of 11,584,000 tons was over 12 per cent of the total output of coal in the country. In 1937 this percentage will be raised to over 13. By the end of the Second Five Year Plan the output of the Kuzbas coal-field will nearly equal that of pre-war Donbas—the leviathan of the coal industry of old Russia. 'Kuzbas must be made a second Donbas'—this is the task set by Stalin before the country.

Fuel. Coke. Electric current. Oil from coal. Chains of new pits.

The boundary of the distribution of the cheap first-class Kuznetzk coal has extended to the Volga. In the depths of Siberia the Kuzbas has rallied round itself a gigantic group of new industries, which sprang up in the short space of five years: ferrous and non-ferrous metallurgical centres, machine-building works, chemical works, electric power stations. Half a million persons inhabit the new towns of the Kuzbas.

The vast resources of coal of the Karaganda in Kazakstan were hidden by the desert steppe. Karaganda, which lies comparatively near the iron ores of the southern Urals and the copper ores of the Kounrad (on the Lake Balkhash) and possesses good coke-forming coal, is planned to become the third coal centre, after the Donetz and the Kuzbas coal basins of the country. So far, its output is not large—in 1934 it was 1,830,000 tons—but Karaganda is still in process of construction. Shafts are being sunk. During the Second Five Year Plan the output of coal in Karaganda will be made to increase tenfold.

In the Urals the old Kizel coal-field has been further developed, and new areas have opened up, of which the most important is the Chelyabinsk brown-coal district.

New coal regions have been developed in Central Asia, the Transcaucasus; in Siberia, in the Far East. During the Second Five Year Plan a metallurgical works will be constructed on the newly investigated coal of the Bourein coal-field in the Far Eastern Area. Not only will Bourein coal satisfy the requirements of the Soviet Far East: to a large extent it can in the future be exported to the Pacific Ocean basin. Far Yakutia is extracting coal. The foundations of the first mines have been laid beyond the Arctic Circle on the tributaries of the Pechora, which falls into the Arctic Ocean. Pechor coal will be used by the industry and the fleet of the North.

Each new industrial region of the U.S.S.R. is creating its own power spring-board.

The centre, which used to burn almost exclusively high-calorific fuel brought from great distances (Moscow-Caucasian oil and Donetz coal; Leningrad-Caucasian oil and imported coal), is now developing its own fuel bases.

In 1913 the Moscow brown-coal district yielded an output of only 300,000 tons—1 per cent of the total output of

coal in the country. Now new methods have been learnt of
burning Moscow coal (coal-dust burning), which facilitate
the partial substitution of it in Moscow for imported Donetz
coal. In 1934 the output of coal in the Moscow coal-field
had increased to 4,906,000 tons, i.e. over 5 per cent of the
coal output of the U.S.S.R. Within the period of the
Second Five Year Plan the output of the Moscow coal-field
is due to increase three and a half times. In 1932 Moscow
coal had already attained a proportion of 16·8 per cent in the
fuel balance of the Moscow Region. Electric power stations
and a large chemical works, Stalinogorsky (formerly Bobriky),
have been constructed in the region of the coal-field.

The extraction of brown coal in the Borovich district near
Leningrad and on the right bank of the Dnieper in the
Ukraine has begun.

But what has happened to the Donetz basin? It has
simultaneously suffered a decline and a growth. It has
grown, if one expresses this growth in tons—it has grown
to more than double its output (in 1913, 25·3 million tons;
in 1934, 60·0 million tons). It has fallen, if one expresses
the dynamics of its relative weight as a percentage. In
growth it has been outstripped by new districts and the
output of the Donbas relatively to the total output of coal
in the country has fallen from 87 per cent in 1913 to 64
per cent in 1934. The Donbas still remains the most
important coal district in the country—but it is no longer
the only important one.

The method of coal-mining in the Donetz basin is changing. Both mining and the distribution of the coal are
planned. Coal that is not used for turning into coke is set
aside for burning in furnaces; and shaft-sinking is moving
towards the eastern regions of the Donbas, where anthracite
—'fuel' coal—is found.

In the oil industry in Tsarist Russia geographical narrow-
ness was even more pronounced than in the coal industry.

The predominance of the Caucasus was undisputed. The
word 'Baku' was synonymous with petroleum. The largest
Baku oil centre (on the south side of the mountain range)

COAL-MINING BY BASINS

Basins	1913		1927-8		1934		1937	
	In thousands of tons	Per cent	In thousands of tons	Per cent	In thousands of tons	Per cent	In thousands of tons	Per cent
Don Basin	25,288	87·2	27,330	77·0	60,016	64·2	80,000	52·5
Kuznetzk Basin	774	2·6	2,618	7·4	11,584	12·4	20,000	13·1
Karaganda Basin	—	—	—	—	1,830	2·0	7,000	4·6
Moscow Basin	300	1·0	1,135	3·2	4,906	5·1	10,000	6·5
Ural Basin	1,217	4·1	1,989	5·6	5,507	5·9	13,000	8·5
East Siberian Basin	822	2·8	884	2·6	3,454	3·7	4,500	3·0
Far Eastern Basin	373	1·3	1,073	3·0	2,995	3·2	6,500	4·4
Central Asian Basin	158	0·5	228	0·6	999	1·1	3,000	2·0
Transcaucasian Basin	70	0·2	85	0·2	239	0·2	1,400	0·9
Undistributed and Minor Basins	115	0·8	143	0·4	1,950	2·2	7,100	4·5
U.S.S.R.	29,117	100·0	35,485	100·0	93,480	100·0	152,500	100·0

NOTE.—The distribution by basins for 1934 is based on the report of the People's Commissar of Heavy Industry Orjonikidze at the VIIth Congress of Soviets (1935).

yielded 83 per cent of Russian oil; the Grozny wells (on the north side of the mountain range) provided 13 per cent. The output of the other regions—Emba on the north-east coast of the Caspian Sea, the Fergan Valley in Central Asia, Sakhalin in the Far East—was quite insignificant.

In oil output the U.S.S.R. occupies the second place in the world. Primitive methods have been replaced by the most perfected methods. In the electrification of the oil industry the U.S.S.R. is ahead of every other country.

OUTPUT OF PETROLEUM (GAS INCLUDED)
(millions of tons)

1913	.	.	.	.	.	9·2
1920	.	.	.	.	.	3·8
1927–8	.	.	.	.		11·7
1932	.	.	.	.	.	22·3
1934	.	.	.	.	.	25·5
1937	.	.	.	.	.	46·8

The First Five Year Plan made changes in the distribution of the oil industry. A chain of new oil districts, traversing the country from north to south and destroying the monopoly of the Caucasus, appeared on the map. It starts in the northern taiga. In 1931 the foundations of the most northerly oil centre in the world were laid on the River Ukhta in the Arctic Pechora basin. There were no roads in this region; no one lived here. Derricks sprang up amidst the firs, followed by a workers' settlement, a mechanical factory, an electric power station and a wireless station.

The second link in the chain is the new Choussov oil districts in the northern Urals.

The third is the Sterlitamak oil industry in Bashkiria. Petroleum first gushed out here in 1932. Both banks of the White River are now covered with derricks. The district is becoming the oil base of the Urals, which till quite recently had been importing oil from Caucasus. During the Second Five Year Plan a petroleum combine will be constructed in Bashkiria.

The fourth link in the chain is Emba on the north-east coast of the Caspian Sea. During the period of the Second

PRODUCTION OF PETROLEUM

(including gaseous by-products)

	1913		1927–8		1933		1937	
	In thousands of tons	Per cent	In thousands of tons	Per cent	In thousands of tons	Per cent	In thousands of tons	Per cent
Transcaucasian S.F.S.R.	7,669	83·1	7,591	65·2	15,939	70·8	29,950	64·0
North Caucasian Region	1,208	13·1	3,606	31·5	5,161	22·9	9,750	20·8
Azov-Black Sea Region	87	0·9	107	0·9	766	3·4	1,800	3·9
Kazak A.S.S.R.	118	1·3	251	2·1	198	0·9	1,700	3·6
Bashkirian A.S.S.R.	—	—	—	—	36	0·2	1,350	2·9
Far Eastern Region	—	—	—	—	197	0·9	800	1·7
Central Asia	152	1·6	87	0·8	206	0·9	1,450	3·1
U.S.S.R.	9,284	100·0	11,592	100·0	22,508	100·0	46,800	100·0

Five Year Plan the oil output of Emba will grow nearly sevenfold

The fifth, most southerly, link is the new oil district of West Turkmenia.

The oil industry of the northern part of the island of Sakhalin in the Far East has made rapid progress. During the First Five Year Plan its output increased eighteen times.

By the end of the Second Five Year Plan the proportion of oil output in the new non-Caucasian oil districts will increase from 2·5 per cent to 11·3 per cent.

Baku and Grozny are still the most important petroleum districts, but they are losing their monopoly. In Transcaucasia the petroleum industry is no longer limited to Baku; petroleum is also extracted near Tiflis.

In the Pre-Caucasus the oil industry has spread beyond the boundaries of Grozny. Oil is now being extracted in several places along the northern foot of the Caucasian range, of which the most important is the Maikop district.

The manufacture of the crude oil into petroleum products has increased. At the beginning of the First Five Year Plan 65 per cent of Baku oil went through the process of distillation; by the end of the Five Year Plan, 100 per cent. A reorganization of the oil-refining industry, rationalizing the oil supply, has taken place. The Far East, for instance, which extracts its own oil, used to export it in the crude state, at the same time getting oil products by sea from the Black Sea via the Suez Canal and the Indian Ocean. Now a new oil distillery is working in Khabarovsk in the Far East.

The peat industry, which scarcely existed before, and the shale industry, which was completely non-existent, have now appeared on the map.

The country possessed great resources of peat, but before the Revolution the output was quite insignificant. During the Civil War, when the central industrial regions were cut off from their coal base, the Donbas, Lenin encouraged the extraction of peat as a local fuel. With his encouragement the peat industry made rapid progress. During the Second Five Year Plan the output of peat will be nearly doubled. The mechanized part of the output is now 65 per cent of the total output. Peat has taken an important place in the fuelling of the country; it has lessened the dependence of the northern half of the U.S.S.R.—the Moscow, Leningrad, Ivanov, Kalinins (formerly Tver) and Western Regions, White Russia, and the Gorky Area—on fuel brought from afar. During the Second Five Year Plan peat works will be greatly developed in the east of the country, especially in the Urals.

PRODUCTION OF PEAT

	1929		1934		1937	
	Million tons	Per cent	Million tons	Per cent	Million tons	Per cent
Moscow Province . .	2·9	52·8	5·9	34·3	6·7	26·8
Leningrad Province .	0·6	10·9	2·1	12·2	3·4	13·6
Ivanovo Province .	0·8	14·6	2·4	13·9	3·6	14·4
Gorky & Kirov Regions	0·5	9·1	1·5	8·7	2·6	10·4
Western Province .	0·1	1·8	0·8	4·7	1·4	5·6
Kursk and Voronezh Provinces . . .	0·1	1·8	0·6	3·5	0·9	3·6
Kuibyshev Region and Oryenburg Province	0·1	1·8	0·5	2·9	0·6	2·4
Sverdlovsk Province .	0·1	1·8	0·7	4·1	1·8	7·2
Chelyabinsk Province .	—	—	0·1	0·6	0·2	0·8
Ukrainian S.S.R. .	0·1	1·8	1·1	6·4	1·5	6·0
White Russian S.S.R. . .	0·2	3·6	1·4	8·1	2·1	8·4
Other regions . .	0·0	0·0	0·1	0·6	0·2	0·8
U.S.S.R. .	5·5	100·0	17·2	100·0	25·0	100·0

The shale industry is a new development in the U.S.S.R. It is not yet very extensive, but it is growing rapidly. It is being made a large-scale mechanized industry straight away. Shale strata are found in the Leningrad Region and the Povolzhie. Fuel consumption in the U.S.S.R. is increasing, and is changing its structure. The proportion of mineral fuel is increasing, while the proportion of timber burnt decreases. Local mineral 'poor-quality' fuel is playing a more and more important role in the fuelling of the country.

III. ELECTRIFICATION

It was not electricity but steam which turned the pulleys of the machines in most pre-revolutionary Russian factories and pulled the trains. It was not electricity but kerosene which lighted up all but the more or less large towns in old Russia.

Electric power stations in Tsarist Russia were few and not powerful. Only a small number of stations, situated in the large towns—in Leningrad and Moscow, in Baku—were of industrial importance.

The high-calorific petroleum of the Caucasus and Donbas coal were their main fuels. The furnaces swallowed up these valuable products which could have been used as chemical raw material and fuel for blast-furnaces. Even the Baku stations were fuelled by oil, though they might have been worked by gas. Tsarist Russia knew nearly nothing of hydro-electric power stations. The mighty power of the waters of the Russian rivers, the greatest in the world, was utilized to grind the grain by means of village millstones.

Socialist society cannot base itself on muscular strength and steam-power—the energy of the past. The growing country requires electric current—which is easily transmitted over long distances, is universal, economical, and powerful.

Electrification was a means of placing the economy of backward Russia on the firm technical foundation of large-scale socialist production. 'Communism is the Soviet power plus electrification of the whole country,' said Lenin.

The U.S.S.R. is rapidly providing itself with the most up-to-date electric power stations. They are being constructed both in the urban centres and in mountain villages.

The national economy of the Soviet Union can be electrified with greater facility than the national economy of capitalist countries. The socialist State can easily concentrate capital investments in accordance with its plan and erect giant electric power stations, which are the most profitable. A State where private ownership of the land is non-existent can easily choose the best site for the construction of the electric station and utilize natural power resources in the best possible way. A State whose economic life knows no competition and develops according to plan, can set up transmitting wires in any direction it likes, and connect with them any enterprise it likes, the economic interests of the country as a whole being uppermost in its thoughts.

In 1934 the output of electricity in the U.S.S.R. was over ten times greater than in Russia in 1913. The coefficient of electrification of productive processes in industry had already exceeded 69 per cent by 1932. During the Second Five Year Plan the electrification of industry will in the main be completed. As regards thermification, the U.S.S.R. will occupy the foremost place in the world.

OUTPUT OF ELECTRICITY
(billions of kilowatt hours)

1913	1·9
1921	0·5
1928	5·0
1932	13·5
1934	20·5
1937	38·0 (approx.)

Electric poles are appearing all over the land. Wires are hanging above the whole country. They are becoming an element of its scenery.

In the U.S.S.R. preparations are systematically being made for the creation of a unified high-voltage power network which will connect all the electric power stations in the country. This will permit the whole of the industry of the country to be supplied by electricity, make it possible to utilize the power resources of the country independently of their location, decrease the unevenness of pressure on the stations, and considerably reduce the transport of fuel by replacing it by the transport of power. The unified electric-power network will be the skeleton of the distribution of the country's productive powers over the land.

Electric power stations in the U.S.S.R. do not belong to

private owners, but to the socialist State, and it is therefore easy to abolish the difference in tension and frequency. There are no social obstacles in the U.S.S.R. to prevent the union of electric power stations into one system. Each station in the U.S.S.R. is, in point of fact, a station which

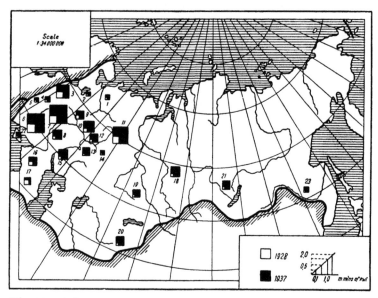

14. CHANGES IN THE TERRITORIAL DISTRIBUTION OF ELECTRIC POWER STATIONS. CAPACITY OF ELECTRIC STATIONS ACCORDING TO DISTRICTS (*see table opposite*)

is utilized by all. Even factory electric power stations give current to the general system. The electric power station of the Magnitogorsk works, for instance, supplies the town and the surrounding settlements with current.

Several powerful high-voltage regional rings have already been created. The electric power stations of the Moscow Region have united into one system which supplies all the industrial centres of the region. This is the most extensive system in Europe. The stations of the Ivanov Region and of the Gorky Area, over 300 kilometres apart, have been connected. The electro-transmission of Svir, Leningrad, has a tension of 220 kilovolts, i.e. the highest in the world.

FIXED POWER OF ELECTRIC STATIONS

	In 1928		1937	
	In thousands of kilowatts	Per cent	In thousands of kilowatts	Per cent
1. Northern Region . .	14·3	0·7	52·0	0·5
2. Karelian A.S.S.R. . .	3·6	0·2	41·2	0·4
8. Leningrad Province .	286·7	15·2	994·7	9·1
4. Western Province . .	35·6	1·8	147·0	1·4
5. White Russian S.S.R. .	17·7	0·9	125·3	1·2
6. Ukrainian S.S.R. . .	463·9	24·5	2,385·5	21·8
7. Moscow Province . .	401·9	21·1	1,572·1	14·4
8. Kursk and Voronezh Provinces . . .	26·7	1·4	208·9	1·9
9. Ivanovo Province . .	102·6	5·4	350·4	3·2
10. Gorky & Kirov Regions	54·0	2·8	497·6	4·6
11. Former Ural Province .	135·6	7·1	1,302·7	11·9
12. Tartar A.S.S.R. . .	11·4	0·6	125·4	1·2
18. Kuibyshev Region and Oryenburg Province .	21·7	1·1	180·3	1·7
14. Bashkirian A.S.S.R. .	8·9	0·4	51·0	0·5
15. Saratov and Stalingrad Regions. . . .	29·9	1·6	312·7	2·9
16. Azov-Black Sea & North Caucasian Region .	79·9	4·2	517·8	4·8
17. Transcaucasian S.F.S.R.	141·5	7·5	657·2	6·0
18. West Siberian Region .	19·2	1·0	441·2	4·0
19. Kazak A.S.S.R. . .	4·2	0·2	194·8	1·8
20. Central Asia . . .	16·0	0·8	368·0	8·3
21. East Siberian and Yakutsk A.S.S.R. . .	8·9	0·4	131·3	1·2
22. Crimean A.S.S.R. . .	10·0	0·5	83·8	0·8
23. Far Eastern Region .	11·2	0·6	147·7	1·4
Undistributed . . .	—	—	11·4	—
U.S.S.R. .	1,905·4	100·0	10,900·0	100·0

During the period of the Second Five Year Plan the linking up of stations within regions will in the main be completed, and the creation of super-powerful inter-regional power systems begun. By means of high-voltage wires

Moscow will be connected with Ivanov and Gorky, the northern and southern Urals with the central Urals, the Donbas with the Dnieper district—the latter system, it should be noted, will be the most powerful in the world (nine milliard kilowatt-hours a year).

Subsequently all these inter-regional systems will form the unified power-saturated system of the country.

Reorganization of the lines of connexion between electric power stations and their fuel bases is now taking place. New stations are working on local fuel. In the north this is peat. Near Moscow it is peat and brown coal. In the Donbas it is coal-dust. In Baku, petroleum gas. Coke-forming coals are allocated to metallurgy, petroleum is turned into petroleum products, transport is economized.

THE IMPORTANCE OF DIFFERENT SOURCES OF POWER
IN THE SOVIET UNION
(per cent)[1]

	1913	1932
Petroleum . . .	60·0	17·3
Coal brought from a distance	40·0	18·7
Peat	—	21·0
Local Coal . . .	—	30·7
Other Local Fuel . .	—	3·9
Water-power . . .	—	8·4
	100	100

Industry will be built up on local fuel of inferior quality transformed into electric current in regions where, the level of technique being what it was, industry could not develop because of the absence of high-quality fuel. Poor regions are becoming rich. Thus electrification assists in the even distribution of industry corresponding to the political and economic ideals of the country.

The power of falling water is being utilized for the first

[1] Power output of regional power stations.

time on a wide industrial scale. The first plants are working on the energy of the wind (in Crimea and in Turkmenia). The new country is served by new kinds of power.

The First Five Year Period saw the completion of the first plan of electrification, drawn up in 1921. It was the plan elaborated by the State Commission for the Electrification of Russia (G.O.E.L.R.O.) under the direction of Lenin. It provided for the construction, within ten or fifteen years, of a number of large electric power stations with a total capacity of 1,700,000 kilowatts. The first electrification plan, called by Lenin 'the second programme' of the Communist Party, was at the same time the first plan of restoration and reconstruction of the national economy of the U.S.S.R.

The fulfilment of the G.O.E.L.R.O. plan meant, above all, the restoration and extension of the power base of the central regions.

The fulfilment of the plan under the Second Five Year Plan period will signify the creation of a power base of great capacity in the east.

The Revolution introduced many powerful electric stations into the economy of the country. They entered into the economic configuration of the regions and transformed them.

The old electric power stations of the centre have been reconstructed. They have been entirely rebuilt and their capacity has increased. The plant installed in the Leningrad electric power stations after the Revolution amounts to over 80 per cent of their equipment. Such 'reconstruction' is colloquially described in the U.S.S.R. as the process of 'sewing on a new coat to a button'.

In addition, new stations have been constructed in the centre.

Near Moscow—in Kashira—a new electric power station is working: it is one of the largest fuel stations in the country. The perfected furnaces use brown coal which formerly was considered almost valueless. A huge station in Stalinogorsk, which is already partially functioning on Moscow brown coal, is in process of construction.

Not far from Moscow the powerful Shatoura electric power

station has been erected on the unsteady soil of the peat bogs. This building, with its smoking chimneys and huge windows, thrusts itself upon the dreary landscape of stagnant lakes and meagre woods like a crowning symbol of the industrial rebirth of the land.

A hydro-electric station, which is at the same time a monument, stands near Leningrad on the Volkhov. The first of the Soviet electric power stations, it was built by the whole country in the face of superhuman difficulties during the difficult years of civil war and economic collapse. The Volkhov station is esteemed in the U.S.S.R. as a memorial to Lenin, even though its total capacity is only equal to the power of each of the aggregates of the new station on the Dnieper.

The peat-fuel electric power stations 'Red October' and Kirov ('Doubrovka'), and the hydro-electric power station on the Svir are constructed near Leningrad. A second hydro-station is being built on the Svir. The water raised by the hydro-stations has covered the rapids and facilitated navigation.

Thermo-electric stations are being constructed in Moscow, Leningrad, and other towns. They transmit electric current, carrying motive power to machines; and steam, which means warmth to houses and factories.

The Niva hydro-station in Karelia, which borders on the Leningrad Region from the north, is the most northerly hydro-station in the world. It lies far beyond the Arctic Circle, amidst the tundras and forests of the Kola peninsula. In the winter the concrete froze with the temperature at 40° C. below zero, and the iron tools were blunted in the frozen earth. In the summer the builders stood up to their waists in mud when setting up the masts of the electro-transmitters. The Niva station will supply energy to the new mining and chemical industry of the Kola peninsula. Still farther to the north, nearly on the shore of the Arctic Ocean, the Toulomsk hydro-electric power station is in process of construction.

The powerful Zouyev and Shterov stations which have been erected in the Ukraine utilize anthracite-dust. Their

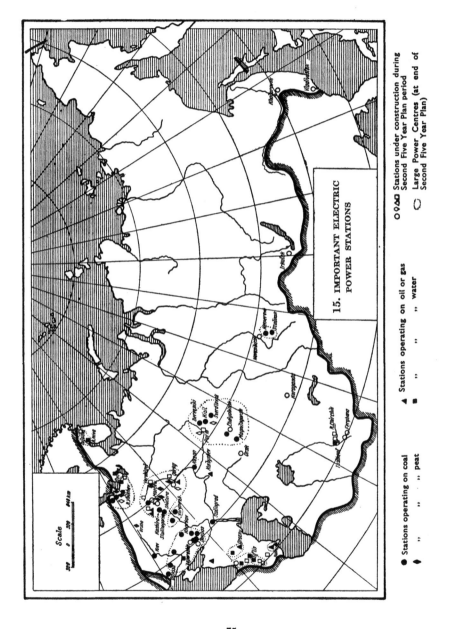

Scale
300   0   300   600 km

15. IMPORTANT ELECTRIC
POWER STATIONS

● Stations operating on coal
◗ „   „   „   peat
▲ Stations operating on oil or gas
■ „   „   „   water
○○◐◐ Stations under construction during
Second Five Year Plan period
◯ Large Power Centres (at end of
Second Five Year Plan)

75

wires have penetrated into the Donbas, a highly important industrial region densely built over with towns, factories, and coal-pits.

The famous Dnieper hydro-electric power station, with a total capacity of 558,000 kilowatts, stands in the Dnieper Region.[1]

The south-western crystalline massif crossed the Dnieper and for 90 kilometres blocked up the course of the river with rocks. Only a skilful pilot was able to steer his boat through the rapids. Geographically there was one Dnieper. Economically there were two Dniepers—two absurd stumps.

Plans for utilizing the energy of the waters of the Dnieper had long ago entered men's minds, but the flooding of the rapids entailed flooding the banks at the same time, and the great landowners opposed the accomplishment of this plan. Considerable capital was required—and there was little to be found. There were no consumers of electric power of any great importance in the Dnieper region. It was only after the Revolution that the Dnieper dam could be constructed.

It traverses the river in the form of a concrete wall three-quarters of a kilometre long, has raised the level of the water 37 metres and forms a lake which floods the islands, the rapids, and the shores. The pressure of the water reaches the town of Dniepropetrovsk 97 kilometres up the river.

Side by side with the dam a canal and a three-sectioned sluice—a stairway for steamers—have been constructed. The Dnieper has become a single navigable river.

Colossal aggregates, constructed in the U.S.A. and U.S.S.R., with a capacity of 62,000 kilowatts each, have been set up in the station. During the Second Five Year Plan the Dnieper station will be functioning to its utmost capacity. The cost of each kilowatt-hour of current will work out at 0·6 copecks.

The current of the Dnieper will rally round itself the works of the huge Dnieper combine.[2]

[1] The capacity for January 1st 1935 was equal to 435 thousand kilowatts.
[2] Cp. further, p. 111.

In the northern Urals, high above the ash trees, tower the chimneys of the new Berezniak and Kizel electric power stations. The new Chelyabinsk and Magnitogorsk stations rise amidst the steppes of the southern Urals. The Urals of the horse-capstans, water-wheels, and cheap semi-serf labour are now traversed by the sharp lines of the high-voltage transmitters.

Powerful electric stations—the Kuznetzk and Kemerov stations—have been built in the Kuzbas, the new industrial region of far Siberia. Powerful electric power stations are in process of construction in the Far East.

The power of the mountain rivers of the Transcaucasus has been harnessed. Near Tiflis, where the Rivers Kura and Araks meet just at the foot of a rock crowned by the ruins of an ancient monastery, there stands the concrete structure of the Zemo-Avchalsk hydro-station.

The electric locomotives of the Souramsk Pass and the Zestafon ferro-manganese works are supplied with current from the new hydro-station on the River Rion. The Allaverd copper-smelting works and the Karaklis chemical works receive current from the hydro-station constructed in the gorge of the River Dzoraget.

They are covering the whole country—these long open-work masts, stepping over the widest rivers and above the highest mountains, carrying powerful humming wires with them. The map is dotted over with new stations: the Gorky station in the Gorky Area, the Kazan station in the Tartar Republic, the Shakhty station in the Azov-Black Sea Area, the Gizel-Don station in the North Caucasus, the Karaganda station in Kazakstan, the Chirchik station in Central Asia. These are only a few out of the long list of electric power stations which have been constructed or are in process of construction.

The U.S.S.R. has started on the reconstruction of the Volga—the longest river in Europe. This mighty river traverses growing industrial regions, but does not give them a single kilowatt of electric power.

Dams, some of which will be amongst the largest in the world, will block up the Volga and its tributaries. The hitherto idle river will be transformed into a gigantic stair-case with concrete steps. The weight of the Volga will become a productive force. Every year the river will produce up to 38 milliard kilowatt-hours of power. The magnitude of this figure will become clear if one remembers that the Dnieper-Donbas power system in the Ukraine, which is one of the largest in the world, will be producing 9 milliard kilowatt-hours during the years of the Second Five Year Plan.

The first Volga electric power stations are already being constructed: the Yaroslav station on the Volga and the Perm station on the Kama, a tributary of the Volga. Plans of the next constructions are being worked out. The reconstruction of the Volga will be of a complex character. The Volga will not only become a source of electric power, but will also be a source of irrigation for the vast dry expanses of the south and a magnificent waterway as well.[1]

Mountain lakes are important reserves of potential hydro-energy. The Lake of Sevan (Gokcha), about 1,400 square kilometres in area, lies in the mountains of Armenia at a height of 2 kilometres above sea-level. Twenty-seven small rivers and seven streams flow into Sevan, whilst only one small river, the Zanga, flows out of it. Through the Zanga Lake Sevan loses something like 30 million cubic metres of water a year, while approximately 1,200 million cubic metres are evaporated.

The rapidly growing industry of the Transcaucasus requires electric power, and Lake Sevan allows water to disappear into the air—40 cubic metres a second are thus wasted.

A tunnel or a pumping station along the Zanga will let the water from the lake down into the valley. A hundred kilometres along the Zanga waterfall, which falls from a height of 1,000 metres, a chain of 9 hydro-electric power stations will be constructed. The construction of one of them—the Kanakir station—is already in progress. In the valleys 130,000 hectares of land under cotton and vines will be irrigated.

[1] Cp. further, pp. 129, 184, 186.

Within fifty years the level of the lake will be lowered 50 metres. The surface of the lake will decrease to 239 square kilometres. The decrease of the area of the lake will greatly decrease evaporation, i.e. the useless waste of valuable power.

A grandiose plan of utilization of the water resources of Eastern Siberia is at present being considered in the U.S.S.R. Huge rivers flow from the 'ancient body of Asia', from a high elevation along the rocky bed: the Angara, regulated by the Lake of Baikal, the Yenisei, and others. Hydro-electric power stations could produce a prodigious quantity of power: approximately 100 milliard kilowatt-hours a year.

In addition to its mighty reserves of exceptionally cheap water-power (between 0·25 and 0·30 copecks a kilowatt-hour), Eastern Siberia possesses great resources of coal (the Cherem-kov, Kan, and other coal-fields). All this will permit of the concentration in a formerly barren region of a rich aggregate of power-utilizing industries (steel, aluminium, liquid fuel, chemical works).

At the present time the Irkutsk-Cheremkov fuel electric power station is in process of construction in Eastern Siberia. Geological investigation is proceeding. By the end of the Second Five Year Plan a detailed working hypothesis of the solution of the Angara-Yenisei problem must be ready and a technical plan of one of the hydro-stations must be elaborated. The contours of an industrial region of fantastic dimensions are being traced.

IV. FERROUS METALLURGY

Fifteen works were distributed over the Donbas and the Dnieper district; this was the metallurgical south—74 per cent of Russia pig-iron, the metal base of old Russia. Here was geographical one-sidedness once again: the country depended altogether on the blast-furnaces of the south.

For one cannot seriously consider the Urals with their 21 per cent of the total, with their output which consisted, not of girders and of beams, but of roofing iron, nails, and frying-pans. The times had long since passed when the Urals—a region where serfdom reigned—supplied the whole of Europe with metals. The region remained at the technical level of the eighteenth century. Its toy forges, working on cold blowing and charcoal, are 200 years old. Shackled by feudal survivals, it was speedily surpassed by the capitalist metallurgical south which developed later.

The small works of the centre extracted the other 5 per cent from poor ores with the aid of coal brought from other districts; although it was the centre which used the greater part of Russian metal. The Caucasus, Central Asia, Siberia, and the Far East either imported metal from afar or did without metal altogether.

Smelting of pig-iron increased two and a half times in the U.S.S.R. in comparison with 1913. This increase is a result both of the reconstruction of old works and of the construction of new works and the consequent new distribution of metal production.

PRODUCTION OF PIG-IRON
(millions of tons)

1913	4·2
1920	0·1
1927–8	3·3
1932	6·2
1934	10·4
1937	16·0

The metallurgical south has been re-born. The old works have acquired new blast-furnaces and open-hearth furnaces, which are incomparably more powerful than the old ones. At the Makeyev works in the Donbas a new blast-furnace department, for example, has been constructed consisting of three mechanized powerful furnaces.

The largest blast-furnace in Europe is in process of construction as well as a new huge hearth-furnace department. At the oldest works in the south (the former

Youzovsky works), which are now called the Stalin works, the last open-hearth furnaces left over from pre-Revolutionary times have been taken down and replaced by new ones. Blooming plants have been installed in two of the works in the south. On the surface things are the same. Factories have remained where they were before. But in fact they have been re-created.

The majority of the metallurgical works of the south were concentrated in the Donbas coal-field. They received iron ore from Krivoi Rog, 500 kilometres away. Empty trucks returned to Krivoi Rog. A new metallurgical works has been constructed in Krivoi Rog. Part of the formerly empty trucks are now loaded with coal from the Donbas to Krivoi Rog. The lack of proportion in railway traffic is disappearing. On the south coast of the Sea of Azov, in the iron ore district, the Kerch metallurgical works have been 'renewed' or rebuilt. A metallurgical works—Azovstal—has been constructed in Mariupol on the north coast of the Sea of Azov. Steamers carry iron ores from Kerch to Mariupol and coal from Mariupol to Kerch on their way back. It is thus that the metallurgical industry of the south is extended and rationalized.

The output of metal in the south has increased, but this increase is insufficient to satisfy the demands of the growing country. The Soviet East, a huge region with an entirely new structure of industry, requires its own metal. And therefore in accordance with the decision of the XVIth Congress of the Communist Party on the basis of a report by Stalin in 1930 the second metallurgical base in the east was created—the Ural-Kuznetzk Combine (U.K.C.), a combination of Ural iron ores and Kuznetzk coal. This was not mere reconstruction. This was the creation on an almost barren tract of a new industrial region.

Ural ores lie at a distance of 2,000 kilometres from Kuznetzk coal. New smelting factories are already functioning at the two extremities of this long road. Truck-loads of ore meet loads of coal being carried in the opposite direction. Is it profitable to transport metallurgical raw material such great distances by train?

6

PIG-IRON PRODUCTION

Regions	1913 In thousands of tons	1913 Per cent	1927-8 In thousands of tons	1927-8 Per cent	1934 In thousands of tons	1934 Per cent	1937 In thousands of tons	1937 Per cent
Ukrainian S.S.R.	—	—	2,361	71·9	6,333	60·7	9,040	56·5
Azov-Black Sea Region	—	—	30	0·9	59	0·6	48	0·3
Crimean A.S.S.R.	—	—	—	—	326	3·1	368	2·3
Southern Total	3,108	73·7	2,391	72·8	6,718	64·4	9,456	59·1
Moscow Province	—	—	58	1·8	220	2·1	656	4·1
Gorky and Kirov Regions	—	—	48	1·5	72	0·7	64	0·4
Voronezh Province	—	—	83	2·5	184	1·8	656	4·1
Central Total	195	4·6	189	5·8	476	4·6	1,376	8·6
Sverdlovsk Province	—	—	532	16·2	870	8·3	1,616	10·1
Chelyabinsk Province	—	—	133	4·1	1,418	13·7	2,208	13·8
Bashkirian A.S.S.R.	—	—	26	0·8	87	0·8	80	0·5
West Siberian Region	—	—	6	0·2	855	8·2	1,200	7·5
East Siberian Region	—	—	5	0·1	4	0·0	64	0·4
Eastern Total	913	21·7	702	21·4	3,234	31·0	5,168	32·3
U.S.S.R.	4,216	100·0	3,282	100·0	14,028	100·0	16,000	100·0

82

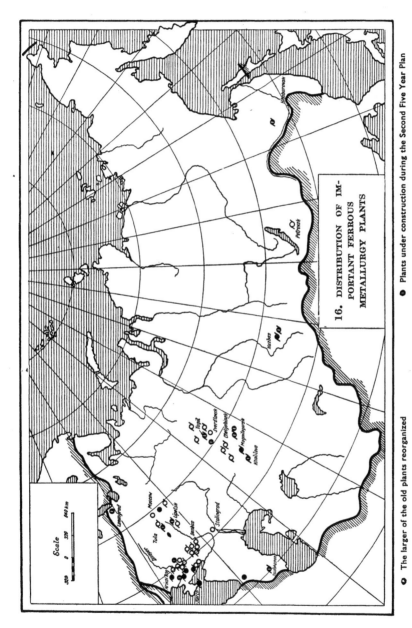

16. DISTRIBUTION OF IM-
PORTANT FERROUS
METALLURGY PLANTS

○ The larger of the old plants reorganized

● New plants which have been launched entirely or in part

◐ Plants under construction during the Second Five Year Plan

⟋ Plants having blast-furnace processes

83

1928

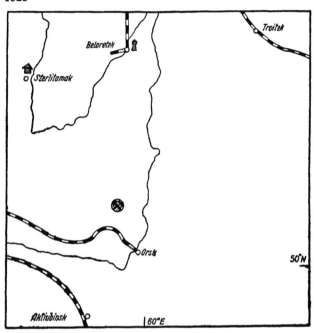

17. THE INDUSTRIALIZATION OF THE
Large enterprises indicated.   Shaded figures functioning enterprises.

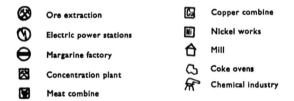

⊗	Ore extraction	Cu	Copper combine
Ⓥ	Electric power stations	Ni	Nickel works
⊖	Margarine factory	⌂	Mill
▨	Concentration plant	⌣	Coke ovens
▣	Meat combine	⚒	Chemical industry

But what kind of raw material is it? The ore of Magnet
Mountain, one of the richest in the world, extracted from
the upper surface, and with a low cost of production. The
coal of Kuzbas, one of the best in the world, easily extracted
and capable of producing first-class coke and, in part, even
of being used in its natural form in the blast-furnaces. Such
raw material can easily stand the costs of transportation
for 2,000 kilometres, especially as its extraction, transport,

1935

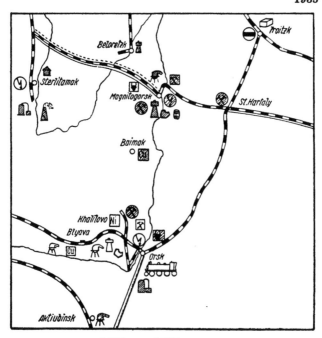

SOUTHERN URALS 1928 AND 1935

Unshaded figures enterprises under construction during Second Five
Year Plan period.

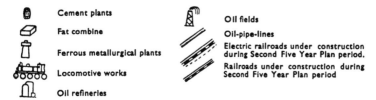

and consumption are previously calculated, adjusted, and
entered into a single plan. (*See Map No. 18.*)

At the Ural pole of the Ural-Kuznetzk Combine the
Magnitogorsk metallurgical works, the second most powerful
in the world, are in process of construction. Eight blast-
furnaces will stand at the foot of Magnet Mountain in the
desert, treeless, and hilly steppe of the southern Urals.   Four
are already constructed and are producing cast iron.   The

steppe is full of noise, smoke, and the planned chaos of technique. During the Second Five Year Plan the works will be completed. It will yield an output of 2,700,000 tons of pig-iron a year, a third of what all the metal industry of Great Britain produced in 1929.

In addition to Magnitogorsk, the following works are being constructed in the Urals: a smelting factory in the north—the Novo-Tagilsky works; in the centre—the First Ural tube-rolling works; in the south—the Bakal and Khalilov works. An iron foundry has been built in Chelyabinsk.

The old Ural works, which worked on charcoal only, stood in the forests by the side of navigable rivers. They were unable to leave the forest zones, although the most valuable ore-deposits in the Urals lay in the treeless southern regions. But now the shackles which bound the metallurgical works to the Urals have been torn asunder. Now that the new works are using mineral coal brought from other parts, the rich ores of the treeless regions can be utilized.

Two Kuznetzk metallurgical works are being built at the Siberian pole of the Ural-Kuznetzk Combine. One of them is operating already; it is nearly completed. Siberia is already getting its own metal. The rails of the Moscow Underground Railway were made in these Siberian works. The output of the Kuznetzk and Magnitogorsk foundries will equal the output of all the metallurgical works of old Russia.

The charcoal metallurgy of the Urals has not at all been neglected: six of the best of the old works have been reconstructed. They are smelting extremely valuable steel of the highest quality on charcoal, and are becoming a base of highly skilled machine-building.

Thus the Ural-Kuznetzk Combine is created, forming an amalgamation not only of ferrous metallurgy, but of non-ferrous metallurgy, the chemical industry, machine-building, and allied industries.

The movement of metallurgy to the east continues. The old Petrovsky works in Eastern Siberia are being reconstructed and extended. From the point of view of the private owner their reconstruction would be unprofitable. But the economic life of the U.S.S.R. is not moved by considerations of the profitableness of single enterprises, but by the interests of the whole State. Eastern Siberia, formerly a backward colonial region, stands in need of an industrial base of its own. The extension of the Petrovsky works tallies with the political principles of the Soviet State and is therefore being accomplished.

The Far East of the U.S.S.R., whose shores are on the Pacific Ocean, never produced metal of its own. At the present time railway construction, machine-building, and shipbuilding are all developing there. The Far Eastern Area must have its own metal.

The raw material has been found: rich resources of coke-forming coal in the basin of the Bourei, a tributary of the Amur, and of iron ore in the region of the Little Khingan mountain range, on the left bank of the Amur. During the Second Five Year Plan in the unused taiga district the construction of a metallurgical works will commence on the basis of these resources.

During the Second Five Year Plan the Dashkesan metallurgical works will be constructed in the Transcaucasus, which hitherto depended for its metal on the Ukraine.

The new distribution of ferrous metallurgy is a means of attaining economic uniformity in the country.

The centre, by utilizing Moscow coal, peat, coke, pyrites (sulphide of iron), metal scrap, and local ores, is extending its metallurgical base and diminishing its metal deficit. New metal works are being constructed in Toula and Lipetsk. Leningrad and Moscow are increasing their output of steel. The newly discovered iron ores of the Kursk magnetic anomaly (which are already being exploited) and of the Kola Peninsula are on the point of becoming the basis of a great metallurgical industry situated near the centre. The production of metal is drawing geographically near to its consumption.

V. NON-FERROUS METALLURGY

Old Russia: a few small works, nine-tenths of which are the property of foreign capital; dependence for non-ferrous metals on imports; a marked discrepancy between the map of industry and the map as yet incomplete of mineral resources.

The U.S.S.R.: Huge non-ferrous metal works, completed and in construction; new branches of non-ferrous metallurgy —aluminium and nickel. The task of the Second Five Year Plan is to satisfy completely the requirements of the country in non-ferrous metals.

The new distribution of non-ferrous metallurgy in the U.S.S.R. is characterized by the transference of the greater mass of capital investments (73 per cent during the Second Five Year Plan) to the basic regions of raw material—copper, lead, zinc, and nickel—i.e. the eastern regions: Kazakstan, Central Asia, the Urals. And here again the movement to the east combines industrial expediency with the policy of the industrial development of backward regions.

Up till the Second Five Year Plan the Urals mined the greater part of the copper output. Kazakstan possessed considerably larger resources, but its output was insignificant. Central Asia, which has rich copper deposits, had no copper industry at all.

Copper-mining is increasing at the present time, during the Second Five Year Plan in the Urals, and the Urals still retain first place in the copper industry. The new and powerful Krasno-Ural combine, with its model technique, has already been constructed, and the Central-Ural and Bliav Combines are in process of construction.

But copper-mining in Kazakstan will develop at a greater rate than that in the Urals. Soon the Pribalkhashsky Combine (Kounrad)—one of the largest enterprises of the copper industry in the world—will be working there.

Central Asia will have its own copper industry for the first time in its history. The building of the Almalyk Combine, a large-scale enterprise, will begin there (in the region of Tashkent).

METAL-WORKING INDUSTRIES

	Output of the Metal-working Industries under the People's Commissariat of Heavy Industry.				Capital investments in the Machine-building Industry according to 2nd Five Year Plan (in per cents of total)
	1932		1937		
	Millions of Roubles	Per cent	Millions of Roubles	Per cent	
Northern Territory . .	6	0·1	8	0·1	0·1
Karelian A.S.S.R. . .	9	0·1	22	0·1	0·2
Leningrad Province . .	1,931	26·8	2,765	18·8	7·2
Moscow Province . .	1,862	25·9	3,650	24·8	19·9
Ivanovo Province . .	268	3·7	470	3·2	4·7
Gorky and Kirov Regions	369	5·1	1,245	8·5	11·0
Western Province . .	169	2·4	330	2·3	1·2
Kursk and Voronezh Provinces	73	1·0	200	1·4	1·4
Tartar A.S.S.R. . .	17	0·2	50	0·3	1·5
Kuibyshev Region and Oryenburg Province .	130	1·8	255	1·7	4·7
Saratov and Stalingrad Regions	242	3·4	440	3·0	4·3
Azov-Black Sea and N. Caucasian Regions .	206	2·9	410	2·8	8·1
Crimean A.S.S.R. . .	28	0·4	35	0·2	0·3
Former Ural Province .	305	4·3	1,115	7·6	12·9
Bashkirian A.S.S.R. .	21	0·3	110	0·8	2·0
Kazakstan . . .	2	0·0	13	0·1	0·2
West Siberian Region .	28	0·4	130	0·9	6·9
East Siberian Region .	12	0·2	45	0·3	1·6
Far Eastern Region .	26	0·4	150	1·0	3·0
Various in R.S.F.S.R. .	—	—	477	3·3	1·8
Ukrainian S.S.R. . .	1,409	19·5	2,575	17·5	11·1
White Russian S.S.R. .	42	0·5	80	0·5	0·3
Transcaucasus S.F.S.R. .	28	0·4	75	0·5	0·3
Central Asia . . .	16	0·2	43	0·3	0·3
Various	54	—	1,057	—	—
U.S.S.R. .	7,253	100·0	15,750	100·0	100·0

The Chimkent Polymetallic Combine has been constructed in southern Kazakstan. New spelter-works have been built in the Urals, Western Siberia, the Ukraine, and the North Caucasus.

New aluminium works are functioning on the Dnieper and near Leningrad. During the Second Five Year Plan aluminium works will be constructed in Karelia and in the Urals. By the end of the Second Five Year Plan the U.S.S.R. will produce 30 per cent of the total world output of aluminium.

A nickel works is operating in the Urals—the first in the country.

During the Second Five Year Plan two works will be constructed for the production of magnesium, and the production of tin will be developed. Tin ore is extracted in the mountains of Eastern Siberia and Central Asia, where recently a tin-mine was laid at a height of 4 kilometres.

The U.S.S.R. possesses the largest resources of gold in the world—both in auriferous sands and in ores. The east of the country is the richest in gold—Siberia, the Urals, Altai, the Far East. Untold treasures lie in the taiga. Every year brings new discoveries of gold deposits. Many of them possess scores of tons of the metal whose extraction can be done by open mining.

The gold industry of the U.S.S.R. is developing rapidly. The former semi-manual gold-fields are being transformed into large-scale industrial enterprises. Special machine-building works in Irkutsk and Krasnoyarsk (Siberia) are being constructed to provide the gold industry with the necessary equipment. Gold-mining in 1913 was mechanized to the extent of 20 per cent; in 1933 70 per cent of production was mechanized.

In his interview with the correspondent of the *New York Times*, W. Duranty, Stalin said in December 1933:

'We have many gold-bearing regions and they are being developed rapidly. Our gold output is already double that of Tsarist Russia and amounts to more than one hundred million roubles a year. In particular during the last two years we have perfected the methods of our work of investigation and have struck on new deposits. But our industry is still young, not only as regards the output of gold, but also as regards iron, steel, copper, and all metals, and our young metallurgy is as yet incapable of giving the necessary aid to the gold industry. The rate of progress is considerable but the volume of production small. We could increase the output of gold four times if we only had the necessary machinery.'

VI. MACHINE-BUILDING

The backwardness of Russia was characterized by feeble development of machine-building. Agricultural machines were made, but amongst them there were neither combines nor tractors. Half the agricultural machines were imported: even scythes were almost entirely bought in Austria. Locomotive engines were made, but in comparison with world models they were pygmies drawing little box-like carriages. Ships were built, but they were propelled for the main part by engines imported from abroad. The erection of factories was reduced to building walls and assembling machines which were bought abroad.

The distribution of such machine-building industry as existed was even more confined than the assortment. Machine-building was limited to the centre and part of the Ukraine. The whole of the east remained a country not only without machine-building but practically without machines.

In the U.S.S.R. machine-building became the main lever of the reconstruction of the whole of the national economy. The machines made in the country are the basis of its economic power and independence.

New branches of machine-building have been created: tractor-building, motor-car construction, aeroplane construction, etc. The country has learned not only to build but also to exploit its new factories. The U.S.S.R. can now construct any machine it wants.

In comparison with 1913 the output of machine-building and metal products had increased sixteen times in the U.S.S.R.

TOTAL MACHINE-BUILDING PRODUCTION
(billions of roubles at 1926–7 prices)

1913	0·7
1928	1·6
1932	7·6
1934	11·1

Machine-building in the U.S.S.R. in the Second Five Year Plan period will grow at a higher rate than heavy industry as a whole. In 1937 not less than half the means of production in the whole country will consist of those which began to be used during the years of the Second Five Year Plan. A rapid development will take place in the production of complex automatic machines, the newest models of machine tools, complete metallurgical equipment, prime movers, and so on. Laborious and heavy processes in industry will be extensively mechanized.

TOTAL METAL PRODUCTION (INCLUSIVE
OF REPAIR) at 1926–7 prices
(billions of roubles)

1932	9·4
1937	9·5

The placing of machine-building has been carefully considered and altered. The centre, which is far from the chief metallurgical bases, but possesses the most advanced technical knowledge, experience, and trained workers, is giving up the production of heavy metal machines for the production of more complex and exact machinery requiring more skilled labour. Its old factories have been newly equipped and new ones have been constructed. (*See Maps Nos. 18, 19.*)

Moscow, formerly the 'calico city', has become a machine-producing centre.

A huge factory has been erected in Moscow which produces 24,000,000 ball-bearings annually. Its departments resemble a clean and bright exhibition of new machines. All the wheels in the country are revolving on Moscow ball-bearings.

An automobile works has grown out of a small workshop just outside Moscow. Moscow sends out railway-trucks loaded with lorries to every corner of the U.S.S.R. The standard grey-green car has become an indispensable item in the stock of Soviet factories, kolkhozes, and institutions. The same trade-mark, 'Stalin Works', is seen in the forests of Siberia and in the sands of Central Asia. It is a symbol of aid sent by Moscow to the outlying districts.

First-class works have been constructed in Moscow and near Moscow for the manufacture of cutting and measuring instruments, electrical equipment, every kind of machine-tool machinery.

Powerful steamers, timber ships, and ice-breakers are built in the Leningrad wharves. The electro-technical works in Leningrad are making huge hydro-generators, including aggregates for the Dnieper-Petrovsk hydro-electric power station. The largest automobile works in Europe have been built in Gorky.

The industrial centre manufactures watches and binoculars, arithmometers and microscopes, gondolas for stratosphere balloons, and escalators for the underground railway.

During the Second Five Year Plan the works of the centre will be extended. The centre has become the basis for the industrial development of the outlying districts, the arsenal of the industrialization of the country.

The Ukraine, which formerly sent out the greater part of its metal, now possesses a large-scale and many-sided metal industry, and is being transformed into an industrial region of the highest value. Kharkov used to be a town of merchants and landowners. Now it is a city of workers, engineers, and scientists. A huge tractor works and a boring machine works have been constructed there. The new Kharkov electro-technical works are equipped with powerful

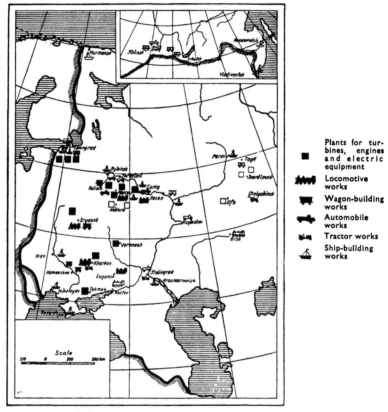

18. IMPORTANT MACHINE-BUILDING WORKS

Black figures functioning enterprises. White figures enterprises
under construction in Second Five Year Plan.

machines, which have made it possible to master the production of gigantic generators—with a capacity of up to
160,000 kilowatts in each aggregate, a whole electric station
according to the old standards. In Lougansk, where Voro-
shilov, the leader of the Red Army, once worked as a fitter,
a locomotive-building works has been constructed whose
size almost equals that of the great Baldwin works in the
U.S.A. It is able to produce 1,080 powerful locomotives
annually. One of the largest metallurgical equipment works
in the world (150,000 tons output) has been constructed in

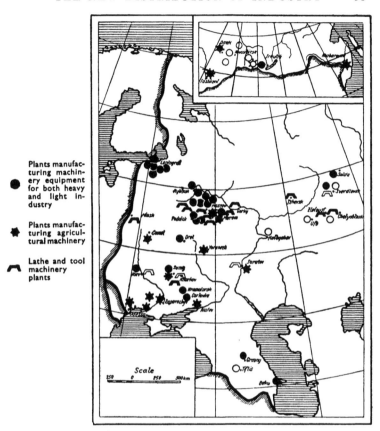

19. IMPORTANT MACHINE-BUILDING WORKS
Black figures functioning enterprises. White figures enterprises
under construction in Second Five Year Plan.

Kramatorsk. This giant works, together with the new town
which was built for the workers and engineers, occupies an
area of 1,000 hectares. Hundreds of powerful machines—
the best that world technique could give—stand in its
departments. The works produces other works. Its annual
output is able to equip completely three modern metallurgical works. The Ukraine will now be building blast-furnaces
open-hearth furnaces, and blooming plants out of its own
parts.

The most notable of all the geographical movements in

the U.S.S.R. is the construction of machine-building works in the backward regions. Former purely agricultural regions are not only receiving machines, but are making machines of their own. This industry revolutionizes provincial modes of life and raises culture to a high level. A man who yesterday knew only how to turn up the earth and scatter handfuls of seed over it, now works up inert metal by the most modern methods and according to the laws of modern technique.

Machine-building giants have been erected in the former purely agricultural regions of the Volga and the North Caucasus: a tractor works in Stalingrad, a combine works in Saratov, an agricultural machinery works in Rostov. A works for building narrow-gauge locomotives is being constructed in Novotcherkassk, and a wagon-building works is being constructed in Kazan. The Second Five Year Plan has seen the beginning of the construction of automobile works in Kuibyshev (Samara) and in Stalingrad.

It is this creation of machine-building in new regions which guarantees the radical transformation of the country.

The U.S.S.R. could construct, for instance, one or two large automobile works during the Second Five Year Plan. But it is constructing four in order to provide a greater number of industrially undeveloped regions with industrial enterprises.

Of the total amount devoted to machine-building in the U.S.S.R. the proportion of the centre and the Ukraine fell from 67 per cent to 64 per cent during the First Five Year Plan. The proportion of the new regions of machine-building increased accordingly. In 1937 the eastern regions will produce a tenth part of all the machines. Heavy machine-building has been shifted to the east, to the Urals and Siberia (U.K.C.). This movement means, not only the rational approximation of the metal industry to metal extraction, but the industrial development of new regions as well.

In the Urals, which produced metal but had no machine-building industry, there have been constructed a tractor works in Chelyabinsk (40,000 caterpillar tractors a year), and a metallurgical equipment works in Sverdlovsk (the Ural-mash works with an output of 100,000 tons). A wagon-building works in Tagil, a chemical apparatus factory and an electrical machine-building works in Sverdlovsk, a motor works in Ufa, and a locomotive and a Diesel engine works in Orsk are all in process of construction.

Machine-building has penetrated into Siberia and has thus removed from it its former unfortunate reputation of being a region of criminal hard labour, taiga, and uncivilized people. During the Second Five Year Plan the building of a huge automobile works is to begin there. A mining-equipment works is springing up in Novosibirsk, locomotive-and wagon-building works in Stalinsk, a mining-equipment works in Irkutsk, a locomotive-repairing works in Oulan-Oudeh (former Upper Oudinsk), shipbuilding docks and a motor-car assembling works in the Far East, and so on.

Even Central Asia, the classical agricultural colony of Tsarist Russia, has its own engineering industry now. An agricultural machinery works has been constructed in Tashkent.

During the Second Five Year Plan nearly a hundred new machine-building works will start operating. Only the largest enterprises have been enumerated here.

But, to name a place at random, there is Semipalatinsk, a small town in the steppes of Kazakstan. It lies 4,000 kilometres from the capital. It is almost indistinguishable on the map of Asia. Dust, fairs, one-storied little houses. Dostoevski lived here in exile.

During the Second Five Year Plan a works manufacturing equipment for the flour-milling industry will be built in Semipalatinsk. Heavy industry will be erected amidst the steppes. What does this mean? The clang of metal—and transformation in the mode of living. The assemblage of parts—and new professions. The organization of industrial labour—and opportunities for cultural development.

Tagil in the Urals can serve as an example of the planned connexion of metallurgy and machine-building: the last department of the metallurgical works which is being built

7

there will become the first department of the new wagon-building works. In the U.S.S.R. machine-building works are not functioning for a capricious free market: they know where the plan will send their products. And therefore even geographically separated enterprises are in close co-operation. The former universal enterprises are becoming specialized workshops firmly bound to each other.

Agricultural machine-building has been developed in the regions which play the most important part in the development of agriculture.

Machine-tool construction and instrument-making works are being built in regions of the most intensive development of machine-building.

Textile engineering is situated in regions with the most highly developed textile industry.

Petroleum machine-building is developing in the main oil regions; metallurgical and mining machine-building in the principal mining and metallurgical regions, and so on.

VII. CHEMISTRY

In Russia chemistry was more of an outlandish curiosity, an artifice of the foreigner, than a branch of industry. By means of its natural resources, the country might have supplied the whole world with nitrogen, potassium, phosphorus, and sulphur, but the cheap chemicals of Germany and the absence of constructive initiative stood in the way of the development of the chemical industry. If a 'home' chemical industry did exist at all, it was founded by foreign capital and worked on imported raw material—sulphur pyrites from Italy, phosphorites from Morocco, and rubber from Brazil. This determined its geography: chemical works were to be found in the ports, on the external frontier of Russia. Not one out of every four chemical works coincided with the geographical centres of raw material.

During the years of the First Five Year Plan the chemical industry of the U.S.S.R. grew into a powerful branch of national industry. The nitrogen, coke-chemical, aniline dye, pharmaceutical, timber-chemical, potassium, and apatite branches of the chemical industry were new creations, as also were the production of artificial fibre, plastic masses, synthetic rubber, and so on. The difficulties of mastering branches of production quite new to the country have been overcome. The chemical industry in the U.S.S.R. was, in point of fact, newly created: one must speak in the case of chemistry of the creation of a new industrial map, rather than the alteration of the old.

The greater part of the new chemical works have grown up in the regions where chemical raw materials are to be found. Geological investigation has extended the raw material base of chemistry from the Arctic Circle to the southern deserts of Central Asia.

The extraction and concentration of apatite—phosphoric raw material—is proceeding in the extreme north of the Leningrad Region in latitude 68° N., in the barren Khibin mountains of the Kola peninsula. These apatite mountains —ensuring abundant harvests for hundreds of years to come —are already supplying all the fields of the country with fertilizers, thus relieving the U.S.S.R. of imported phosphates. Part of the apatite is exported.

Near Moscow the Stalinogorsk Combine has been erected on the basis of brown coal and clay, producing synthetic ammoniac, nitric acid, etc., while the Voskresensk Combine has been built up on phosphorites and manufactured super-phosphates.

In the northern Urals in the region where coal, potassium, limestone, salt, sulphur, pyrites, and phosphorites lie close to each other, the Bereznikov Combine has been constructed —a whole tribe of works manufacturing synthetic ammoniac, acids, soda, and so on. Not far away lie the new Solikamsk potassium works, perhaps the largest in the world. A chemical combine based on the great deposits of phosphorite is being constructed in Aktiubinsk (in Kazakstan). New sulphur works are operating in the sandy deserts of Turkmenia.

The bay of Kara-Bougaz is in the Caspian Sea. Formerly its shores were lifeless. They were surrounded by the sandy desert of Kara-Kum. But the bay has rich resources of mirabillite (Glauber's salt). Its exploitation was begun only under the Soviet power, and now, amidst the deserts, a chemical combine is in process of construction and vast quantities of salts are extracted.

A number of new works are situated in the regions of vegetable chemical raw material: such are the timber-chemical combines of the north, and the synthetic rubber works in Yaroslav, Voronezh, and Yefremov, which are working on alcohol derived from potatoes. Synthetic rubber is produced extensively only in the U.S.S.R. This socialistic industry, unimpeded by the competition of cheap imported natural rubber, was able to endure the painful periods of investigation and experiment—which were crowned by signal success. The great motor-race through the Kara-Kum desert in 1933 proved the high quality of tyres made of artificial (or synthetic) rubber.

CHEMICAL INDUSTRY

Regions	Gross Production of Heavy Chemical Industry in per cent of total for 1933	Capital Investments in the Chemical and Coke-chemical Industry under the supervision of the People's Commissariat of Heavy Industry according to Second Five Year Plan in per cents of total
Central Region . . .	58·9	34·1
Volga Region . . .	5·7	2·2
Ural Region . . .	6·1	14·2
Ukrainian S.S.R. . .	17·6	26·7
Transcaucasian S.F.S.R..	1·0	3·3
Central Asia . . .	0·1	6·5
West Siberian Region .	0·7	5·8
Other Regions . . .	9·9	7·2
	100·0	100·0

In 1931 Stalin had thus every reason to say, 'We have everything in the country, except perhaps rubber. But in a year or two we shall possess rubber as well. . . .'

Some of the chemical works are situated in the regions of that industry whose by-products serve as raw material for

them. Such are the coke and benzole plants in the metallurgical regions of the Ukraine, the Urals, and Kuzbas,
and the sulphuric acid plants in the regions of the copper
industry of the Urals.

New centres of attraction for the chemical industry are
springing up. In Central Asia, during the Second Five Year
Plan, a nitrogenous fertilizer works is to be built which will
work on the electrolysis of water by the current of the hydro-
electric power station erected on the River Chirchik near
Tashkent.

During the Second Five Year Plan the eastern regions
will receive 28 per cent of all the capital investments in the
chemical industry of the U.S.S.R.

Chemical combines are scattered over the whole territory
of the U.S.S.R. in order to ensure the successful application
of chemistry to all the industries of the country.

VIII. LIGHT INDUSTRY AND FOOD PRODUCTION

The geographical distribution of industrial enterprises
producing articles of consumption in old Russia was as
uneven as the geographical distribution of the production
of the means of production.

The centre of Tsarist Russia developed as a producer of
cotton fabrics. Within it were concentrated 99·5 per cent
of all the looms in the country, although it possessed not an
ounce of cotton. Part of the cotton it received from abroad
and part from its south-eastern provinces.

Bales of cotton came to the centre from Central Asia and
the Transcaucasus, three or four thousand kilometres away.
On the journey they would meet bales of fabric travelling
the other way.

Cotton fabrics raised the Russian centre above the east;
cotton fabric became the foundation of its economic might
in Asia.

All this has changed. A union of peoples in the U.S.S.R.
has taken the place of relations as between master and man.
There is no reason to impede the industrial development of
the regions of raw material; there is no need to carry cotton

backwards and forwards. Fabrics are produced in the cotton-producing regions. The U.S.S.R. is able altogether to do without imported cotton.

The first textile mills have been constructed in Central Asia—in Ashkhabad, Fergan, and Tashkent. During the

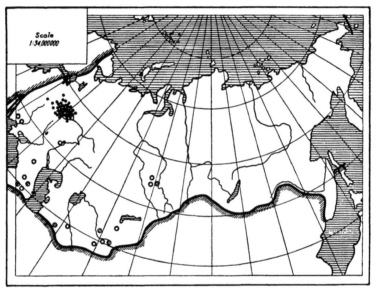

20. THE MOST IMPORTANT ENTERPRISES OF THE COTTON CLOTH MANUFACTURING INDUSTRY

- Old enterprises
- Newly built enterprises
- To be built during Second Five Year Plan

Second Five Year Plan cotton combines will be constructed in Stalinabad, Khojent, Charjouje.

Textile mills have been constructed in Ganje and Leninakan in the Transcaucasus. Several cotton combines will be constructed in the Transcaucasus during the Second Five Year Plan. The Ukraine will for the first time acquire a powerful cotton industry.

The proportion of the produce of the cotton industry in the cotton-growing regions to the total produce of the U.S.S.R. is increasing: in Central Asia, for instance, from

0.5 per cent in 1932 to 3·1 per cent by 1937. By the end of the Second Five Year Plan Central Asia will, in the main, be supplying itself with the produce of its own textile industry. The capacity of the textile mills which are being constructed in the new regions during the Second Five Year

MANUFACTURE OF COTTON FABRICS

	1932		1937	
	In millions of metres	Per cent	In millions of metres	Per cent
Leningrad Province . . .	117	4·6	250	5·6
Moscow Province	1,262	49·8	2,125	47·5
Ivanovo Province	1,093	43·1	1,769	39·6
Saratov Region	11	0·5	27	0·6
North Caucasus	—	—	1	0·0
West Siberian Region . . .	—	—	40	0·9
Ukrainian S.S.R.	—	—	10	0·2
White Russian S.S.R. . . .	6	0·2	11	0·3
Transcaucasus	32	1·3	100	2·2
Uzbekistan	8	0·3	120	2·7
Turkmenian S.S.R. . . .	5	0·2	10	0·2
Tajik S.S.R.	—	—	10	0·2
U.S.S.R. .	2,584	100·0	4,473	100·0

Plan will be about 20 per cent of the total capacity of the cotton industry of the U.S.S.R.

The construction of a textile combine in Barnaul in Western Siberia will be completed. There is no cotton in that district, but it will be brought in the empty railway trucks that bring timber and grain to Central Asia from Siberia. Thus it will be seen that the transference of productive industry to the actual regions of raw material is far from being a fetish in itself. Raw material may be brought if this favours economy and leads to greater productivity of social labour.

The relative decline of the textile centre is accompanied by its absolute expansion. The reconstructed mills of the

centre have increased their output. They are being transferred to the production of high-quality, complex, technical
fabrics.

The flax industry in Russia was concentrated in the
Ivanov Region, though the principal flax-growing districts
were in the Western and Kalinin Regions, White Russia, and
other regions.

The geographical deconcentration of the manufacture of
linen fabrics is in progress. During the Second Five Year
Plan flax-mills will be built outside the Ivanov Region (in
western regions and White Russia). The capacity of these
new enterprises will equal the capacity of the flax industry
of the Ivanov Region itself. The new flax industry will cover
the whole north of the U.S.S.R.

The wool industry of Russia gravitated towards the central
regions. During the Second Five Year Plan the process of
its transference to the regions of raw material will be continued. New wool factories will be erected in the North
Caucasus, the Ukraine, Central Asia, and Siberia.

Before the Revolution the silk-producing regions—Central
Asia and the Transcaucasus—had nothing but a handicraft
silk industry. A few factories in the centre worked partly
on imported silk. Silk-spinning works have already been
constructed in Central Asia and the Transcaucasus, amongst
which one is considered to be, so far, the largest in the
world. The Second Five Year Plan will increase their
number.

The clothing industry existed only in the centre. Now
it can be found in nearly every region, including the outlying
districts—in the Transcaucasus and the Far East, for
example. Formerly a handicraft trade, the clothing industry has now become a large-scale technically developed
industry.

Half the leather and footwear industry in Russia was
situated in the centre. It is now being moved to the
south-east of the Soviet Union, to the regions of raw
material.

The paper industry of wooded Russia worked on raw
material brought from Germany and Finland and therefore

kept close to the north-west frontier of the country. The U.S.S.R. is erecting its new paper mills in the regions of timber industry—in the north, in Siberia, and the Urals.

Sugar was supplied to Russia by the Ukraine and to a lesser extent by the Kursk Region. The distribution of the sugar industry was confined within these boundaries. The limited quantities of sugar allowed to be put on the home

PRODUCTION OF GRANULATED SUGAR

	1932		1937	
	Thousands of tons	Per cent	Thousands of tons	Per cent
Moscow Province . . .	7·4	0·9	17·5	0·7
Western Province . . .	1·6	0·2	10·0	0·4
Kursk and Voronezh Province	280·9	27·9	540·0	21·6
Kuibyshev Region and Oryen-burg Province . . .	—	—	12·5	0·5
Saratov Region . . .	—	—	21·5	0·9
Azov-Black Sea Region . .	16·0	1·9	44·0	1·7
North Caucasus Region . .	—	—	2·5	0·1
Bashkirian A.S.S.R. . . .	—	—	2·5	0·1
Kazakstan	—	—	33·0	1·3
West Siberian Region . .	4·3	0·5	50·0	2·0
Far Eastern Region . . .	—	—	11·5	0·5
Ukrainian S.S.R. . . .	559·7	67·6	1,700·0	68·0
Transcaucasian S.F.S.R. . .	—	—	15·0	0·6
Kirghiz A.S.S.R. . . .	8·3	1·0	40·0	1·6
U.S.S.R. . .	828·2	100·0	2,500·0	100·0

market, which were determined by the Government, artificially hampered the development of sugar-refining in other regions to the advantage of the monopolist sugar-refiners. The intensive erection of sugar-refineries in new regions is taking place: in the Moscow Region, in Bashkiria, Western Siberia, Kazakstan, Kirghizia, the Azov-Black Sea Area, the Transcaucasus, in the Far East, and other places.

The Second Five Year Plan is continuing the distribution of the sugar industry over the territory of the U.S.S.R. Of twenty-five new refineries twenty will be constructed in new regions.

The tinned-food industry has developed to a very great extent. Within the First Five Year Plan its output was increased ten times. Its boundaries have been extended. New factories were built, not only in the old regions—the Ukraine, Crimea, the North Caucasus—but in new ones as well—the extreme north, the Far East, the Transcaucasus, and so on. During the Second Five Year Plan the Volga Region will contain an important tinned-food industry.

The tobacco industry of Russia was concentrated in Moscow and Leningrad. For the purpose of aiding the industrial development of backward regions, after the Revolution a number of tobacco factories from the centre were taken to the south, to the tobacco-growing regions. Subsequently a number of new factories were also built in the south.

The oil industry (production of sunflower seed oil) was situated mainly in the North Caucasus and the Voronezh Region. Now the erection of oil mills is proceeding in new regions of raw material—in Kazakstan and Siberia.

Large-scale, technically perfect meat combines, some of which are already partly functioning, are being constructed in the regions of the raw material—Kazakstan (Semipalatinsk), the Orenburg Region (Orsk), and in Bouriat-Mongolia (Oulan-Oudeh), formerly Verkhneoudinsk).

In accordance with the decisions of the XVIIth Congress of the Communist Party, light industry and the food industry —the branches of industry which manufacture articles of general consumption—will develop at a higher rate during the Second Five Year Plan than during the First Five Year Plan. This is the result of the fact that unemployment has been abolished, of the increase in the well-being of the kolkhoz peasantry, and the higher level of culture amongst the working class.

By the end of the Second Five Year Plan the light industry of the U.S.S.R. must, as regards technical equipment, occupy one of the foremost positions in the world.

The food industry will be the first in Europe as regards output by the end of the Second Five Year Plan.

THE GROWTH OF THE LIGHT AND FOOD INDUSTRIES
DURING THE SECOND FIVE YEAR PLAN

(in billions of roubles at the prices of 1926–7)

	1932	1937 (plan)
Light industry . .	7·8 . .	19·5
Food	5·7 . .	14·4

This growth of the light and food industries will make it possible to fulfil one of the principal current tasks of the country—to double or treble consumption during the Second Five Year Plan.

IX. THE TIMBER INDUSTRY

There are a billion hectares of forest-land in the U.S.S.R. —a third of all the forests in the world. The north and east of the country are covered by forest. The forests extend for thousands of kilometres—tangled and impassable. Under the cold sky the wood grows up close-grained, strong, and resilient.

The U.S.S.R. possesses vast resources of timber, but they have so far been little investigated. The trees grow up twice as rapidly as they are felled. The uneven geographical distribution of timber exploitation in old Russia led to the result that in some places the forests are dying of decrepitude, whilst in others they have to be planted artificially.

The forests in the old timber regions—the most densely populated—lying near the centre, the Leningrad, Moscow, and Western Regions, and White Russia, and even in the southern well-populated regions, as for instance the Kursky and Voronezh Regions, were cut down extensively. In Siberia and Yakutia, the outlying districts, with a feebly developed railway network the forests were not touched.

The timber industry of the U.S.S.R. is growing quickly. The export of timber is developing. Olonetsk pinewood, Vologda firwood, Caucasian walnut, and Far Eastern cedar are put on the world market. Motor saws, timber-cutting

Regions	Total area of Forests on Jan. 1st 1934, in millions of hectares (excluding minor Forest Land)	Percentage of Forest Lands to general Area of Districts	Percentage of Timber Products in proportion to total timber resources	
			1928–9	1937
Northern Region . . .	66·3	41·2	14·3	15·8
Karelian A.S.S.R. . . .	11·3	47·5	6·7	5·4
Leningrad Province . .	18·8	22·5	10·6	7·3
Western Province . . .	3·3	13·7	7·5	4·4
Moscow Province . . .	2·9	13·0	5·5	2·1
Ivanovo Province . . .	3·6	23·4	5·9	3·5
Gorky and Kirov Regions .	11·1	33·4	11·1	11·4
Former Ural Province . .	70·5	15·6	10·0	14·8
Bashkirian A.S.S.R. . .	4·2	23·4	1·9	1·5
Tartar A.S.S.R. . . .	0·9	12·2	0·2	0·5
Kuibyshev Region and Oryenburg Province . .	2·7	8·5	5·2	3·5
Kursk and Voronezh Province	0·8	3·3	1·7	0·9
Saratov and Stalingrad Region	0·5	0·8	0·3	0·1
Azov-Black Sea and North Caucasian Region . .	1·9	4·3 }	0·8	1·1
Daghestan A.S.S.R. . .	0·1	1·7 }		
Crimean A.S.S.R. . . .	0·2	6·2	0·0	0·0
Kazak A.S.S.R. . . .	23·8	5·4	0·1	0·7
West Siberian Region . .	60·1	22·6 }	7·6	{ 6·2
East Siberian Region . .	250·8	27·9 }		{ 6·5
Yakoytsk A.S.S.R. . .	277·2	37·9	0·0	0·5
Far Eastern Region . .	112·3	18·4	3·1	7·1
Ukrainian S.S.R. . . .	2·5	4·0	2·9	2·9
White Russian S.S.R. . .	3·1	16·8	4·4	3·1
Transcaucasian S.F.S.R. .	3·6	15·1	0·0	1·1
Uzbek S.S.R.	1·4	4·9 }		
Turkmenian S.S.R. . .	2·9	5·5 }		
Tajik S.S.R.	2·2	6·8 }	0·0	0·1
Kirghiz A.S.S.R. . . .	2·3	4·8 }		
Kara-Kalpakian A.S.S.R. .	10·0	— }		
Undistributed . . .	0·2	—	—	—
U.S.S.R. .	951·5	21·5	100·0 55 mlns. cm.	100·0 170 mlns. cm.

machines, automobiles, and tractors have come to the aid of the axe, saw, and horse. Forest roads are made.

The distribution of the timber industry is changing together with its growth. From the central regions the timber industry is moving to the north, the north-east, and the east —the regions of untouched forest districts. By this means the production of timber is made to correspond more closely to the natural growth of the forests, the new industrial centres of the east are provided with timber, and centres of technical culture are being created in the backward taiga regions. In the Western Region timber collections increased only by 25 per cent during the First Five Year Plan, whereas they increased by 70 per cent in the Urals, by 110 per cent in Eastern Siberia, by 210 per cent in Western Siberia.

Huge wood-working enterprises are springing up in the new regions: the Kondopozh Cellulose and Paper Combine in Karelia, the Kama Combine in the northern Urals, and the Krasnoyarsk Combine in Eastern Siberia, and a timber combine has been constructed in Igarka, a new town lying on the lower Yenisei, beyond the Arctic Circle.

Europe has become a customer of that identical old Siberian taiga which had been for her merely a symbol of Russian savagery and desert isolation.

Soviet ice-breakers discovered the forests of Siberia. The timber is floated along the Yenisei to the Arctic Ocean. Every year it is met by the caravan of the Kara expedition —timber-carrying ships accompanied by ice-breakers and aeroplanes. They carry the timber to Europe via the Kara Sea, formerly called 'the ice-bag of the north'. In 1933 the passage was extended farther to the east past Cape Cheliuskhin to the mouth of the Lena. This made it possible for the vast forests of Yakutia to find an egress into Europe. The larch of these forests is as durable in water as metal.

X. COMBINES

Hitherto we have considered the geographical distribution of the industry of the U.S.S.R. branch by branch. But at the present level of development of the productive powers this method is not exhaustive. Though we may examine them one by one and as isolated objects, in reality the threads cross on the map. They are tied in knots. These knots are the inter-branch combines. Most of the enterprises enumerated above are either combines or parts of combines. Amalgamated production makes it possible to attain the highest productivity of labour and the best utilization of natural resources.

The concentration of the whole of industry in the hands of a socialist State and the planned method of economy open up quite different prospects before amalgamation in the U.S.S.R. from those in the most advanced capitalist countries. And still less, naturally, are they comparable with those possibilities which existed in backward Tsarist Russia.

The following fact is an example of the anarchy of productive processes in bygone Russia: at the Upper Ufalei metallurgical works in the Urals there was a blast-furnace and a metal frame; at the Lower Ufalei works, which lay at a distance of 22 kilometres from the first, there were an open-hearth furnace and a roofing frame. Cast iron from Upper Ufalei was carried to Lower Ufalei; steel from Lower to Upper Ufalei; metal sheets from Upper to Lower Ufalei; and finally the roofing was carried past Lower Ufalei to the railway station. . . .

The idea of amalgamation pervades Soviet industry and its distribution. Amalgamation makes for the territorial linking up of enterprises. The distribution of those which play a subordinate part in the combine is determined by the distribution of the principal leading branches of the combine. For example, sulphuric acid, a by-product of the copper industry, is manufactured in the same place as copper is produced. Therefore the development of amalgamation leads to a shift in the geography of industry, although the distribution of the combines themselves in the U.S.S.R. is determined by the general principles lying at the root of the formation of the new geography of the country—the policy of an even distribution of industry, of approximation to the raw material, of the development of the national outlying districts, and of the abolition of the differences between the village and the town, the intensification of the productivity of social labour.

Soviet combines are based on the many-sided utilization of raw materials or on the combination of consecutive stages of the working-up of the product.

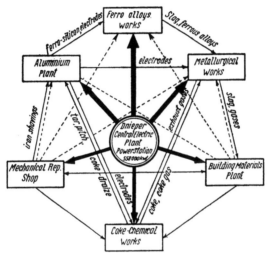

21. THE DNIEPER COMBINE

In one and the same combine a material can be used both as a substance and as energy. Brown coal gives synthetic ammoniac and electric current. Electric power causes motors to move and aids the process of electrolysis.

The most remarkable combine in the U.S.S.R. is the Dnieper Combine, which has not its equal in the whole world. The cheap power of the Dnieper hydro-electric power station, which is equal to the accumulated power of sixteen million human beings, has rallied round itself a knot of industries bound to each other by strong economic and technological threads—an aluminium works, consisting of a works manufacturing aluminium oxide, a works manufacturing electrodes, and an electrolysis works; a metallurgical works with an electric steel department; an iron foundry,

manufacturing ferro-manganese, ferro-silicon, ferro-chrom-
ium, and ferro-tungsten; a coke-chemical works; a number
of works manufacturing building materials (bricks, lime,
fireclay, silicon, dolomite). This industrial monster, this
town of factories, is already functioning. Soon its construction will be fully completed.

The newest ferrous metallurgical works—those of Magnitogorsk, Kuznetzk, and others—are combines. They combine
the production of cast iron, steel, rolled iron; they possess
electric power stations; coke-benzole and slagged-cement
works; and reckon on the utilization of the coke gases in
the metallurgical departments. Some of them possess a
mining industry as well.

The non-ferrous metallurgical works—the Krasno-Ural,
Pribalkhash, and other works—are also combines. They
possess mines, ore-concentration works, by-products such as
sulphur, sulphuric acid, zinc, and so on.

All the large-scale chemical works built in the U.S.S.R.
are complex combines. Each manufactures a large number
of products.

Machine-building works in the U.S.S.R. merge with metallurgical works, paper mills with wood-working factories,
weaving mills with spinning mills and cotton-purifying
works, and so on.

Different branches of national economy meet at almost
every geographical industrial point.

Inter-regional combines are being constructed, as, for
instance, the Ural-Kuznetzk Combine, the basis of industrialization of the Soviet East, whose construction will be
completed during the Second Five Year Plan.

The whole of the U.S.S.R. is becoming a combine of
combines.

Chapter 5

THE NEW DISTRIBUTION OF AGRICULTURE

THE peasant drew the map of the agricultural development of Russia with his plough. From century to century the ploughland encroached on the virgin soil, but its geographical contour was laid down unevenly and charily.

Farming in Russia took the line of least resistance. The isolated ploughman, armed with medieval technique, was powerless to till difficult soil: he could only wrench away the best earth from the country. Agricultural areas alternated with huge expanses of waste land which, had they been cultivated in an organized manner, might have become fertile.

The ploughman disregarded the boundless tundra and the elemental taiga. He encroached on the wide belt of the marshes, but he pulled up before the immensity of the deserts. He tilled but a small area of the podzol soil. Agriculture was attracted towards the Central South and black earth regions. Excess of heat and insufficiency of moisture did not permit the farmer to go to the extreme south. Excess of moisture and insufficiency of heat prevented him from going farther north.

The plough left vast areas untouched; and at the same time, frequently within the boundaries of the cultivated territory, land poverty caused the peasant to till the meadows and grass lands and to destroy the last forests for the sake of an extra pood of grain.

The agricultural specialization of the different regions of Tsarist Russia, which was distinguished by the extreme diversity of its economic structure, proceeded in an uneven and preposterous manner.

In many regions the poor peasant, oppressed by the survivals of serfdom, farmed on a semi-subsistence basis. The owner of a small piece of land, bearing in mind the unexpected blows of a cruel economic law, sowed, to be on the safe side, rye and flax and oats. Thus unspecialized farms grew up over large areas with complete disregard of agronomy and of the nature of the soil. There was no certainty of the morrow, and the distribution of agricultural products remained confused.

But where capitalism progressed and wherever the imperious demand of the market made itself felt, it subjugated the will of the farmer and forced him to sow the same commercial crop year in, year out; again with complete disregard of agronomy and of the nature of the soil. Thus excessively specialized regions grew up—cotton here, flax there, or some other crop—monocultural regions, where correct rotation of crops was unknown and where the soil was speedily exhausted. The cultivation of crops was artificially hemmed in by narrow geographical boundaries. The vagaries of the market bore heavily upon the single-crop cultivator; for they led to complete dependence on the part of the cultivator, uncontrolled fluctuation of prices, and constant vacillation between the hope of getting rich and the fear of being ruined.

The anarchy of production and the anarchy of geographical distribution went hand in hand.

Seventeen years have elapsed since the October Revolution changed the agriculture of the country beyond recognition.

In Russia nearly half the land belonged to the landowners, the monasteries, and the Imperial family. The rest was parcelled out amongst millions and millions of peasant farms. The abolition of private ownership of land in the U.S.S.R. was a guarantee that a rational geographical distribution of agriculture would come into being there.

After the Revolution nearly all the arable land was leased to the peasants for their utilization. But the development of backward agriculture and—connected with this—the general industrial development of the country could not be achieved on the basis of petty individual peasant farming, which was incapable of utilizing and mastering new technique, raising the productivity of labour, and increasing its profitableness to a sufficient extent. Socialist development of agriculture could only be achieved by the consolidation of agriculture: by the creation of large-scale State agricultural enterprises—'sovkhozes'—and the amalgamation of the scattered households of the peasant toilers into large-scale collective farms—'kolkhozes'.

THE PLACE OF THE U.S.S.R. IN THE WORLD'S PRODUCTION OF MAIN AGRICULTURAL PRODUCTS.[1]

Items	1928	1932	1937
Wheat	2	2	1
Barley	2	2	1
Oats	2	2	1
Cotton	5	4	8
Flax	1	1	1
Sugar Beet	2	2	1
Horses	1	1	1
Cattle	2	4	8

Collectivization as the keynote of agricultural development was adumbrated at the XVth Congress of the Communist Party (1927). It was put into practice under Stalin's guidance. The fierce resistance of capitalist elements in the villages was overcome. The achievements of socialist industry, which sent agricultural machines to the country-side, the organization of the sovkhozes, which served as models to the peasants of large-scale socialist agriculture, and the financial support given by the State all combined to fulfil this most difficult task.

COLLECTIVIZATION OF PEASANT HOUSEHOLDS
(in per cents)
(By 1, VI)

1913 . . . . —
1928 . . . . 1·7
1932 . . . . 61·5
1934 . . . . 73·0 (by 1, X)
1937 . . . . Completion of collectivization (plan)

[1] U.S.S.R. figures for 1932 and 1937 compared with figures for capitalist countries in 1928–9.

At the present time the collectivization of agriculture in the U.S.S.R. is in the main complete. By the beginning of 1935 four-fifths of the peasant households had united into large collective farms on the basis of collective labour and collective ownership of the means of production. Individual farming in the village has become a secondary factor—which must be subordinated and adapted to the system of collective farming. Capitalist elements in the agriculture of the U.S.S.R. have been stamped out. Nearly five thousand sovkhozes—great grain and meat factories—have been organized. Nine-tenths of the sowing areas are in the hands of the kolkhozes and sovkhozes. Agriculture in the U.S.S.R. is conducted on a larger scale than anywhere else in the world. This facilitates the alteration of its location.

SOWING AREA OF THE SOVKHOZES
(million hectares)

1913	.	.	.	.	.	.	—
1928	.	.	.	.	.	.	1·7
1932	.	.	.	.	.	.	13·4
1934	.	.	.	.	.	.	15·0
1937	.	.	.	.	.	.	16·8

In Russia petty peasant agriculture was on a barbarically low level of technique: the peasants tilled the soil with wooden ploughs and sowed out of bast baskets. Technical progress in the great landowners' farms was undermined by the cheap labour of the peasant drudges. The number of tractors could be counted on one's fingers. In the U.S.S.R. by the end of 1934 there were already 278,413 tractors. In order to introduce the most up-to-date technique into the kolkhozes there have been created three and a half thousand State socialist enterprises of a particular kind in the U.S.S.R.— machine-tractor stations (M.T.S.). These stations provide the kolkhozes with technical and organizing help, and are the economic and political organizers of agriculture.

During the Second Five Year Plan the mechanization of agriculture in the U.S.S.R. will, in the main, be completed.

Technical equipment helps to build up the distribution of agriculture on a rational scientific basis.

NUMBER OF MACHINE TRACTOR STATIONS
(M.T.S.)
(By 1, VI)

1913	—
1928	—
1932	2,115
1934	3,326
1937	6,000 (to the end of year)

TRACTOR PARK

(wear and tear accounted for; at the end of the year, millions of horse-power)

1913	—
1928	0·3 (by 1, X)
1932	2·2
1934	4·5
1937	8·2

Agriculture in Tsarist Russia was backward and unproductive. Feudal survivals hampered its development. The peasants in the central regions suffered from land-hunger and leased land from the landowners on serf-like conditions. The competition of cheap wheat from the gratuitously colonized lands of the south-east increased the impoverishment of grain farming in the centre. The landowner, who received a high rent and utilized the cheap labour of the peasant drudges, did not trouble to intensify his agricultural enterprise. It was only in West Ukraine, in the sugar-beet regions, that the farms of the great landowners attained a comparatively high technical level. The colonized regions in the south-east were more profitable. Agriculture there was a predatory commercial enterprise which overtaxed the soil and rendered it barren. Vast areas in the Asiatic part of Russia were occupied by primitive nomad cattle-breeding.

'The immense difficulties of uniting scattered petty peasant households into kolkhozes, the difficult work of creating a great number of large-scale grain and cattle-breeding farms on almost empty spaces, and also the period of time required for reconstruction and transition of individual farming to the new kolkhoz path, a re-organization that demanded some expense; all these factors inevitably predetermined both the slow rate of development of agriculture and the comparatively lengthy period of decline in the growth of the available stock of cattle.'[1]

In 1933, when the reorganizing process in agriculture was nearing completion, a noticeable increase commenced in the yield of grain and technical crops. The year 1934 was a turning-point in the development of cattle-breeding.

Sowing Area	Output of Agriculture
In million hectares	In billion roubles at 1926–7 prices
1913 . . 105·0	1913 . . 12·6
1928 . . 113·0	1928 . . 14·7
1932 . . 134·4	1932 . . 13·1
1934 . . 131·4	1934 . . 14·8
1937 . . 139·7	1937 . . 26·2

The agriculture of the U.S.S.R. is gaining strength. It is developing in accordance with a single State plan. Its planned distribution corresponds to planned production. The alteration of the agricultural map follows the alteration of the industrial map.

During the period of reorganization the geographical boundaries of agriculture extended mainly towards the south and the east of the country: by the end of the First Five Year Plan the area under crops in the U.S.S.R. had increased by 28 per cent in comparison with the pre-War area. During

[1] Stalin.

the period of the Second Five Year Plan the area will increase by another 3·9 per cent only—chiefly in the north and the centre: shrubberies will be cleared away, forests stubbed up, and marshes dried. One of the main tasks of the Second Five Year Plan is to secure an increase in the productivity of the cultivated areas, and therefore a comparatively small increase in the area under crop will be accompanied by a double yield of agricultural products.

The structure of agriculture in Tsarist Russia was backward. Grain cultivation occupied the chief place. In the U.S.S.R. an ever-increasing proportion of technical and fodder crops is being sowed. Less valuable are being replaced by more valuable grains: for instance, rye by wheat.

The land is being conquered, not by an unarmed solitary peasant farmer, but by the State through collective bodies, who are working in accordance with a single plan and armed with the latest technique. As they cultivate the more difficult lands—the waste lands of yesterday—they destroy the old contours. This is a correction of physical geography, not adaptation to it.

Together with the alteration of the structure of the sowing areas in the U.S.S.R. there is proceeding a planned agricultural specialization, and the agricultural map is being re-made. Each region cultivates the crops which suit its nature and economics and give the best results under the given conditions. Thus, for example, the north of the Moscow Region specializes in flax, the south in grain, and the centre in vegetable produce and dairy farming. The peasant newspaper of the Moscow Region *Towards Collectivization* is published in three editions. The grain, flax, and vegetable regions read issues of their own. Agricultural distribution is organized in accordance with the newest discoveries of science.

The corn problem is solved. A planned supply of corn is guaranteed, and therefore where the soil is particularly convenient the peasant now sows not corn, but technical crops. Vast areas of valuable plants are coming into being.

But specialization in the U.S.S.R. does not mean uncontrolled development in one region of a single crop, which

AREA UNDER CULTIVATION

	1918		1934		1937	
	In thousands of hectares	Per cent	In thousands of hectares	Per cent	In thousands of hectares	Per cent
Northern Region .	1,088	1·0	1,213	0·9	1,448	1·0
Karelian A.S.S.R. .	54	—	62	—	85	0·1
Leningrad Province .	1,751	1·6	2,210	1·7	2,785	2·0
Moscow Province .	4,585	4·1	5,924	4·4	6,548	4·7
Ivanovo Province .	2,005	1·8	2,419	1·9	2,910	2·1
Gorky and Kirov Regions . . .	5,603	5·0	6,540	5·0	7,090	5·1
Western Province .	4,197	3·7	4,506	3·4	5,300	3·8
Kursk and Voronezh Provinces . .	9,971	8·8	10,727	8·2	11,110	8·0
Tartar A.S.S.R. .	2,718	2·4	3,290	2·5	3,280	2·8
Kuibyshev Region and Oryenburg Province . .	7,417	6·6	9,754	7·4	10,020	7·2
Saratov and Stalingrad Regions. .	6,398	5·7	8,231	6·3	8,964	6·4
Azov-Black Sea and North Caucasus .	9,533	8·4	11,324	8·6	12,095	8·7
Crimean A.S.S.R. .	704	0·6	1,063	0·8	1,000	0·7
Former Urals Prov.	5,216	4·6	6,528	5·0	7,000	5·0
Bashkirian A.S.S.R.	2,626	2·3	3,380	2·6	3,500	2·5
Kara-Kalpakian A.S.S.R. . .	—	—	108	0·1	150	0·1
Kazak A.S.S.R. .	4,475	3·9	5,100	3·9	5,350	3·8
West Siberian Reg'n	—	—	9,052	6·8	8,870	6·4
East Siberian Region	9,357	8·3	2,160	1·7	2,235	1·6
Yakutsk A.S.S.R. .	—	—	83	0·1	100	1·0
Far Eastern Region	1,512	1·3	994	0·7	1,190	0·8
Ukrainian S.S.R. .	24,929	22·0	26,027	19·9	27,000	19·3
White Russian S.S.R.	3,398	3·0	3,864	2·9	4,060	2·9
Transcaucasian S.F.S.R. . .	2,137	1·9	2,481	1·9	2,550	1·8
Uzbek S.S.R. . .	1,767	1·6	2,435	1·8	2,815	2·0
Turkmenian S.S.R. .	332	0·3	383	0·3	480	0·3
Tajik S.S.R. . .	545	0·5	592	0·4	705	0·5
Kirghiz A.S.S.R. .	674	0·6	929	0·8	1,100	0·8
U.S.S.R. .	112,992	100·0	131,379	100·0	139,740	100·0

would exhaust the soil. Other crops are introduced into the rotation which has been worked scientifically, side by side with the leading crop, in order that their alternation may renew the fruitfulness of the soil. Thus, lucerne is cultivated in cotton-growing regions and clover in flax-growing regions. Within the next few years the introduction of a rational rotation of crops in every region in the U.S.S.R. will be completed.

The extremely varied natural conditions of the U.S.S.R. make it possible to cultivate the most varied plants—it is necessary only to distribute them rationally. Only a planned socialist economy is able to create a rational and rich distribution of the flora. An exact organization of agriculture in accordance with nature is carried on together with the active transformation of the physical conditions.

II. RECLAMATION OF MARSHLANDS

Agricultural plants require a certain measure of moisture, but the location of the water system in the U.S.S.R. is uneven. Soil moisture in cultivated areas is extremely unevenly distributed in the different regions. Near Batoum in Georgia the atmospheric precipitations amount to 2,600 millimetres a year; in White Russia to 600; on the left bank of the Volga to 300; in the lower Amu-Darya Regions only to 80.

In the north of the U.S.S.R. there is a belt of marshes. In the extreme south there is an arid belt. 'You may expect disaster where there is a great deal of water,' runs a proverb of the north, while the saying in the south is 'Who dreams of water may expect success.'

A reasonable amount of moisture is needed, and in the U.S.S.R. the water system of different regions is being altered: here marshes are drained; there dry lands are irrigated.

The Soviet North is humid and cold. The soil, which dries with difficulty, is swollen with the water of the frequent rains. Water becomes stagnant at the watersheds and in the lowlands, and is grown over with sedge and moss.

A belt of marshes stretches right through the whole country—from White Russia to the Far East. They extend over huge areas; in White Russia, for example, the peat bogs

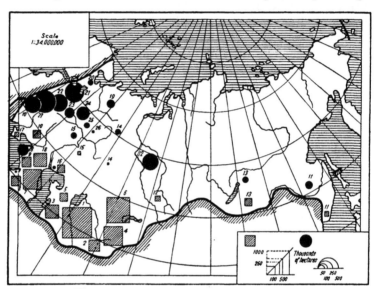

22. IRRIGATED AND DRAINED TERRITORIES

As on January 1st 1933.   Shaded square =irrigated.   Black disk =drained.

1. Uzbek S.S.R.	15. Kuibyshev Region and
2. Tajik S.S.R.	(Orenburg District)
3. Turkmenian S.S.R.	16. Saratov and Stalingrad Regions
4. Kirghiz A.S.S.R.	17. Crimean A.S.S.R.
5. Kara-Kalpakian A.S.S.R.	18. Azov-Black Sea and North
6. Kazak A.S.S.R.	Caucasian Region
7. Azerbaijan S.S.R.	19. Northern Region
8. Armenian S.S.R.	20. Karelian A.S.S.R.
9. Georgian S.S.R.	21. Leningrad District
10. Ukrainian S.S.R.	22. Western District
11. Far Eastern Region	23. Moscow District
12. West Siberian Region	24. Ivanov District
13. East Siberian Region	25. Gorky and Kirov Regions
14. Former Ural District	26. Tartar A.S.S.R.
	27. White Russian S.S.R.

alone, not counting the marshy mineral soils, occupy one-fifth of the territory.

Peat bogs, sloughs, and quagmires are far from being suitable for sowing, but even where it is possible to sow corn, it often becomes sodden, rots, and perishes. Wheeled tractors stick in the damp earth.

Ninety million hectares of marshland in European Soviet Russia alone have to be drained.

Within seventeen years 2 million hectares in the U.S.S.R. have been drained. This is twice as much as during the whole history of Russia; but this, of course, is only a beginning of the mighty work of transforming the surface of the huge land. During the Second Five Year Plan two million three hundred thousand hectares will be drained.

The trencher follows the caterpillar tractor, leaving behind it a ditch one metre deep. The ameliorative system dries up the marsh like a sponge. The machines turn up, roll out, and fertilize the soil, which only yesterday was soaked through with putrid stagnant water, and to-day is ready to be tilled.

The harvests on marshy land are abundant: they are bigger than harvests on mineral soil, especially in the case of vegetables and grasses.

Scores of thousands of hectares have been drained intensively, i.e. the subsoil waters, as well as the surface waters, have been regulated. In former Russia intensive drainage was hardly known at all.

The ameliorative works in the U.S.S.R. are a complex system. They include not only new meadows and ploughlands but new waterways, new fisheries, and new peat-works.

Before the Revolution the drained lands were utilized mostly as grass-lands and meadows. Now they are more and more frequently sown with flax, hemp, vegetables, and wheat.

The main region where drainage is in progress is White Russia. The appearance of many places in White Russia has quite changed. Formerly there were impassable uninhabited jungles, swarms of mosquitoes, and miasmal winds. Now the ground is hard and dry, the air is healthy, and the soil is sown with hemp and fodder-grass. There are sovkhozes, which possess many thousand hectares of land, and are the largest agricultural enterprises which have ever been created on drained marshes. There are kolkhozes, electrical power stations, hemp works, hospitals, schools, cinemas, and new roads. The change of the area is followed by a change of the map.

Next in order of area of marshlands drained come the Leningrad District, the West Siberian Area, the Moscow District, and others.

The whole of the newly created agriculture of the Far North is based on the cultivation of drained marshes.

In the Azov and Black Sea Area the Kuban marshes are being drained: they are low-lying marshlands situated along the Kuban River.

Thousands of hectares of land which formerly were quite barren and were merely hotbeds of malaria are now being made healthy and sown with valuable agricultural crops, including rice.

In the Transcaucasus, along the east coast of the Black Sea, there is a lowland which is an area of frequent rains, red soil, and warm winters. This is Colchis, the legendary land of the Argonauts who sought the Golden Fleece.

Alluvions raise the beds of the Colchis rivers. The sandbanks which have been built up by the wash do not permit the waters of the flooded rivers to enter the sea. The waters form enormous marshes, become putrid, and poison the close atmosphere. Wild growth hides the ruins of the villages which have been wiped out by malaria. A quarter of a million hectares of the most fertile soil are lying waste which can yield three or four harvests a year; the most valuable sub-tropical plants can be cultivated on them.

At the present time great drainage works are proceeding in Colchis. Within the next few years the malarial swamps and jungles will be transformed into the largest sub-tropical region of the U.S.S.R. and also into a region of health resorts.

Excavators and earth-pumps are creating, in accordance with a definite plan, a new, healthy, and flourishing land 150 kilometres in length. The country is only now being created but the map already exists.

The first main canal, 43 kilometres long, has already been constructed. The construction has begun of a second canal which will exceed the first in length.

By 1935 nearly 16,000 hectares were drained in Colchis.

Lemons, tangerines, and tea have been planted in the new soil.

III. THE CULTIVATION OF THE DESERTS

A seventh part of the U.S.S.R.—the plains of Central Asia, the south of the Left Volga Region, and of Kazakstan —is bounded by a belt indicating 200 millimetres of atmospheric precipitation a year. Within this vast area the figures of the atmospheric precipication fall to nearly zero. There is no rain in summer. This is the desert zone whose area is more than twice that of the whole cultivated area of the U.S.S.R.

The few and scanty rivers do not flow into the ocean, but peter out at the bottom of a gigantic flat basin. The swift waters disregard the parched and hot soil, giving it no moisture, and, falling into the closed basins of the Caspian, the Aral, and the Balkhash, they evaporate under the pitiless sun.

Desert lands cover 50 per cent of the territory of Uzbekistan and Kazakstan, 85 per cent of Turkmenia, 90 per cent of Kara-Kalpakia.

Amidst the sand wastes and great saline tracts there are many places with very fertile loess soil. There is a cloudless sky here and an abundance of solar energy. The air is dry, and favourable for agriculture. On loess soil the poplar becomes an adult tree in three or four years. The cotton crop is capable of the highest yield per acre. There may be as many as seven harvests of lucerne in one year. Fruit grown in these regions has a very high sugar content. Here can also be grown hibiscus cannabinus, kendyr, ramie, abutilon aricennac, southern hemp, the castor oil plant, sesame, eucalyptus, rubber-bearing plants, grapes, apples pears, peaches, apricots, melons, walnuts, figs, and so on.

This region possesses incredible potential fertility, which can be fully revealed only in conditions of artificial irrigation. The region needs new rivers.

Settled life is limited to the rare oases. The oases are pierced by a network of irrigation canals, which take their water from the rivers. The rivers flow from the mountains.

Eight million persons inhabit the smooth bed of a dried-up sea of Central Asia, because snow and rain fall on the mountains which enclose it on the south. The road is slow but sure: snowfall in the mountains, a melting glacier, a turbid river, and finally the channel ('aryk') which feeds the cotton stem.

Before the Revolution, 4¼ million hectares were under irrigation in Russia, mainly in Central Asia. This figure is insignificant in comparison with the area which requires to be irrigated and watered. The greater part of the territory was irrigated by primitive native methods, which had remained unchanged since the days of Alexander the Great. At the river sources—where the banks are low— the water was let into the fields through narrow ditches dug by the ketmen, the native hoe pickaxe. Downstream, where the banks are high, the water was scantily poured into the fields by means of chigirs, wooden wheels with earthenware jugs.

A complete reconstruction of the old irrigation systems in the U.S.S.R. and a speedy construction of new systems is proceeding at the present time.

By 1933 irrigation channels—constructed by the most advanced technical methods—were irrigating 1½ million hectares of new lands. This is equal to the area of the whole of the ploughland of Latvia. At the present time the newly irrigated land is being cultivated. During the Second Five Year Plan another million hectares of land will be irrigated. But this is only the beginning of the mighty work of transforming the deserts into flourishing countries.

As far back as 1921 Lenin, referring to the Transcaucasus, wrote:

> 'Particular attention must be paid to white coal irrigation. Irrigation comes first: it will regenerate and raise our economic system, it will re-create the land, and facilitate the passage to socialism.'

In common with every other work of amelioration, irrigation in the U.S.S.R. is a complex system: not only are

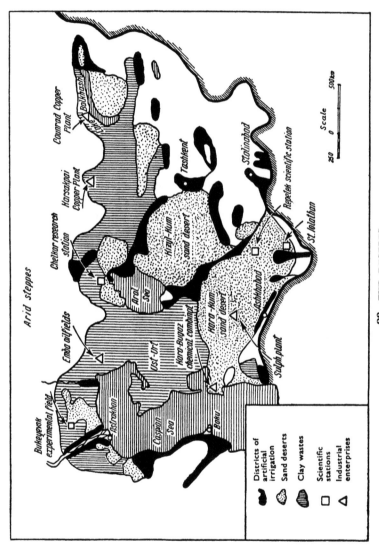

Arid steppes

Berezyevsk
experimental field

Astrakhan

Emba oilfields

Chelkar research station

Harsakpai Copper Plant

Konrad Copper Plant

Balkhash

Tashkent

Stalinabad

Repetek scientific station

St. Iolathan

Aral Sea

Kara-Bugaz chemical combinat

Ust-Urt

Kizil-Kum sand desert

Kara-Kum sand desert

Ashkhabad

Sulph plant

Caspian Sea

Baku

Scale

250   0   500 km

Districts of
artificial
irrigation

Sand deserts

Clay wastes

☐ Scientific
    stations

△ Industrial
    enterprises

23. THE DESERTS

127

new irrigated ploughlands created, but water transport, the fishing industry, and the water supply of industrial enterprises and towns are improved, and hydro-electric stations are constructed. The complexity of the works is ensured by the fact that all branches of economy are united under one plan.

Half of the newly irrigated territory is in Central Asia. A large number of powerful irrigation systems have been constructed here: the Dalverzin, the Golodno-Steppe, and the Chardaryin on the Syr-Darya, the Chouisk on the River Chou, the Koum-Kourgan on the Soukhan-Darya, and so on. Their channels are many kilometres long and irrigate vast expanses of land.

In the lower Amu-Darya 70,000 ancient wooden wheels—chigirs—are being replaced by mechanical irrigation.

The construction of a great irrigation system on the river Vakhsh in Tajikistan is nearing completion. It is already partly being utilized. This system will irrigate during the Second Five Year Plan 41,000 hectares of land for the sowing of the best cotton in the world—Egyptian cotton. The work is being carried on by the newest excavators in a desert country, where the wild littoral jungles are three times the height of a man. The river has taken an artificial course, in some parts cut out of the solid rock. The Vakhsh—fed by the melted ice of possibly undiscovered Pamir glaciers—glides along its ferro-concrete bed through seven windows with iron sectoral sluice-gates which allow 120 cubic metres of water to pass per second, and flows into a network of small channels, the total length of which is nearly equal to the earth's meridian. A powerful hydroelectric station will be built at the confluence of the water. What was but a desert yesterday is now traversed by telephone wires and macadamized tar motor-roads, and is becoming inhabited. By the autumn of 1934, 8,450 households had already settled in the Vakhsh valley. Cotton-cleaning works and oil mills will be constructed here.

In the Transcaucasus there have been constructed the Little Sardarabad, the Alazan, and the Tiripon systems, the Orjonikidze Canal, and other systems.

Marvellous hypotheses, which have become tangible plans, are on the point of being translated into reality.

On the lower Volga—at Kamyshin—conditions are being studied for the construction of a hydro-electric station dam with a capacity of approximately 8 billion kilowatt hours

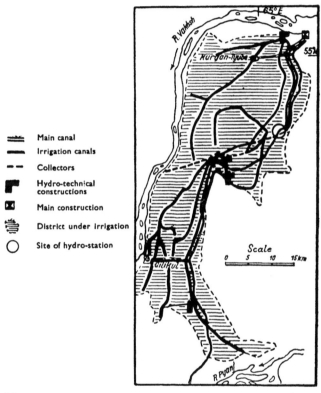

Main canal
Irrigation canals
Collectors
Hydro-technical constructions
Main construction
District under irrigation
Site of hydro-station

24. THE IRRIGATION SCHEME IN THE VAKHSH BASIN (TAJIK S.S.R.)

per year. Channels will lead the present idle waters of the Volga into the steppes of the Left Volga Region. There will be created an unbroken irrigated wheat-field of approximately 4 to 4·3 million hectares with a constant yield of 50 million centals of grain a year. The temperature will be lowered and the humidity increased within the surface stratum of air over this territory, which is equal in area to

9

Switzerland. Drought will be dealt a decisive blow. The importance of the irrigational works in the Volga Region was emphasized by Stalin in his speech at the last Congress (the XVIIth) of the Communist Party.

A plan is being worked out for utilizing the waters of the Dnieper for the irrigation of the southern Ukrainian steppe over an area of $2\frac{1}{2}$ million hectares and the northern part of the Crimean peninsula over an area of a million hectares.

After the construction of the canal which, within the period of the Second Five Year Plan, will connect the Volga with the Don, the Kalmuck steppe will be irrigated.

The Caspian and Black Seas will be connected by the Manych Canal, which is in course of preparation. The canal will irrigate a huge land of dry and desert steppes.

The unchained waters of the mountain lake Sevan will irrigate 130,000 hectares in Armenia.

In Azerbaijan a vast flat, sun-parched Caspian lowland stretches by the lower part of the Rivers Kura and Araks. In climate this land resembles Egypt. Hundreds of thousands of hectares of valuable cotton might be growing here. But only about a tenth part of this area has been cultivated. Nine-tenths are dead—there is no moisture. In the winter there are pastures here and in summer it is desert. There are malarial salt marshes in the low-lying parts.

In the future, after the period of the Second Five Year Plan, a dam, more than 60 metres in height, will be constructed on the Kura at the village of Mingechaur. An artificial reservoir, 13,000,000 cubic metres in volume, will be created—a new lake on the map of the country. Canals, each more than 100 kilometres in length, will traverse the dead steppes and irrigate a million hectares of land—10,000 square kilometres! Several hydro-electric stations will be constructed. The Kura will be dammed. Floods will be abolished. The fishing industry will develop. Malaria will disappear.

To-day the silt waters of the Amu-Darya, which are more fertile than the waters of the Nile, flow into the Sea of Aral, while around lie boundless deserts parched by the fierce sun. To-morrow the course of the greatest river of Central

Asia will be altered. Part of the Amu-Darya will fall into the Caspian Sea near the town of Krasnovodsk in the place where fresh water is brought from Baku, from the opposite shore of the sea. The waters of the Amu-Darya will flow over an additional 600 to 800 kilometres and will traverse the Kara-Kum desert. Beds of valuable plants will take the places of the moving beds of quicksand.

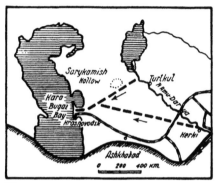

25. PROJECTS FOR NEW BEDS OF THE
RIVER AMU-DARYA, TO DIVERT IT INTO
THE CASPIAN SEA

At the present time the State Planning Commission is working out the course of a new river—the invention of man—in accordance with the work of special expeditions. It had been intended to take the river through the great Sarykamish hollow, which lies to the north of the desert, and to create a new sea there which would be nearly as big as the Sea of Aral. But scientific expeditions have pointed out the inexpediency of filling up the hollow in view of the presence of salt there which would make the water bitter, salty, and unsuitable both for drinking and for technical purposes. Moreover, the filling of the hollow would take too long a time. The water can pass by the Sarykamish hollow and utilize the Uzboi, the old dried-up beds of the Amu-Darya, which flowed, many centuries ago, into the Caspian Sea.

The bifurcation of the river is not a Utopian scheme. An experiment has already been made. From year to year the Amu-Darya waters are thrown out on the sand at a point 30 kilometres up the Bassag-Kerkinsk Canal in Turkmenia, which was constructed in 1927.

The new river is taking possession of kilometre upon kilometre of the desert. The spade of the irrigator is helping it to wash away the sandhills. The river is slowly moving forward. Within four years 475 million cubic metres of water have been poured on to the sand. The river flowing through the Kara-Kum desert is already 107 kilometres long.

At first the sand absorbs all the water. Then it is covered by a layer of fertile silt half a metre thick. Reeds shoot up. Birds fly to the oasis and settle in it. Crops of wheat, lucerne, and cotton spring up. Poplars murmur in the desert.

In the U.S.S.R. 5·6 million hectares[1] have been irrigated. Further irrigation work can increase this figure threefold and fourfold.

But the desert plains are vast: they cannot be made fertile by mountain rains and melting glaciers alone. Sooner or later there will be a lack of river water. Already the Chou and Zeravshan Rivers, in contrast to ordinary rivers, are growing shallower, and not deeper, the further they flow. They are used up for irrigation, die away in the sands, and arrive nowhere. Besides, there are high-lying regions, which it is difficult to supply with water.

In the U.S.S.R. there are 300 million hectares of sandy, clay, salt, and stone deserts—a quarter of the whole of the desert area of the world. Will they remain deserts? A dead patch on the map of a flourishing country? A symbol of human impotence?

Clouds without rain. Springs without brooks. Rivers without mouths. Lakes without a flow. Plants without leaves. . . .

The parched sand smokes under the burning wind. The whirlwind is saturated with suffocating dust. The sun is hidden by a yellow haze. The horror and the majesty of the desert.

[1] For 1, I. 1933.

But is the desert dead?

The sand deserts seem to be the apotheosis of sterility. And indeed it could not be otherwise. Life in vegetable tissue is extinguished at 54° C., while the sand is heated to a temperature of 70°. Yet it is easier to cultivate these sandy deserts than any other.

The sand greedily absorbs and filters winter and spring water, but because it is possessed of a weak power of capillarity it does not evaporate the water. There is always a stratum of water under the sand for a plant with a sufficiently long root.

The sandy desert, covered by crumbling sandhills and not by vegetation, is a product, not of nature, but of man. The savage cut down the saksaul, tended his cattle irrationally and wastefully, and the hooves of the nomad herds broke up the sand.

If man loosened the sands, he is capable of putting them together again.

Sand deserts are easier to cultivate than any other, and it is just this type of desert that prevails in the U.S.S.R.

The sand desert of Kara-Kum (35 million hectares) adjoins the desert of Kizil-Kum (20 million hectares), and together they form the largest sand desert in the world. Sand-covered expanses lie on the north coast of the Sea of Aral and in the region of the Lake of Balkhash. Sandy tracts are wedged between the fertile soils of U.S.S.R. in Europe—in the lower parts of the Dnieper, in the lowlands of the Don, and in the lower parts of the Volga.

Is the desert dead indeed?

Where the sand is not broken up it is covered by a peculiar kind of dry vegetation, on which camels and sheep feed. Some of the desert plants are highly nutritious.

Rare groups of Turkmens and Cossacks wandered about the desert with their herds from well to well. They lived a nomad life. They never laid in fodder and were always dependent on the desert pastures. The sand desert is not dead, but the utilization of it is in need of great improvement.

The 'Desert Cultivation Bureau', connected with the

Lenin Academy of Agricultural Sciences, is working out methods of utilizing the deserts in accordance with the newest discoveries of science and planned economy.

Cattle-breeding is the chief method by which those deserts, which are not yet transformed into agricultural regions by means of irrigation, will yield a return. The poorest pasture-lands in the country will be giving (and yield already) the most valuable products. Sand deserts are most suitable for the breeding of Astrakhan sheep, a very profitable occupation. The desert pastures are capable of feeding as many as 70 million head of cattle.

A planned regulation of the pasturing of kolkhoz and sovkhoz cattle, possible only in a socialist economy, the choice of pastures, their rational alternation, and a correct formation of the herd, all this will greatly increase the production of the valuable wool of the Astrakhan sheep.

This will not be a slavish adaptation to the desert. Motor-mowing stations will for the first time introduce mowing and ensilage into the desert, and sheep will be provided with fodder for winter. Nomads will become settled.

The flora of the desert will be changed. The problem is to replace under-productive or inedible plants by edible ones. Such plants have been found and tested: the yerek, a perennial cereal which in nutritiousness resembles bran, and is extremely hardy, and drought-enduring; sand barley, which possesses in high degree the power of strengthening the sands; sand oats, which are less nourishing, but are able to endure drought and heat; melilot, yellow lucerne, and others. It is easy to sow the seeds of these plants from aeroplanes. Selection makes it possible to deal even with clayey and saline soils.

The productivity of artificial grasses is many times higher than that of wild vegetation, to say nothing of the difference in the quality of the hay. On the Boukey experimental field (the Lower Volga), the yield of yerek under particularly good conditions has attained 20 centals a hectare.

Artificial grass-sowing in the northern part of the desert is easily accomplished. It is more difficult in the south, which is the driest and hottest part.

In addition to cattle-breeding, forestry will be developed in the desert. The 'tree of the desert', the saksaul, provides good fuel, strengthens the sands, and can serve as a decorative plant. The reserves of fuel in the black saksaul groves yield as much as 40 tons a hectare. This is a large figure for deserts. Artificial sowing of saksaul seeds from aeroplanes will renew the greatly thinned forests of the deserts. Drought-enduring trees will penetrate into the desert—the pistachio tree, the fig tree, and the almond tree.

The desert plants are revealing unexpected value. Some of them are capable of producing potash, alkaloids, gum, magenta, dyes, starch, and sugar. They are already being utilized.

Cultured civilized settlements are beginning to spring up in this wild desert land of nomad shepherds. The demands of the nomad of yesterday are increasing. Formerly, the consumption of bread per unit in the desert was as low as 50 kilograms a year. The nomad never even saw vegetables or fruit. The desert must be tilled.

Large industrial enterprises are springing up in the desert. Chemical combines in Aktiubinsk and Kara-Bougaz, coal-mines in Karaganda, a vast copper-foundry works on the banks of the Balkhash, and a sulphur works in Kara-Kum. The desert towns must be made green. Hundreds of thousands of workers live amidst the deserts, and they must be provided with vegetables.

Soviet horticulture comes to their aid. Its task—undreamt of in old Russia—is to cultivate potatoes, grain, roses, and grapes in the sand desert.

Year after year Jevinsky, a railwayman, is carrying out his marvellous experiments in the clayey and sand desert at Chelkar (Kazakstan), by the Sea of Aral. His little plot of land is irrigated by the water taken from under the sand-hills. His kitchen-garden yields crops which indicate the possibilities of horticulture in the desert.

Each square metre produces 12 kilograms of carrots. His cabbages attain a weight of 4·4 kilograms each. Each potato-plant gives 5·3 kilograms of potatoes. Many of the onions attain a weight of 380 grammes. One

square metre yields as much as 2 kilograms of straw-
berries. Beetroot, cucumbers, tomatoes, radishes, capsicum,
gooseberries, black currants, barberries, water-melons, and
ordinary melons all grow here.

The vines, which are protected from the winds and
covered by straw, survived the winter with its frosts of
40°. The pears were destroyed by the frost, but the apples
survived it. It has been proved that it is possible to grow
in irrigated areas wheat, millet, sorghum, rice, and maize.
An immense quantity of flowers has been cultivated there,
including twenty varieties of roses.

A kitchen-garden, of industrial importance, has been
created in Chelkar in accordance with Jevinsky's experiments. In 1932 the area of the irrigated land cultivated as
a kitchen-garden, and situated by the artificially damned
lake of Chelkar, was 150 hectares. In autumn the village
was fully provided with vegetables.

In 1933 an experimental station known as the 'Desert
Cultivation Bureau' was organized in Chelkar.

The desert can be made to bloom: water is the main
question. But desert plants do not use more than 50 per
cent of the moisture—the rest is lost. Wells have to be dug
to reach the subsoil water, which should then be raised to
the surface by means of the energy of the wind and the sun.

In Repetek, at the sand research station in the Kara-
Kum desert, three varieties of water-melon out of sixty
grew up without irrigation. For this most terrible sand
desert in the world, the ratio three to sixty is a great victory.
Some of the vines that had been planted there took root.
The railwaymen of Repetek, watering their plots in the
usual way, grow cucumbers, radishes, beetroot, salad,
melons, and water-melons. In 1933 two hundred varieties
of plants, collected from nearly every desert in the world,
were planted in Repetek. Only five survived, but amongst
these was a most valuable North African plant, the pennise-
tum, which does not require to be watered.

The Chernishev experimental improvement forestry
station on the Don sand terraces obtained crops of wheat,
sorghum, maize, and sunflower seeds which were no smaller

than those of the clayey black soil areas. The lupin not only grows and develops here, but increases the yield of grain crops by 70 per cent. The usefulness of lucerne here has been proved. The sands of the Lower Don are particularly valuable for vines. Valuable vineyards have already been laid out here. The importance of this cultivated area, until recently a desert tract, is specially great because it is situated near great industrial centres—the Donetz basin, Stalingrad, and Rostov-on-Don.

Forest gardens, producing apricots, pears, and cherries, have been artificially created amidst the sands of Dagestan. The cultivation of rye has been successfully accomplished in north-west Kazakstan. But the following fact is perhaps the most remarkable of all.

Barley has ripened on the sand without being watered at a scientific station in Yolotan in the south-east corner of the Kara-Kum desert. No fertilizers were used, but the yield was 3·5 centals from each hectare. The areas which were fertilized with nitrogen and phosphorus produced a crop of 4·8 centals.

Clearly, the struggle with the desert is not an easy one. It is not surprising that natural selection was impotent in the face of the desert. And yet the driest and hottest part of the desert gave man bread, barley bread though it was. Does this not speak of the approaching end of the desert?

IV. THE STRUGGLE WITH DROUGHT

The region of dry, parched, blazing-hot deserts is surrounded by the concentric circles of isohyets of 200, 300, and 400 millimetres of atmospheric precipitation a year. They cover the Volga Region, the North Caucasus, the east and the south of the Ukraine, North Kazakstan, and part of Western Siberia. These are not deserts: agriculture is carried on here without artificial irrigation. But they are zones of periodic droughts. They are scorched by the hot breath of the desert. Together with its source of origin— the desert—the dry zone occupies more than a third of the territory of the U.S.S.R., and is equal in area to the whole of the United States.

Drought was the constant curse of Russia. A general drought was an inevitable occurrence at regular intervals. A partial drought devastated different parts of the land every year.

Drought signifies the destruction of grain, famine amongst the people, and millions of deaths.

The life and death of the peasant used to be in the hands of this arbitrary and pitiless visitor. The figures of yield fluctuated feverishly: in the Volga Region 22·7 centals a hectare in 1919, 5·5 in 1920, 0·5 in 1921, 15·1 in 1922, 9·8 in 1923. The instability of the harvest was a constant menace to the national economy.

During years of partial drought Russia had a deficiency of ten to twelve million centals of grain. During years of general drought Russia was deprived of no less than 100 million centals.

Droughts attained the dimensions of a State calamity in Russia owing to the peculiarities of its geography.

The desert zone is surrounded by a wide strip of black soil. The zone of black soil from the Dniester on the west to the Ob on the east was the basic and decisive region of agriculture. Here, in these black soil steppes, there was concentrated the great mass of the population of Russia— an agrarian country. On the map the black soil zone and the zone of the greatest density of the population coincide. But to a great extent the drought zone also coincides with them. Similarly to the black soil region, the drought zone surrounds the deserts of Central Asia. The drought attacked the very granary of the country, and was therefore a national catastrophe.

The petty individual peasantry of Russia stood helpless before the drought. If old Russia struggled at all, it was not with the droughts, but with their result—famine. In order to destroy drought one had to deal with the climate itself; the physical geography of the country had to be altered. The struggle must be carried on over great areas subordinated to one will, and not in separate plots. Only a socialist State whose whole work is based on a plan, and a State which rests on a collectivized peasantry, can start a real struggle with age-long, hitherto unconquered, natural calamities.

In the north, in the zone of excessive humidity—beyond the drought sphere—the Soviet Union is for the first time creating a wheat-growing area.

In the drought zone itself, in the driest regions, a change of crops and the introduction of varieties is taking place with the aid of science. New drought-enduring crops are being introduced—sorghum, millet, maize, sunflowers, melilot, and French lentils. New drought-enduring varieties of old crops are being introduced, such as wheat. Agriculture is being made to suit the climate within a short period over an area of many million hectares.

The collectivized peasantry, equipped, owing to the Machine Tractor Stations, with the latest agricultural technique, is making use of the most perfected methods of husbandry in the drought zone. In order to preserve the surplus moisture in the soil, the land is tilled, not only in spring before sowing, but in autumn as well before the snow falls. Snow is retained over an area of millions of hectares: shields and coulisses of stalks are disposed all over the sowing area, dried branches are strewn about, and snow heaps are made. The melting of the snow in the fields is retarded and the spring is lengthened.

In order that the plant might develop before the commencement of the driest and hottest season, early sowing in the mud is effected from aeroplanes. A few days' accelerated ripening of the crops preserves millions of centals of grain from drought.

Over large areas woods are cultivated along the edges of the fields. The trees which are planted in woodless steppes protect the field from dry and hot winds, retard the melting of the snow, and condense the moisture. In 1933, for example, trees were planted in the Central Volga Area (now Kuilysher Area, and Orenburg Region), over a territory of 12,000 hectares.

Preparations are being made for the introduction of artificial rain, which was quite unknown in former Russia.

The kolkhozes of the left bank of the region dam up the local streams—the Kinel, Solianka, and others, and make the water flow into the fields. Some dams have been constructed which are 400 metres long and over 10 metres high. The water collected in the reservoirs is of importance not only for the immediate irrigation of the fields. It increases, at the same time, the humidity of the air and augments the local rotation of moisture, i.e. the rainfall. During the Second Five Year Plan 130,000 hectares will be irrigated in the left bank of the Volga Region. The productivity of watered wheat exceeds that of non-watered wheat about six times.

For intensity of drought and dry and hot winds, the year 1933 was the worst for the last fifty years. Yet in spite of this the total harvest in the Central Volga Area amounted to 22·7 million centals, whereas in 1931 only 11 million centals were gathered.

The radical method employed to abolish drought on the left bank of the Volga Region is the process of irrigating the area with the waters of the Volga.

V. SOIL-IMPROVEMENT

The area of naturally poor earth in the U.S.S.R. which has to be radically improved is enormous. In many regions the soil has deteriorated as a result of the predatory methods of husbandry in old Russia. The fields, which were leased for a certain term, and knew neither artificial fertilization nor correct crop-rotation, became exhausted. Artificial fertilization was made use of only in some noblemen's farms and on the land of some rich peasants.

Even manure was often allowed to putrify behind the cattleshed in the backward villages. But in any case there was not much manure, because cattle-breeding was little developed in agricultural regions.

Now, steps have been made to improve the earth's surface. In addition to direct fertilizers, which supply the soil with new nutritive substances, indirect fertilizers which 'liberate' nutritive substances already in the soil are used.

Thus calcification, which neutralizes acid soils and greatly increases productivity, will have been carried out over an area of 5 million hectares by the end of the Second Five Year Plan, and will facilitate the cultivation of the central and northern regions of the U.S.S.R.

Gypsum is being used for the first time to fertilize the vast saline regions in the south and south-east of the U.S.S.R., which up till now have been lying waste. In Kirghizia, for example, the soil sown with sugar-beet is fertilized with gypsum.

The black soil plain is dissected by ravines. The fields are full of them. The roads have been undermined. The level of the subsoil water has fallen.

Former Russia knew nothing about combating ravines: on the contrary, it widened them year after year—the plough of the peasant, who struggled against his land-poverty, loosened the surface of the ground, the melted snow and rain washed it away, the ravines multiplied and widened, swallowing up the ploughlands, and extending over regions millions of hectares in area.

The Soviet collective and State farms were the first to start a systematic struggle against ravines. The chief means of struggle is the planting of forests. Trees, whose roots strengthen the soil and prevent the widening of ravines, are being planted over immense areas in the south. In 1932 the struggle against ravines was carried on over an area of 14,000 hectares. During the Second Five Year period the work will be continued over an area of 500,000 hectares.

Foremost among 'inconvenient' soils is sandy soil. The sand, blown about by the wind, buries beneath it oases, roads, and villages. For thousands of years the 'tongues of the desert' have been licking whole centres of civilization off the face of the earth in the south of Russia. But it is only now that an organized struggle against sand has been started. The sandy soil is being planted, partly with the aid of aeroplanes, with the seeds of grasses and bushes which make the soil firm. During 1932 and 1933 the cultivation of sandy soils was effected in an area of over 39,000 hectares.

During the Second Five Year period it is intended to check and cultivate over 500,000 hectares.

The term 'waste lands' will be abolished in the U.S.S.R. The flaws of nature are being rectified.

VI. TOWARDS A BALANCED AGRICULTURAL DISTRIBUTION

A line ran from Kiev to Sverdlovsk, through the whole of European Russia, dividing it into two parts. The line lay on the map for hundreds of years, and was felt to be indisputable and eternal.

To the south of it lay the black soil region, tilled steppes, surplus grain. This was called the 'productive' region.

To the north lay podzol soil, copses, swamps, insufficiency of grain. This was called the 'consuming' region.

In the consuming region the harvest of rye was eaten up in the winter. Beginning with spring, the north became the dependant of the south: it ate imported bread, whose price was raised by railway tariffs and the profits of the merchant. As to wheaten bread of its own, the north hardly knew it at all. Why?

Because there is not enough land in the north? No. In the southern black soil regions 90 to 97 per cent of the arable land has been tilled, while only 25 per cent of the arable land in the northern non-black soil regions has been tilled. The remaining 75 per cent lies idle. As much as 30 million hectares of land which might be turned into wheatfields is overgrown with bushes and rotten stumps and covered with hillocks.

Is the soil in the north so bad? Not at all. In the north of Russia the soil is no worse than that in Denmark, and Denmark produces the largest crops in the world. Alaska, which lies in the Arctic Circle, has its own grain industry, which is built up, by the way, on the selection of Russian Siberian varieties.

Is the climate so bad in the north? Not at all. There is not as much heat as in the south, but, on the other hand, the deadly breath of the drought, which often destroys the harvest of the south, does not reach the north.

Is productivity in the north so low? Not at all. The relative yield of wheat in the northern regions is approximately 25 per cent higher than in the south.

But what is the matter then? The matter is that the soil of the north is more difficult to cultivate than the soil of the south. It is sufficient to till the forestless black soil of the steppes, but ordinary soil must, in addition, be freed of trees and bushes, it must be dried and fertilized. The small Russian peasant farmer living in the non-black soil regions had neither the money nor the technical means to extend his sowing area.

During the First Five Year Plan large-scale industry grew up amidst the southern agricultural steppes. Large towns sprang up amidst the boundless wheatfields.

The sowing area in the south has greatly increased, but now the south cannot give away all its bread; and the north, whose consumption of bread has also increased, has had to build up its own stable agricultural base. What poor and isolated farms could not do can be done by collective farms working according to plan and equipped with machinery and fertilizers.

And so the map of wheat-distribution is being re-drawn. Wheat is sown not only in the south but in the north as well, and on an increasing scale each year.

Collective farms, with the aid of machine-tractor stations are introducing wheat into the 'consuming' region.

The caterpillar tractor crawls over the thick brush-wood, breaking it down and flattening it to the earth. The heavy brushwood plough turns up the layers of soil. The branches and leaves are ploughed up—the soil is turned. The bush-cutter cuts down the young woods. The remains of the trees are burnt. There is no more forest. In its place stretches a field enriched with ashes.

Stubbing machines tear the stumps out of the ground. The land on which the forest stood, covered now by the burnt and mutilated roots of the trees, is ready to be sown with wheat.

Thus forests are replaced by ploughlands. During the

Second Five Year Plan 5 million hectares of virgin soil, at present covered by forests, will be tilled. This area is equal to twice that of the whole of the arable land in Denmark.

During the period of the First Five Year Plan it was mainly the southern black soil regions which were supplied with agricultural machinery. But during the Second Five Year Plan the northern non-black soil regions will be supplied with machines at a greater rate than the southern regions. The geographical distribution of the mechanization of agriculture is altering.

Wheat is growing on clayey soil. Before the Revolution only 226,000 hectares of wheat were sown in the non-black soil region—in the White Russian and Tartar Republics, in the Gorky and Northern Areas, in the Western, Moscow, Ivanov, Kalinin, and Leningrad Districts. In 1937 the area sown will exceed 3 million hectares. 'The consuming zone which specializes in flax and productive cattle-breeding is increasing its grain production at the same time.'

THE EXTENT TO WHICH THE NON-BLACK SOIL REGION
IS PROVIDED WITH ITS OWN GRAIN

	1928	1937
Town .	. 0 per cent	60 per cent
Village .	. 92 ,,	100 ,,

Formerly the corn loads were carried by rail, an average distance of approximately 950 kilometres (1928); now (1934) 650 kilometres. The fact that the 'consuming' region will be supplying itself with corn lowers the average distance and lightens the excessive overloading of transport.

The line of demarcation of dependence, high prices, and under-feeding which ran across Russia dividing it into two parts—the corn region and cornless region, the 'productive' region and 'consuming' region—within the next few years this division, which has existed for so many centuries, will disappear.

Just as agricultural colonization of the west was the historic fate of the United States, so the ploughing of the

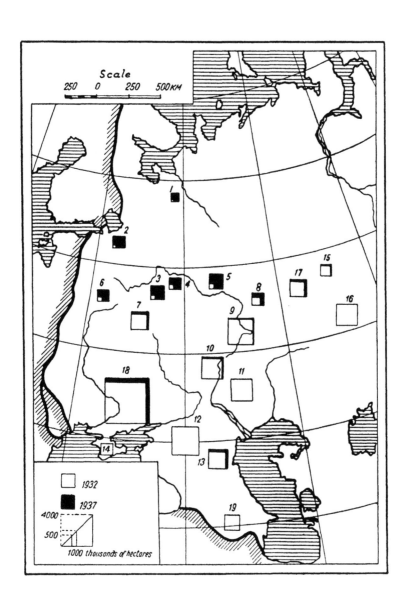

26. THE NORTHWARD MOVEMENT OF WHEAT CULTIVATION

(see table on pp. 146-7)

	Wheat (Winter		
	1928		1932
	In thousands of hectares	Per cent	In thousands of hectares
1. Northern Region . . .	25	0·1	24
Karelian A.S.S.R. . . .	—	—	—
2. Leningrad Province . .	16	0·1	35
3. Moscow Province . . .	20	0·1	68
4. Ivanovo Province . . .	61	0·2	63
5. Gorky and Kirov Regions .	71	0·3	112
6. Western Province . . .	50	0·2	77
7. Kursk and Voronezh Provinces	487	1·8	1,019
8. Tartar A.S.S.R. . . .	106	0·4	253
9. Kuibyshev Region and Oryenburg Province . .	1,948	7·0	2,838
10. Saratov Region . . ·⎫	2,334	8·4	⎰ 1,866
11. Stalingrad Region . ·⎭			⎱ 1,955
12. Azov-Black Sea Region . ·⎫	4,013	14·5	⎰ 3,840
13. North Caucasus Region . ·⎭			⎱ 1,215
14. Crimean A.S.S.R. . .	401	1·4	470
Former Ural Province .	2,025	7·2	2,215
15. Including Sverdlovsk Province	—	—	356
16. Including Chelyabinsk Province	—	—	1,815
17. Bashkirian A.S.S.R. . .	583	2·1	888
Kazak A.S.S.R. . . .			2,820
Kara-Kalpakian A.S.S.R. .	2,830	10·2	10
West Siberian Region . ·⎫			⎛ 3,686
East Siberian Region . ·⎬	4,869	17·6	⎨ 614
Yakutsk A.S.S.R . . ·⎭			⎝ 15
Far Eastern Region . .	575	2·1	399
18. Ukrainian S.S.R. . . .	4,736	17·1	6,949
White Russian S.S.R. . .	95	0·4	111
19. Transcaucasian S.F.S.R. .	1,022	3·7	1,095
Uzbek S.S.R. . . .	645	2·3	778
Tajik S.S.R. . . .	322	1·1	470
Turkmenian S.S.R. . .	134	0·5	186
Kirghiz A.S.S.R. . . .	352	1·2	483
U.S.S.R. . .	27,720	100·0	36,675

and Summer)						Rye	
1932	1934		1937			1934	
Per cent	In thousands of hectares	Per cent	In thousands of hectares	Per cent	In thousands of hectares	Per cent
0·1	66	0·2	220	0·5	285	1·0
—	—	—	—	—	18	0·1
0·1	146	0·4	460	1·1	478	1·9
0·2	361	0·9	670	1·6	1,365	5·4
0·2	218	0·6	500	1·1	495	1·9
0·3	360	0·9	745	1·7	2,342	9·2
0·2	175	0·5	450	1·1	1,250	4·7
2·9	1,144	3·0	1,260	2·9	2,933	11·6
0·7	450	1·2	505	1·1	1,219	4·7
8·2	3,042	8·1	3,100	7·2	2,259	8·9
5·4	1,689	4·5	1,977	4·5	1,070	4·2
5·7	1,708	4·5	1,759	4·1	828	3·2
11·1	2,705	7·2	3,510	8·1	726	2·8
3·5	1,052	2·9	1,370	3·1	80	0·3
1·4	470	1·3	480	1·1	3	—
6·4	2,284	6·1	2,401	5·6	1,339	6·1
1·0	426	1·1	526	1·2	703	2·8
5·3	1,802	4·8	1,819	4·3	579	2·3
2·6	968	2·6	1,110	2·4	938	3·6
8·2 }	2,873	7·6	{ 2,808	6·6	} 235	0·9
—			25	0·1		
10·7	4,945	13·2	4,987	11·5	653	2·6
1·8	715	1·9	760	1·7	480	1·9
0·0	20	0·1	30	0·1	30	0·1
1·2	373	1·0	410	0·9	37	0·1
20·1	6,500	17·4	8,083	18·8	3,746	15·0
0·3	197	0·6	370	0·9	1,213	4·7
3·2	992	2·6	1,022	2·4	4	0·0
2·3	886	2·3	907	2·1	—	—
1·4	305	0·9	311	0·8	—	—
0·4	121	0·3	127	0·3	—	—
1·4	482	1·3	483	1·1	—	—
100·0	37,475	100·0	42,885	100·0	25,308	100·0

virgin steppes of the east—the Trans-Urals, Western Siberia, Kazakstan—was for many years the fate of Russia.

In the U.S.S.R. the movement of agriculture towards the east continues, but its causes and its form are quite different from before.

It was the settler from the old agricultural centre who colonized the eastern border of old Russia. The lonely pioneer of Russian Asia came here from the landless village of the centre. The development of the east was one-sided—it was merely agricultural.

In the U.S.S.R. great industrial centres have for the first time sprung up in the east. They are new consumers of agricultural products and have caused the creation of new centres of agriculture. New soils have been tilled, mainly by the newly organized large-scale and mechanized State agricultural enterprises, the sovkhozes. A huge grain industry has sprung up on the former desert steppes. A host of tractors and combines have taken the place of wandering herds of semi-wild beasts. The process of settling has begun amongst the nomads, who have for the first time started cultivating the land.

Agriculture is developing in the Far East. During the Second Five Year Plan the grain deficit, which has hitherto been the rule in the Far Eastern Area, will no longer exist.

The plan has interfered with the previous distribution of wheat in the far south of the U.S.S.R. as well—in Central Asia. Wheat, which was a consumption crop, was often sown there on irrigated soil, thus reducing the cotton crop. The cotton-grower, in order to avoid dealings with merchants, endeavoured to provide himself with his own corn.

The planned supply of the peasants of Central Asia with corn has made it possible for the collective farms to utilize fully the irrigated lands for that extremely valuable crop, cotton. But this does not mean either a transition to the single cultivation of cotton, which would exhaust the soil, or a complete banishment of wheat from Central Asia. The necessary proportion of lucerne enters the crop-rotation of the sowing area side by side with cotton; and wheat is sown in the non-irrigated soil, the so-called bogar lands at the foot-hills where there is sufficient rainfall.

Thus the geographical distribution of wheat is being altered in the U.S.S.R. The significance of this process for the agriculture of the country will be understood if one remembers that wheat occupies no less than a quarter of its sowing area.

In Western Georgia, in the Rion Valley, the most fertile district in the U.S.S.R., where oranges, lemons, tea, ramee, and bamboo can grow, only maize used to be cultivated. It occupied 95 per cent of the most valuable soils.

Now the plan is extending the area of maize out of the kolkhoz fields of the Transcaucasus in other regions, while the valuable soil is used for sub-tropical crops.

The distribution of beet in Russia used to be absurd. The sugar-beet fields were wholly concentrated in the south-western corner of the country—in the Ukraine and the Kursk Region.

It was here that the distribution of the sugar industry was enclosed. The demands of the sugar factories led to an unreasonable extension of sugar-beet sowing. Sugar-beet took possession of all the fields in a narrow territorial circle, which were often unsuited to it, and around stretched an immense country suited to the cultivation of beet, but whose population did not even know about it.

In the U.S.S.R., simultaneously with the change in the geographical map of the sugar industry, a change is taking place in the map of beet sowing.

Sugar-beet has broken its former boundaries, which limited it to the 'old natural sugar-beet zone', and is extending far towards the south, the east, and the north.

In its movement towards the south it has reached Georgia. For the first time thousands of hectares have been sown with sugar-beet on soil which is more favourable to the beet than the soil of the Ukraine.

Moving towards the east, the sugar-beet reached the shores of the Pacific Ocean; it is now being sown in the Far Eastern Area. For the first time the sugar-beet has appeared in

Kirghizia and in the south-east in new regions less populated than the west.

The cultivation of the cotton-plant in Russia of the old days was limited to Central Asia and to the eastern Trans-caucasus. It was believed that cotton would grow only

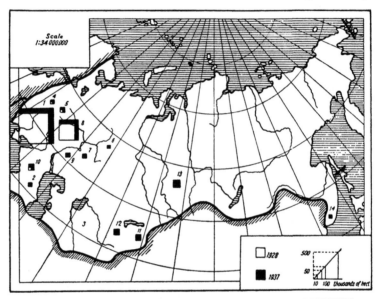

27. THE SPREAD OF BEET CULTIVATION INTO NEW DISTRICTS
(*see table opposite*)

on the sun-saturated irrigated oases of the extreme south, which were scattered here and there at great distances from each other. The cotton zone had settled itself against the southern boundary of Russia and remained stationary for many, many years.

Half of the cotton consumed in Russia was bought abroad. This cost the country 100 million gold roubles a year. The Soviet Union endeavoured to base its rapidly developing cotton industry on its own cotton. And thus there arose the need to double the acreage under cotton within the next few years.

But the increase of sowing areas was obstructed by the

old geographical distribution of cotton. In Central Asia and the Transcaucasus—the regions of irrigated agriculture —new sowing areas were prepared at the cost of the construction of expensive and complicated irrigation systems. The tendency towards cotton independence overstepped

AREA UNDER SUGAR BEET (FACTORY)

	1928		1934		1937	
	In thousands of hectares	Per cent	In thousands of hectares	Per cent	In thousands of hectares,	Per cent
1. Ukrainian S.S.R. .	647·1	84·1	821·7	69·4	927·0	67·2
2. Transcaucasian S.F.S.R. . .	—	—	5·7	0·5	9·0	0·7
3. Uzbek S.S.R. .	2·5	0·3	—	—	—	—
4. Western Province .	2·7	0·4	6·0	0·5	7·0	0·5
5. Moscow Province .	5·5	0·7	9·7	0·8	11·0	0·8
6. Bashkirian A.S.S.R.	—	—	1·3	0·1	4·0	0·3
7. Kuibyshev Region	—	—	1·7	0·1	8·0	0·6
8. Kursk & Voronezh Regions . .	106·6	13·8	276·7	23·5	300·0	21·7
9. Saratov Region .	—	—	1·2	0·1	13·0	0·9
10. Azov-Black Sea & North Caucasian Region . .	5·3	0·7	21·2	1·8	24·0	1·8
11. Kazak A.S.S.R. .	—	—	7·4	0·6	17·0	1·2
12. Kirghiz A.S.S.R. .	—	—	9·6	0·8	17·0	1·2
13. West Siberian Reg.	—	—	18·0	1·5	35·0	2·5
14. Far Eastern Reg'n	—	—	3·1	0·3	8·0	0·6
U.S.S.R. .	769·7	100·0	1,183·3	100·0	1,380·0	100·0

the rapid increase of sowing in the old regions. Cotton sought new regions where it might grow without irrigation and where the sowing areas might be rapidly and cheaply extended.

On the eastern shore of the Sea of Azov and on the northern shores of the Black and Caspian Seas there lies a chain of extensive though sparsely populated, and fertile though dry, lands, stretching from the borders of Rumania to the Lower Volga. Rain is infrequent here, though it falls more often than in Central Asia and the eastern Transcaucasus.

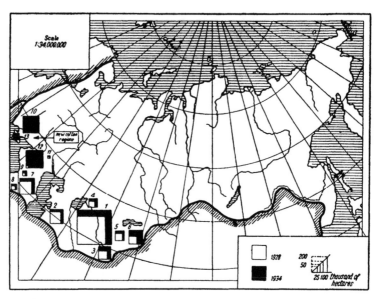

28. THE SPREAD OF COTTON-GROWING INTO NEW DISTRICTS
(*see table opposite*)

These regions required a drought-resisting crop. Such a crop was found: unirrigated cotton.

Thus were formed the circumstances which re-traced the geographical boundary of cotton growing—it was moved sharply to the north: from latitude 43° north to 47°.

The science of selection has revealed new, early varieties for the new, comparatively cold, regions. In 1929 large agricultural enterprises—sovkhozes and cotton motor-tractor stations were created, in the empty steppe kolkhozes were organized, cotton culture was in progress in these thinly populated regions: it had to be completely mechanized. The condition of the land and the soil, and the absence of irrigation canals facilitated the task: ploughing, sowing, and cultivation were accomplished with the aid of the tractors and a large number of other agricultural implements.

The cotton plant speedily became the principal agricultural crop in the new region.

AREA UNDER COTTON

	1928		1934		1937	
	In thousands of hectares	Per cent	In thousands of hectares	Per cent	In thousands of hectares	Per cent
1. Uzbek S.S.R.	568·9	58·1	882·6	45·6	921·0	45·1
2. Turkmenian S.S.R.	111·9	11·5	150·0	7·7	159·0	7·8
8. Tajik S.S.R.	52·2	5·4	91·7	4·7	116·0	5·7
4. Kara-Kalpakian S.S.R.	24·6	2·5	50·0	2·6	52·0	2·5
5. Kirghiz A.S.S.R.	40·1	4·1	63·8	8·3	70·0	3·4
6. Kazak A.S.S.R.	44·7	4·6	115·6	6·0	128·0	6·8
7. Azerbaijan S.S.R.	111·1	11·4	195·3	10·1		
8. Armenian S.S.R.	14·3	1·5	18·6	1·0	230·0	11·3
9. Georgian S.S.R.	6·2	0·6	8·2	0·4		
10. Ukrainian S.S.R.	—	—	156·3	8·1	156·0	7·7
11. Stalingrad Region	0·6	0·1	4·2	0·2	10·0	0·5
12. Azov - Black Sea and N. Caucasian Regions	1·7	0·2	173·1	8·9	168·0	8·2
13. Crimean A.S.S.R.	—	—	27·8	1·4	30·0	1·5
U.S.S.R.	971·3	100·0	1,937·2	100·0	2,040·0	100·0

Uninhabited steppes. A pitiless sun. In the spring, the rustle of brightly coloured flowers. In the summer, the murmur of brown wormwood.

Now the steppe has been tilled. The furrows disappear behind the horizon. Cotton, cotton everywhere. Roads have been made. Cotton-cleansing works have been constructed. A new cotton region has been created within three or four years.

The old regions continue to remain the chief cotton-growing areas in the U.S.S.R., but the proportion of this region to all the cotton-growing areas grew during the First Five Year Plan from zero to 19·7 per cent.

The first attempt to plant cotton on the north coast of the Caspian Sea was made 300 years ago by Tsar Alexis. It is only now that his aim has been accomplished.

The chief task now is to increase the productivity of unirrigàted cotton which is still far behind that of irrigated cotton.

The frontiers of Central Asia and of the Transcaucasus were looked upon as the boundary-line of the cultivation of rice in just the same way as they were looked upon as the boundary-line of the cultivation of cotton. Confined as they were to the oases, these two irrigated crops kept up an ever-lasting dispute over the water, which was so valuable there, and interfered with each other.

Ricefields are covered with water for a hundred days. The rapid growth of cotton-sowing during the First Five Year Plan caused a search for new regions for rice sowing in places where rice would not take the water away from cotton.

Thus started the migration of rice. Science has discovered large tracts of new lands, situated much farther north than the usual rice zone in Russia, but quite suitable for the cultivation of rice. Rice—which is a first-class food product and the most profitable of the grains—has been found to be the only possible crop in many deserted, swampy or saline regions of the Far East, Kazakstan, the North Caucasus, Daghestan, the Azov-Black Sea Area and the Ukraine.

While it has remained in reasonable proportions among the crops of the old regions, rice has speedily begun to settle in new regions. This crop, which from time immemorial has been grown only in small farms, is being cultivated here by newly created sovkhozes, the largest in the world—agricultural enterprises each possessing several thousand hectares of land under crop. The cultivation of rice, hitherto performed by traditional manual labour, is being completely mechanized—from sowing from aeroplanes to harvesting by rice combines. In a large number of new regions—near the Dnieproges in the Ukraine, for example—the harvest of rice has attained world record dimensions. In places where formerly there was no industry of any kind rice-purifying works are being constructed.

The rice crops in the U.S.S.R. extend over a vast territory, which is capable in the future not only of satisfying the internal requirements of the country in rice, but also of producing sufficient grain for export.

Rice is moving towards the north. But it is far from having attained its northern limits. Experience has shown that this 'southern' crop, which is remarkably frost-enduring, survives the winter and ripens perfectly even in the Moscow District—two thousand kilometres to the north of the old rice zone. This gives the country a promise of a complete revolution in the geographical distribution of rice sowing.

Other agricultural crops are also shifting to new regions. For instance, sunflowers and hemp are now being sown in the east. Around the new industrial regions of the east, north, and south, new regions of vegetable farming are springing up.

The successes of crop-shifting are great, chiefly because it is carried out by socialist enterprises—sovkhozes and kolkhozes—which have the most up-to-date technical equipment and work according to plan.

The success achieved in the transformation of crop distribution in the U.S.S.R. is the result of the successful application of Soviet agricultural science. There are 400 scientific research institutions, 1,500 model fields and stations, 10,000 scientists, all united by one plan and a common aim. The names of world-famed scientists are bound up with the problem of transforming the agriculture of the country.

The All-Union Institute of Plant-Culture, of which the Academician Vavilov is director, has collected a huge quantity of seeds, experiments on which open up new perspectives for the geographical transposition of varieties and crops.

The Academician Vavilov has established the fact that the qualitative and quantitative composition of vegetable produce varies greatly according to the geographical factor; for example, exactly the same variety of barley can in one region be suitable for brewing, and in another for fodder.

The famous Russian horticulturist Michurin has produced more than three hundred new varieties of fruit, which are not only remarkable for the perfection of their quality, but also for their exceptional power of endurance of rigorous natural conditions. For this purpose he crosses different varieties (interbreeding of one species) and also completely different plants—for example, cherries with the bird-cherry, the pear with the mountain-ash, the apple with the currant (interbreeding of species).

The place where Michurin carries on his work (the town of Kozlov now renamed Michurinsk) in the Voronezh region has become the centre of scientific fruit-culture. Michurin has under him a large staff of highly skilled scientific workers working in well-supplied laboratories and studies. The Michurin Institute has fifty branches scattered all over the U.S.S.R.

In 1934 Michurin celebrated his eightieth birthday, but he continues his scientific activities. At the present time he is endeavouring to produce a frost-resisting peach and a seedless grape, and at the same time to produce new varieties of plants with the aid of ionization and radiant energy.

The agronomist Lissenko has succeeded in discovering a method of transforming winter crops into summer crops, late crops into early ones, by the action on the seeds of these plants of definite temperatures and light. The artificial curtailment of the vegetation period makes it possible to cultivate plants in regions where they could not grow before on account of climatic conditions.

The achievements of plant-culture are really magnificent. They have enabled southern grapes to ripen in the kolkhozes of the Central Volga Region, the Ivanov District, Bashkiria, and the Trans-Urals; Ukrainian water-melon in the Moscow

District; dessert apples in Krasnoyarsk on the Yenisei, where in winter the temperature falls 50° C. below zero. The mulberry tree has migrated from Central Asia to Bashkiria, and peaches have gone to the Ukraine. The apricot spends the winter in the open near Leningrad.

New regions of agriculture are being created—in the high hills of the Pamirs, in the vast forests of the Birobijan, in the Volga delta, and in the Arctic Circle.

VII. POLAR AGRICULTURE

World agriculture tends towards the temperate and sub-tropical latitudes. The nearer the Arctic Circle, the fewer the ploughlands. Non-agricultural countries lie here.

Thus only the south of Russia was extensively tilled. Beyond the parallel of Leningrad there lay only 1·5 per cent of the sowing area of Russia. The boundless sea of coniferous forests concealed the tiny islands of tilled land, the rare glades tilled by the wooden plough and sown with 'grey corn'—oats and rye.

The extreme north of Russia—the coast of the Arctic Ocean—had no agriculture at all.

The tundra. A swamp of eternally frozen soil overgrown with thin moss. There are neither towns nor villages. Only rare camps of the almost extinct nomad native tribes. For the wandering stag-breeder and fisherman plant-cultivation was an unattainable stage of culture.

A line ran across the map of Russia which was called 'the boundary-line of agriculture', to the north of which lay fully a third of the area of the huge country. For centuries this geographical limit remained immovable.

Within the last five years the extreme north has changed enormously.

Coal, oil, apatite, and polymetals have been found on the barren coast of the Arctic Ocean. A mining industry has grown there. The most northern electric power stations in the world have been built there. Fish-tinning works and timber combines have sprung up. Seaports have been constructed. The north is covered by a network of air lines. Numerous scientific and radio stations have been created there. Large towns have arisen in the land of swamps and stones. Many thousands of new inhabitants have settled on the coasts of the polar basin.

The resuscitated north demanded a huge amount of food, and chiefly, vitaminous vegetables and fresh milk. The anti-scorbutic vitamin 'C' is the basis of the cultivation of the arctic lands.

And loads of agricultural produce had to be carried thousands of kilometres along the roadless lands of the north.

Hundreds of thousands of tons of water—water composes 80 to 90 per cent of the weight of vegetables and potatoes—had to be carried over seas and along rivers.

Hundreds of thousands of cubic metres of air had to be carried to that corner of the continent—the north requires fodder—dry grass. . . .

The rivers are the only way of reaching the extreme north through the impassable belt of the taiga, but loads can be carried on the rivers only in summer. . . . Sledges are the only means of transport in the swampy tundra, but loads can be carried on sledges only in winter. . . . Thus there is always one part or the other of the north which is cut off from the rest of the country. Transport to the extreme north costs dearer than the article which is being transported. In Srednekolimsk, in Yakutia, the production of a kilogram of potatoes would cost 17 copecks. But the transport of a kilogram of potatoes there costs 77 copecks.

The absence of its own food base hampered and held back the economic growth of the extreme north.

Science came to its aid.

Swamps and stones. Eternally frozen soil. In June ice still lies under the moss-heaps. The lowlands are boggy. The summer is short, damp, and cold. The polar winter lasts nine months.

The task seemed beyond human power. It was not a matter of correcting scientifically the age-long experience of a population. There had been no experience. The task was to create a new branch of production in a new country.

The extreme north has been covered by a network of scientific agricultural stations, of which the most important is the Polar Section of the All-Union Institute of Plant-Culture in Khibini and the Kola Peninsula, under the direction of Eichfeld.

The stones have been cleared away from the experimental fields. Swampy tracts have been drained. Acid soil has been neutralized with alkalis and fertilized. The necessary bacterial flora have been planted in the soil. This is not adaptation to circumstances: it is an alteration of Nature.

Year after year seeds brought from every corner of the globe—from Canada, Alaska, South America—were sown there; varieties were selected and crossed. The temperature of the soil was regulated.

The lack of heat was compensated for, as it turned out, by the abundance of light (in Khibini the sun does not set in summer for one and a half months), and the north responded to the energy of the explorer with what in Arctic countries were unprecedented harvests.

In the central zone of the U.S.S.R. the yield of potatoes is 100 centals per hectare. In Khibini it was 300. Subtropical varieties of barley and wheat ripened there. Oats grew to the height of a man. Two harvests of fodder-grass are possible within a year. Beyond the Arctic Circle there now grow cabbages, carrots, onions, swedes and turnips of various kinds, radishes, kohlrabi, peas, cucumbers, pumpkins, and so on.

Numerous large agricultural enterprises—sovkhozes have sprung up on the coast of the Arctic Ocean with the aid of the scientific stations. The Kola peninsula is a new Arctic industrial region with 150,000 inhabitants, and will soon be supplying itself with its own vegetables and milk. The new Siberian town Igarka, which lies 100 kilometres to the north of the Arctic Circle, has its own vegetable supply.

Stable agricultural enterprises (both vegetable and grain) have been created in Kamchatka. The Soviet portion of the isle of Sakhalin has several thousand hectares under wheat and barley, and has a permanent supply of its own potatoes and vegetables. The goldfields scattered over the taiga of Yakutia are also building up their own food base.

The only polar botanical garden in the world has been laid out in the new arctic town of Kirovsk (formerly Khibinogorsk). Along the pavements of the town, which though somewhat warmed by a branch of the Gulf Stream, nevertheless lies on the same parallel as the northern magnetic pole and the world pole of greatest cold, bloom asters, mignonettes, and pinks.

The nomad population of the extreme north—the Nentsi, Evenks, Saams, Chukchi: twenty-six minor nations in all—were entirely ignorant of plant-culture. They only knew the portable ancient reindeer-tent, everlasting wandering in search of new reindeer pastures and fisheries, the absence of all vegetable food. Now, for the first time, the peoples of the north are sowing fodder-grasses and planting vegetables. Artificial grass-sowing has placed the cow side by side with the primordial deer who gets his meagre moss from under the snow. Hay-making and vegetable growing, which supplement hunting, deer-breeding, and fishing, tie the nomad to a permanent dwelling-place, and raise the standard of his life.

The sowing area of the extreme north increased during the period from 1926 to 1933, thirty-three times in the case of vegetables and potatoes, and ten times in the case of grain. Machine-tractor and machine-mowing stations have been organized.

The boundary-line of the distribution of agriculture has been re-traced. Not only has it been pushed up to the very coast of the Arctic Ocean. Hot-house growing and vegetable and flower cultivation are in progress even in the Arctic islands—Franz-Josef Land and Novaya Zemlya. 'Agriculture knows practically no boundaries' (N. I. Vavilov, Member of the Academy of Science).

VIII. THE CULTIVATION OF NEW CROPS

A thousand years have passed since the Russian plains were first tilled, but the assortment of cultivated plants in

Russia has remained extremely poor. Mankind makes no use of over 90 per cent of the different species of plants in the world. In pre-revolutionary Russia the proportion of the vegetable kingdom cultivated was even more paltry. The limited selection of sorts and crops, which had been formed spontaneously, bore the traces of long-bygone centuries. And it found itself in contradiction with the increasing diversity of life.

In U.S.S.R. the development of old and the growth of new branches of industry created a demand for new species of vegetable for technical raw material. There was a demand, in hitherto unheard-of quantities, for rubber, gum, varnish, essential oils, fatty oils, alkaloids, tannin, vegetable dyes, corks, pectins, acids, plastic masses, rayon substances. Agriculture, which before the Revolution existed principally for the purpose of satisfying the needs of nourishment, is now, on an ever-increasing scale, serving the needs of industry. But in the sphere of nourishment as well, the circle of new demands is rapidly growing. The standard of living of the masses is improving, and their cultural demands are increasing. There is a growing need for nourishing vegetables and exotic fruits.

The country was faced with the tremendous task of renewing and enriching its agricultural resources. It was made even more urgent by the fact that agriculture was penetrating into new, formerly desert, regions. There was a need for a thorough revision of the cultivable area, a well thought out change of varieties and crops, and a rapid extension of the range of plants.

By genetic and selective methods the science of plant-culture is successfully creating new varieties out of old, and is effecting the substitution of more valuable for less valuable varieties over huge areas in the country. But this is not enough. Soviet plant-culture is mobilizing and transferring to the U.S.S.R. all the plants of the earth of which it is in need.

The Soviet Union possesses climatic regions similar to those of Florida and California, of Japan and of China, of Alaska and of the Himalayas. The variety of natural conditions corresponds to the variety of national economic needs. The cereals, vegetables, flowers, and fruits of Africa, Asia, America, and Australia are transferred to new geographical surroundings.

Plants are transferred which have long been known to mankind, but because of the isolation of peoples have been shut up within the frontiers of different countries. Plants are also transferred which have been discovered by the numerous Soviet geographical expeditions searching the face of the earth. The plant-seekers from the U.S.S.R., directed by the Academician Vavilov, have collected a large quantity of seeds hitherto unknown to world science and capable of revolutionizing the work of selection. Even a number of new varieties of wheat have been discovered, though wheat has been studied more than any other crop. In the Cordilleras, Soviet expeditions have discovered sixteen new sorts of potato, amongst which are some capable of resisting 8° C. of frost without even the leaves being injured. A particularly large number of new crops have been brought from the foot-hills and mountains of Southern Asia, Africa, Central and South America—from the seats of ancient agriculture. The vegetable species of these mountainous districts which are extremely varied, exactly suit, in view of their frost and drought-resisting qualities, the climate of the extreme north and the deserts of the U.S.S.R.—the climate of the new regions of agriculture.

It was Lenin who first thought of starting this work of renewing the flora of the U.S.S.R., after having learnt of the similar activities of the United States, which imported from other countries all the plants now being cultivated, except maize, tobacco, and cotton. But in contrast to other countries, Soviet scientists are conducting their work in accordance with a single plan; the introduction of crops in the fields is effected by kolkhozes and sovkhozes, which are working in accordance with this plan, and therefore the renewal of the flora of the U.S.S.R. is being conducted in a particularly organized and successful manner.

Agriculture in the U.S.S.R. has been enriched by a large number of new crops. Some of them, both those found in the country and those imported from abroad, have attained industrial significance already. Some are being cultivated by kolkhozes and sovkhozes. Some are still in the experimental stage.

Sorghum has been introduced into the drought regions of the U.S.S.R. It is a grain which is possessed of an exceptional drought-resisting power: it is the 'camel of the vegetable kingdom'. This plant from Palestine has settled in southern Ukraine and Kazakstan.

The soya bean is a Manchurian plant, the only representative of the vegetable kingdom containing albumen which is equivalent to animal albumen, and it occupies now more than 100,000 hectares in the Ukraine and the North Caucasus. It has taken possession of the fields of the U.S.S.R. at a rate unknown to any other crop in the world.

Byzantine oats have become a winter crop in the cotton regions of Azerbaijan; noot (*Cicer arietinum*) in the steppes of the Ukraine and Crimea.

New spinning crops have been introduced: kendyr into Kirghizia and Kazakstan, a wild plant of Central Asia with a stronger fibre than any other spinning plant; kenaf, an Indian plant which replaces jute, has been introduced into Azerbaijan; Egyptian cotton into Tajikistan; sunn into the North Caucasus.

Three exceptionally valuable rubber-plants have been discovered in the southern mountains of the U.S.S.R.: tau-sagiz, kok-sagiz, and krim-sagiz; the last gives a better-quality rubber than the tropical kind. Rubber sovkhozes and works are already functioning. The Mexican guaiula, which yields as much as a ton of rubber per hectare, has been introduced into Turkmenia.

The batata, a native of the West Indies, has been introduced into the south of the Soviet Union. This is similar to the potato but surpasses it for nutritiveness and productivity.

In the Chouisk valley (Kirghizia) Italian hemp attains a height of three metres.

Topinambur is a plant which can be tinned, and from which alcohol, synthetic rubber, and sugar is obtained. Choufa provides flour and oil for confectionery. Melilot is drought-resisting, frost-resisting, and salt-resisting, and is an exceptionally nourishing fodder-plant. Leaf cabbage for fodder can grow on the shores of the Arctic Ocean. The velvet bean increases the productivity of cotton. Sudan grass, American pyrrheus, basil, badan, scumpia, Abyssinian Azhgon, Dolmat camomile. . . .

There are a large number of valuable plants which require a sub-tropical climate. Every year Russia used to import sub-tropical raw material to the value of 200 million roubles, although there are sub-tropical regions in the country.

On the Caucasian coast of the Black Sea the climate is hot and humid, as in a hot-house. The average temperature during the coldest month is only $-5°$ C. There are three or four harvests a year. Roses bloom in January. A wood, ten metres high, grew up within two years on an abandoned maize field. . . . These are the 'humid' sub-tropics—Soviet Florida.

The swamps of the humid sup-tropics are at present in the process of being drained. Plantations are being laid down. The aspect of the country is changing hourly.

The Chinese tree toung-hu, yielding a varnish which preserves metals from corrosion, was unknown in Russia in former days. During the Second Five Year Plan toung-hu plantations will increase from 300 hectares to 10,000 hectares.

The Algerian cork-oak was also unknown in Russia. Now it is growing over an area of 810 hectares.

In 1913 the tea plant, a native of China and India, occupied 980 hectares on the Black Sea coast. That year Russia imported tea to the value of 62 million roubles. During the Second Five Year Plan the sowing area of tea will increase from 31,800 to 48,000 hectares.

The Chinese nettle ramee, from which a very valuable fibre for special fabrics is obtained, did not grow in Russia. During the Second Five Year Plan the area under this crop will increase from 770 to 5,000 hectares.

Russia imported oranges, tangerines, and lemons to the value of more than 12 million roubles every year. During the Second Five Year Plan the area under these fruits will increase from 2,300 hectares to 10,000 hectares.

The sowing of essential oil-bearing plants has completely freed the U.S.S.R. from imports of this product. During the Second Five Year Plan their sowing area will be doubled.

The Japanese date-plum, feihoe, eucomia, Australian acacia, Brazil nuts, peecan loofahs, and bamboo grow in the humid sub-tropics of the U.S.S.R.

The first experimental cocoa plantations are being organized.

In the semi-desert regions of Azerbaijan, in the protected valleys of southern Tajikistan, and in south-west Turkmenia, the climate is hot and dry. In summer there is practically no rainfall, and the winter is mild. These are the 'dry' sub-tropics—Soviet California.

The dry sub-tropics are only now beginning to be cultivated. Tigers still inhabit the jungles of Tajikistan. In 1934 in the sub-tropics of Central Asia there were planted more than a hundred different kinds of sub-tropical plants. Figs, pomegranates, almonds, guaiula, essential oil-bearing plants, olives, citruses, and possibly the sugar-cane can grow here.

The area of the Soviet sub-tropics is not very large comparatively, but the planned method of economy will make it possible to utilize the area rationally.

Florida and California have better climatic conditions than the Soviet sub-tropics. Even the fig palm grows there, liking, as the Arabs say, 'to have its head in fire and its feet in water'. But, according to the Arabian historians, the fig palm once upon a time grew in Termez—Tajikistan—and Soviet scientists might be able to resuscitate it.

The U.S.S.R. is being sown with new crops. They have new names. But it is not only 'new' crops which renew the flora of the country.

Is makhorka, which the scientist has compelled to yield citric acid, a new crop?

Is maize, which now has over a hundred and fifty uses, a new crop?

Is the oldest corn, the patriarch of the agriculture of the world—wheat—from whose stem people have learnt to make soap and paper, a new crop?

IX. IMPROVEMENT OF FAUNA

Cattle-breeding suffered considerably during the re-organization period of agriculture in the U.S.S.R. The total number of cattle diminished particularly in the main cattle-breeding districts of the country, in the east: in Kazakstan, in Central Asia, the slaughter of cattle was a form of resistance by the capitalist elements to the policy of collectivization of the country.

At the XVIIth Congress of the Communist Party in January 1934 Stalin spoke of the improvement of cattle-breeding as of one of the most important current tasks of the nation. This change was achieved. The decay of cattle-breeding is a thing of the past; 1934 became a year of revival.

Cattle-breeding is now proceeding on a yearly State plan, one of its main tasks being the building up of cattle-breeding in the east—in the still backward cattle regions.

According to the Second Five Year Plan the value of cattle-breeding must increase two and a quarter times during these five years. This will be achieved both by the numerical and qualitative growth of cattle-breeding (increase of weight of animal, milk yield, etc.).

The basis of the qualitative growth of cattle-breeding is breeding and selection. Previously this was hindered by an irregular distribution of different breeds of cattle in the country. Now there is a scientific plan of the geographical distribution of different breeds. The map of cattle-breeding is changing.

Artificial grass-sowing will move dairy cattle beyond the Arctic Circle. The creation of a great fodder base will develop pig-breeding in the non-black soil zone. Lucerne, introduced into cotton crop-rotation, will provide beasts of burden for the hitherto poor oases of Central Asia which are being irrigated. Cultivation of the deserts will create new regions of sheep-breeding.

But it is not only the geographical distribution of domestic animals which is being changed: changes have begun in the distribution of all the rest of the country's fauna.

The natural distribution of wild animals is far from perfect. It is not in accordance with the distribution of natural fodder resources. Insurmountable obstacles stood in the way of the transmigration of animals: mountain ranges, wide rivers, barren deserts, and human settlements, and on the fauna map there lay blank spaces—'biological spaces' of unutilized resources.

The steppe zone would not permit the squirrel to migrate to the Caucasus, though she would have found an abundance of food there in the fir forests. The wide steppes of Siberia are not inhabited by the hare, only because its narrow paws stick in the soft snow of the Ural forests which bar its way to the east. The hare could cross the Urals in summer, but at that time he is busy feeding his offspring.

The men who inhabited Russia of the olden times not only did nothing to help nature, but, like beasts of prey, they laid the country waste.

The European red deer has been exterminated. The wild boar has been killed off. The wild goats, which lived near Moscow, have been destroyed. The last aurochs have disappeared. It is seldom that one meets a wild deer.

The taiga of Siberia possessed untold treasure of fur, but with the conquest of Siberia by the Russians it soon began to dwindle. The native hunter killed the animal by shooting pellets into its eye, in order to give the merchant skin after skin in return for the spirits and matches which he had borrowed. Animals were exterminated over great areas.

In the U.S.S.R. hunting is for the first time being combined with science. Protective measures forbid the robbery of the taiga and ensure the rational reproduction of useful animals. The wolf is hunted the whole year round, squirrels are not touched during the forbidden period, while the spotted deer and the egret must not be killed at all. Prohibitive measures saved the useful and beautiful elk, which was nearly extinct, and encouraged its breeding.

But the successes achieved did not consist only in prohibitive measures. Far from it. The forests of the U.S.S.R. hardly know the individual hunter-trader who is ready to exterminate all the beasts of the earth as long as he alone

	Total of Livestock	
	Horses	
	1932	1937
Norther Region	2·0	1·9
Karelian A.S.S.R.	0·2	0·2
Leningrad Province	2·8	2·9
Moscow Province	4·9	5·2
Ivanovo Province	2·2	2·4
Gorky and Kirov Regions	5·0	5·5
Western Province	5·4	6·0
Kursk and Voronezh Provinces . . .	7·2	7·0
Tartar A.S.S.R.	1·7	2·2
Kuibyshev Region and Oryenburg Province	4·3	4·6
Saratov and Stalingrad Regions . . .	2·5	2·3
Azov-Black Sea and North Caucasus Regions	5·8	5·6
Crimean A.S.S.R.	0·5	0·5
Former Ural Province	5·0	4·8
Bashkirian A.S.S.R.	2·8	2·9
Kazak A.S.S.R.	3·7	3·3
West Siberian Region	8·1	8·5
East Siberian Region	4·0	3·9
Far Eastern Region	0·8	0·9
Yakutsk A.S.S.R.	1·0	0·9
Ukrainian S.S.R.	18·6	16·8
White Russian S.S.R.	4·2	4·4
Transcaucasian S.F.S.R.	1·9	2·2
Uzbek S.S.R. ⎫		
Turkmenian S.S.R. ⎬	2·6	2·5
Tajik S.S.R. ⎭		
Kirghiz A.S.S.R.	2·5	2·3
Kara-Kalpakian A.S.S.R.	0·3	0·3
Per cent . .	100·0	100·0
U.S.S.R. in thousands of cattle . . .	19,638	21,800

secures them. Hunting as an occupation is more and more being carried on by co-operative hunters—by collective bodies of hunters, whose activities remain within the limits laid down by the general national-economic plan. This

LIVESTOCK

(in spring of given Year)

Large Horned Cattle		Sheep and Goats		Pigs	
1932	1937	1932	1937	1932	1937
2·6	2·3	1·8	2·2	0·9	1·0
0·3	0·2	0·2	0·2	1·0	0·1
3·3	3·1	2·7	3·3	2·2	2·7
5·0	5·0	5·7	5·0	6·7	5·4
2·9	2·9	2·2	3·3	1·0	1·6
4·9	5·1	7·5	6·8	5·2	5·4
4·8	4·6	5·3	4·6	8·7	5·5
5·7	5·7	4·7	4·0	6·1	8·6
1·4	1·7	2·0	2·1	0·9	1·4
3·6	3·8	3·4	3·5	2·5	3·9
3·8	4·0	3·9	4·5	2·6	3·8
7·8	7·6	9·0	11·8	6·5	6·3
0·3	0·4	0·7	1·1	0·6	0·4
4·9	5·2	3·9	3·5	3·4	4·9
2·4	2·4	2·6	2·1	1·2	1·4
4·8	4·4	5·8	5·8	0·8	1·5
6·6	7·6	6·4	8·4	4·3	8·6
3·2	2·8	2·7	2·5	4·4	3·4
0·6	0·6	0·1	0·1	1·4	1·5
1·5	1·4	0·0	0·0	0·0	0·0
12·3	12·1	4·1	4·4	22·3	22·1
3·8	3·8	4·0	2·8	13·4	7·7
8·6	8·3	8·0	6·8	3·5	2·4
4·1	3·9	9·9	8·3	0·2	0·2
1·1	0·9	3·1	2·6	0·2	0·2
0·2	0·2	0·3	0·3	0·0	0·0
100·0	100·0	100·0	100·0	100·0	100·0
40,651	65,500	52,141	96,000	11,611	43,400

collectivized occupation of hunting has a profound effect on the mind of the hunter, destroying as it does the last elements in it of individual rapacity. State hunting-stations, organized in the form of headquarters in the hunting regions, are centres both for cultural development among the hunters and for the renewal of their technical equipment.

Special hunting-colleges have been created. Beasts and birds are studied, with the result that in the U.S.S.R. people have not only learnt to utilize them rationally, but also to breed them in natural conditions and in captivity and to domesticate them. The mass breeding of sables, silver-and-black foxes, martens, racoons, polar foxes, minks, polecats, and others is in progress in fifteen large sovkhozes of the People's Commissariat for Foreign Trade, which possess over 21,000 valuable pedigree fur-bearing animals.

The correction of the natural distribution of the fauna and the redistribution of animals over the immense areas of the U.S.S.R. are aided by a network of newly created sanctuaries.

The creation of sanctuaries as a reaction to the destruction by man of natural wealth—the tabooing of bits of nature—is well known in history. The sacred white elephants of ancient India, and Yellowstone Park, organized by the U.S. Congress 'for the pleasure and enjoyment of the nation', are illustrations of a common idea.

Pre-revolutionary Russia also had sanctuaries. There were not many of them and they reflected the social character of the country.

The Belovezh thicket, in which there lived a handful of aurochses, the last wild oxen in Europe, was declared to be a sanctuary—for the purpose of solemn royal hunts. In the western valleys of the Caucasus the shooting of deer, wild boars, and roes, was forbidden to everybody except the imperial family. A sanctuary was created in the southern steppes on his private initiative, and at his own expense, by Falzfein, a wealthy amateur. And that was all.

The work of preserving nature in the U.S.S.R. was begun on the initiative of Lenin. It grew to a tremendous extent. Numerous sanctuaries, with a total area exceeding 10 million hectares, have been organized. They cover all the most typical geographical landscapes of the country with their animal and vegetable kingdoms.

The steppe sanctuary of Askania-Nova (50,000 hectares),

which is situated in the south of the Ukraine, consists of a zoological garden steppe preserve, botanical gardens, ponds, and a farm with forests and pastures; it is inhabited by bison, zebra, ostriches, flamingoes, and other species.

The Caucasian sanctuary (350,000 hectares) lies on the northern slopes of the Caucasian range at a height of 325 to 1,900 metres above sea-level. It is inhabited by wild goats, Caucasian deer, chamois, foxes, wolves, bears, badgers, mountain turkey, mountain grouse, the white-headed griffon, the Alpine daw, the green woodpecker, trout, etc. There are glaciers in the mountains, various rich forests (yews, boxes, and others) in the mountainous plateaux.

The Altai sanctuary in Siberia (1 million hectares) lies on the slopes of snow-capped mountains, and is rich in Alpine flora and fauna. The Siberian stag, the musk-deer, the sable, the panther, the lynx, the glutton, the bear, the chipmunk, and other animals live in the sanctuary.

Deer, roe, moufflons, and others live in the Crimean sanctuary (23,000 hectares). Beech-woods are growing here.

The Astrakhan sanctuary (25,000 hectares) lies in the delta of the Volga and protects the places of nesting water-fowl and spawning fish. The lotus grows here.

The Kronotsk sanctuary in Kamchatka has an area of 1½ million hectares—twice as large as Yellowstone Park in the U.S.A. It is situated in a wild mountain-forest region, far from human habitation. It is inhabited by sables, red foxes, ermines, and squirrels—the most valuable fur-bearing animals.

The Ilmen sanctuary (15,000 hectares) lies in the Urals. It is a rare mineralogical museum with mountain lakes and taiga flora and fauna.

The Pechor-Ilich sanctuary (1 million hectares) in the northern Urals possesses twenty-two kinds of industrial animals—sables, kydar, otters, partens, and others.

The Sikhota-Alin sanctuary (1 million hectares) in the Far East is one of the most interesting in the world. Here there is a meeting-point between the southern and northern —Pacific Ocean and Siberian—flora and fauna. Here are found the spotted deer, the racoon dog, the kharza, the tiger, and other animals.

The Central Forest sanctuary in the Western Area, the Lapland sanctuary in the Kola peninsula, the Aksou-Jebogli-sou in Tien-Shan, the Kizil-Agach in Azerbaijan, the Baikal, Sayan, Bargouzin, the Central Volga. . . .

These are only the largest sanctuaries. There are numerous small ones, as, for instance, the Kievo Lake near Moscow where a huge number of gulls dwell under the protection of youthful naturalists; 'The Living Book' near Moscow; 'The Forest in Vorske' in the steppe forest; the 'Pine Grove in Soura', 'The Koziavka Steppe', 'Kivach', and so on.

Compared with other countries, the sanctuaries in the U.S.S.R. have a special method of work. The word 'work' is not used accidentally. The Soviet sanctuaries do work.

In the U.S.S.R. it is considered that human work is a powerful organic and inalienable factor in the evolutionary process of nature, and therefore the idea of non-interference with natural conditions in the sanctuaries has been rejected. The fetish of 'inviolable Nature' has been discarded.

The method is not the passive protection of nature from economic utilization, but the active transformation of nature; not only by observation, but by experiments as well. The sanctuaries are not only preserves of genetic stocks of flora and fauna; they are not only places for relaxation and enlightenment: they are scientific institutions working at the reconstruction of flora and fauna which is subordinated to the economic aims of the nation.

And that is why their role in the alteration of the geographical distribution of fauna is so great.

The experimental biological institute in the Askania-Nova sanctuary is the only one of its kind in Europe as regards its aims and type of work. It works at the acclimatization of llamas, zebra, and the Tibetan yak, at the improvement of breeds of domestic cattle by means of crossing it with its wild kin (the bull with the aurochs, or with the bison, the horse with the zebra), at the domestication of wild animals, and at questions of artificial fecundation. In the sanctuary auroch-bisons have been produced which resemble almost exactly the type of the pure aurochs which has long ago disappeared. Animals have been created which resemble the wild ox. In a few years' time new animals will be replenishing the exhausted stock of fauna in the U.S.S.R.

The acclimatization of the beaver, of which there are only fifteen hundred left in the whole of the U.S.S.R., has been successfully started in the Lapland sanctuary.

The roe, which was long ago exterminated in the Moscow region, is again being bred there.

Whitefish fry have been transported from the Leningrad district to Armenia and bred in the mountain lake of Sevan.

Several kinds of fish have been transported in aeroplanes from the Black Sea to the Caspian Sea.

The sanctuaries are the headquarters for the restoration of the wealth of living nature. The valuable sable is bred in the Pechorsk-Ilich sanctuary—the only place where it is found in the European portion of the U.S.S.R.—and, overstepping the boundaries of the sanctuary, replenishes the hunting-grounds of the neighbouring districts. Great herds of wild oxen, which exist nowhere else in the world, live in the Caucasian sanctuary. The deer and the chamois, which were threatened with complete extermination, are also being successfully bred here. The wild goat has been restored in the Crimean sanctuary. In the Far East the precious spotted deer, with its curative young antlers, has secured a permanent home. Wild reindeer, which promise to be of considerable value when they are crossed with domestic deer, have been saved from extinction in the Lapland sanctuary.

It has been planned[1] to transfer the 600 sea-otters—all that remain—whose skins cost more than 1,000 roubles each, from Kamchatka to the Kola bay in the Barents Sea; the black sable, whose skin is extremely valuable and which is found in very few places, from Siberia to the Urals; the mink from the Urals to Siberia; the racoon dog from the Far East to the Caucasus; the chamois from the Caucasus to Central Asia; the spotted deer from the Far East to the Ukraine; the hare from the U.S.S.R. in Europe to the U.S.S.R. in Asia. And all this is not a form of private initiative on the

[1] On the proposal of Professor Manteuffel.

part of isolated industrialists, but the fulfilment of a general plan uniting into one whole each separate measure. It is planned to transfer the squirrel from the north to the Caucasus, but this plan is interfered with by the fact that her enemy, the marten, lives there. Therefore, together with the squirrel, the lagomys will be transferred from Siberia so that the marten might feed on this and leave the squirrel alone.

Just as it mobilizes plants, so the U.S.S.R. mobilizes all the animals of the world required for the people.

The acclimatization of the musk-rat, which has been brought from North America, possesses a valuable skin and breeds at an unusually high rate, is proceeding in the north of the U.S.S.R. on a huge scale. From 1929 to 1931, 606 musk-rats were bred. By the beginning of 1932 there were 18,000 of them in the forests and swamps. Another 6,000, or thereabouts, were let loose in 1932. Hunting musk-rats has already begun. The economic possibilities of this measure are considerable.

In the Voronezh beaver sanctuary there have been let loose, as an experiment, North American skunks, North American minks, and North American silver-and-black foxes.

Argentine nutrias—'swamp beavers'—were domiciled in the lower parts of the Kura River in the Transcaucasus. These animals, it is interesting to note, were found to have sensitive tails which froze off during frosts.

It is planned to introduce into the U.S.S.R. the musk-ox, the North American racoon, the Himalayan pandu, and the Australian opossum. Dreams of that valuable rodent, the chinchilla, from the Cordilleras of South America, are not unheard-of.

The changes in the animal kingdom form one of the aspects of the new map of the country.

Chapter 6

THE NEW DISTRIBUTION OF TRANSPORT

I. RAILWAYS

TRANSPORT is the overcoming of space. What is far it makes near; it draws remote places, torn away by space and time, into the general life of the country. Transport reflects the geographical shifting of industry and agriculture; but transport itself, when it shifts, creates a new economic geography of the country.

The degree of development of pre-revolutionary railway transport befitted backward Russia: a rare and extremely disproportionate network of railways, low-power locomotives, tiny wagons, hand-brakes.

The economic development of the U.S.S.R. gave transport a huge amount of work. Its goods traffic increased from 1913 to 1932 more than two and a half times. The total number of passengers carried increased even more—more than three and a half times.

LENGTH OF THE RAILWAY SYSTEM

(in thousands of kilometres)

Average

1913	.	.	.	.	.	58·5
1928	.	.	.	.	.	76·9
1932	.	.	.	.	.	81·6
1934[1]	.	.	.	.	.	83·2
1937[1]	.	.	.	.	.	94·0

The length of the railway system increased in lesser proportion. This means that the planned method of conducting the economic system made it possible to utilize the existing system more rationally, and also that the railways grew qualitatively: more powerful locomotives and larger

[1] At the end of the year.

175

wagons are working on them now than formerly, the railway lines have been improved; for the first time in the history of the country electric traction and automatic blocking have been partially introduced. Electrification is the basis of the reconstruction of the transport of the U.S.S.R.

In 1930 already the railways of the U.S.S.R. had taken the foremost position in the world as regards goods turnover (number of tons carried per kilometre).

Nevertheless transport has not kept pace with the growth of the national economy. The Second Five Year Plan, which provides for extensive reconstruction of transport, must do away with this lag. According to plan the goods turnover of the railways will increase 1·8 times.

A student of social phenomena is able to understand the character of a country from a glance at the railway map.

The railway lines of Russia radiated like a cobweb from the centre—from Moscow and Leningrad. Deprived of a food and raw-material base, the centre hung in the air like a voracious spider, clinging to the earth by its web of railway lines. It forced grain, timber, cotton, and metal out of the outlying districts. The manufactured articles of the centre —the means of its enrichment and domination—flowed to the outlying districts along the shining threads of divergent railway lines.

The farther from the centre the wider apart lay the lines: the shining rails became less and less frequent and the outlying districts were plunged in the darkness of roadlessness and savagery. In the European part of Russia there were 11·3 kilometres of railway for every 1,000 square kilometres, while in the Asiatic part there were only 0·6 kilometres. A few lines only penetrated far into the depths of the outlying districts: the Central Asiatic, Transcaucasian, and Siberian railways—the nutrient roots of the centre and the paths of colonization and military conquest. The lop-sided, raw-material economy of the outlying districts was connected by rail with the industrial centre, but there was no connexion between the regions in the outlying districts. Only the mining districts—Donbas and the Urals—possessed a comparatively thick network of railway lines.

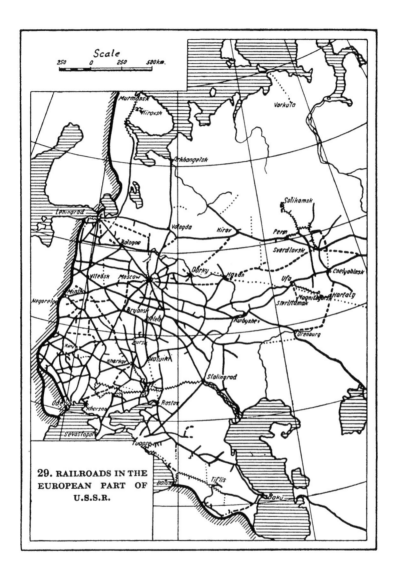

Scale
250   0   250   500km.

29. RAILROADS IN THE
EUROPEAN PART OF
U.S.S.R.

———   Opened before October Revolution

- - -   Opened after October Revolution

.....   Under construction during Second Five Year Plan period

⌇⌇⌇⌇   Electrified railroads (at end of Second Five Year Plan)

Thus the distribution of transport lines betrayed the parasitical character of the old Russian centre, and emphasized the colonial character of the outlying districts.

It is easy to discover on the map other laws in the old distribution of railways.

From the south of the European part of Russia—from the corn-growing regions of the Ukraine, the Kursk, and the Voronezh Regions, and the Volga Region—the railways ran to the ports of the Baltic Sea in the north-west, and to the ports of the Black Sea in the south. These were the routes of grain export.

Thus the railway lines revealed the fact that Russia was a raw-material appendage of industrial Europe.

The western regions of Russia, which were its frontier regions, had the thickest network of railways. Some of these lines showed the influence of foreign capital coming from the west. Some, which had hardly any economic importance and were run at a loss, were of a strategic character.

Thus the railways pointed out the dependence of Russia on the west and unmasked its war aims.

The alteration of the structure and geographical distribution of the national economy of the U.S.S.R. was accompanied by an alteration of the structure and distribution of its goods traffic.

New links were forged between the centre and the outlying districts. The centre is no longer an imperialist mother-country. The centre now sends to the outlying districts not only cotton fabrics and matches, but machines as well, thus industrializing these former colonies of Russia. The outlying districts not only send their cotton, metal, and timber to the centre, but they also use these raw materials themselves for their own industries on an ever-increasing scale.

Nevertheless the importance of the railways which meet in a cluster in the centre and connect it with the outlying districts has not decreased but increased. Centres of manufacture come nearer to the seats of raw material production; but in spite of this, more raw material is carried by rail than before; for the economic structure of the country has greatly developed. Formerly all the cotton was exported from

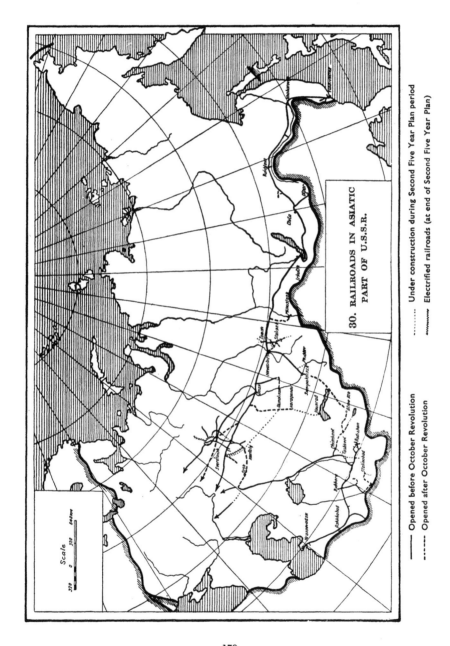

30. RAILROADS IN ASIATIC PART OF U.S.S.R.

——— Opened before October Revolution
- - - - Opened after October Revolution
.... Under construction during Second Five Year Plan period
∿∿∿∿ Electrified railroads (at end of Second Five Year Plan)

Scale

179

Central Asia to the centre. Now only a part is exported, but this part exceeds to a considerable extent the whole output of cotton in the past. The same is true of metal, grain, and timber. The rationalization of the distribution of industry in the U.S.S.R. did not preclude increase of goods traffic; for it was a rationalization of a growing industry. The centre, as a consumer of raw material, is growing, though new industrial centres in the outlying districts are growing even faster.

One more circumstance increases the work of the lines leading from the depths of the country to the centre. Before the Revolution, Leningrad received coal from England. It is only a step from the port to the furnace. Now Leningrad burns Soviet coal, which comes from the Donetz basin, 1,500 kilometres away. Before the Revolution Leningrad worked in great measure on imported metal. The metal works stood close by the port. Now it uses Soviet metal, which it receives from the Urals and the Ukraine, 1,500 kilometres away from Leningrad. Before the Revolution half the spinning looms of the Ivanov Region worked on imported cotton. Now they all work on Soviet cotton, which comes from Central Asia and the Transcaucasus. Such instances can be multiplied.

The transition of Soviet industry to the use of its own raw materials diminished goods traffic on the short western railways which connect Russia with Europe, and increased goods traffic on the long lines connecting the centre with the outlying districts. The total distance travelled by goods increased.

The goods traffic on the lines converging on the centre is enormous. In order to ease it, a new great railway line 1,195 kilometres in length from Moscow to the Donetz basin is being constructed: a part of it is already in use. Two-thirds of it will follow the track, which is being reconstructed, of the Moscow-Valuiki line; the remainder, from Valuiki to Rostov-on-Don, will be newly built. Great loads of coal will flow along it to the north.

A railway semicircle will pass round Moscow from the east, so that goods passing through Moscow from the north to the south and from the south to the north should not encumber the Moscow junction.

Between Briansk and Viasma in the western region (234 kilometres), a line has been constructed which relieves the Donbas-Leningrad line. The Smolensk-Soblango line (253 kilometres) will serve the same purpose.

The Moscow, Leningrad, and Kharkov junctions are being electrified.

The Transcaucasus is connected with the central regions by only one railway, which passes round the Caucasian range along the coast of the Caspian Sea. A second line is now being completed which will pass round the range along the coast of the Black Sea. During the Second Five Year Plan a third railway will be constructed which will cross the Caucasian mountains (170 kilometres). Tunnels and viaducts will raise electric trains to a height of 2,000 metres.

The goods traffic of the centre has increased considerably, but the goods traffic of the eastern, formerly backward, regions, has increased to a still higher degree. This geographical shifting of transport work reveals the geographical deconcentration of economic life—its movement from the centre to the outlying districts. During the First Five Year Plan the goods turnover of all the railways in the U.S.S.R. increased by 71 per cent; whilst in the Urals it increased by 77 per cent, in Western Siberia by 200 per cent, in Kazakstan by 300 per cent.

Transport is the means of developing the outlying districts. New railway lines cross desert roadless expanses and have started the development of industry and agriculture in formerly uncivilized regions. Eighty per cent of the total length of railway constructed during the years of the First Five Year Plan lies in the eastern regions. For instance, the great coal district of Kazakstan, Karaganda, is now connected with the transport system. A new railway passage from the Kuznetzk coalfield to Western Siberia has been constructed. The rails have penetrated to the foot-hills of the Pamirs—they have extended to the capital of Tajikistan, Stalinabad. A railway line, though a short one, has for the first time been built in the Soviet part of Sakhalin in the Far East.

The great Baikal-Amur artery (1,800 kilometres) is being laid across mountains and the taiga in Siberia. It will connect the country on the coast of the Baikal lake with the lower Amur and will emerge on to the coast of the Pacific Ocean. Its track will cross a region where no man has ever set foot and bring new life there. A second track is being railed in the eastern half of the Siberian railway.

During the Second Five Year Plan there will begin the construction of the Lena railway (784 kilometres), connecting the Siberian railway with the basin of the River Lena, i.e. the vast Yakut Republic, which at the present time has no railway connexion whatever with other regions in the country.

The northern part of Kazakstan will be traversed during the Second Five Year Plan by a new latitudinal railway artery: Akmolinsk-Kartali (840 kilometres), the nearest outlet for Karaganda coal to the blast-furnaces of the southern Urals.

At the present time the centre is connected with the Pacific Ocean only by one line, which crosses Siberia. The Baikal-Amur line, the Lena line, and the Akmolinsk-Kartali line are parts of a future second Trans-Siberian railway.

In the regions of everlasting frozen soil in the extreme north a railway line is being laid from the coal-mines of Pechora to the coast of the Arctic Ocean (320 kilometres).

Railways are being constructed from Karaganda to the Lake of Balkhash (504 kilometres), from Ufa to Magnitogorsk (366 kilometres), and others.

Railways in mountainous regions are being electrified (in the Transcaucasus, in the Kola peninsula). In waterless districts the steam locomotive is replaced by Diesel engines (regions in Central Asia and in the North Caucasus). Modern powerful railway arteries are being laid in regions where almost the only means of communication used to be deer teams or camel caravans.

The outlying districts are developing in every direction. They are being connected now not only with the centre but with each other as well. Central Asia (Turkestan) and Western Siberia have been connected by a new railway, 1,442 kilometres long, which crosses the desert and is known as the Turksib. A railway (398 kilometres) connects the Urals with the Central Volga Region (the Troitsk-Orsk line).

The railway system in the mining districts of the Urals and the Ukraine was formed irrespective of any plan. Short lines now being laid mark the direction in which cotton will be carried from the textile combine now under construction.

The rational distribution of railways will correspond to the rational distribution of those branches of industry which they serve.

II. RIVERS

There are mighty rivers in the U.S.S.R.: in length and expanse of water they compare with the longest rivers in the world. The Ob and the Irtysh are together 5,300 kilometres in length; the Yenisei, Angara, and Selenga, 5,200; the Lena, 4,428; the Volga, 3,694; the Amur, 2,946. The majority of them flow slowly along plains. The upper parts of the rivers in European Russia lie close together—they can easily be joined by canals. Although the rivers of the U.S.S.R. freeze in winter and become shallow in summer they are capable of becoming important means of communication—both cheap and capacious.

The competition of the railways hindered the development of river transport in old Russia. Rails took goods away from the water. Steamers were employed on only a quarter of the river system of the country. The length of canals and sluiced rivers was insignificant: 0·7 per cent of the length of the navigable and floatable rivers.

By the end of the First Five Year Plan the freight turnover of the rivers of the U.S.S.R. had increased by 38 per cent in comparison with 1913. Soviet water transport has taken first place in Europe as regards extent of its general freight traffic.

The Soviet Union knows nothing of competition between various forms of transport. All of them constitute the unified transport system of the country and carry out the work which is assigned to them by the plan. But even up till now river transport in the U.S.S.R. is developed less than it could and ought to be. The Second Five Year Plan will see an increase in the share of river transport out of the total goods transport. River freight turnover will increase nearly two and a half times.

The geographical redistribution of industry is another factor influencing river transport: the work of the eastern river basins has developed at a greater speed than the work of the western basins. Navigation has begun on a number of rivers, for the first time, in formerly backward regions.

Ships cross the Arctic Circle on the Pechora River; they sail along the formerly lifeless Koura in the Transcaucasus. Navigation has been introduced on the Kolima in the most remote corner of Siberia. A fleet has made its appearance on the Lake of Issik-Koul, which lies amidst the snowy ridges of Kirghizia.

River-beds are being made deeper. The old and shallow Marinskaya water system, which connects the Baltic Sea with the Volga basin, is being reconstructed, as is the Moscow River water system which connects Moscow with the Oka and the Volga.

III. CANALS

Large and complex hydro-technical constructions are being erected. They will do away with the isolated character of water basins, create a unified system of waterways, give power to hydro-stations, ensure the irrigation of dry lands, improve the fishing industry, and facilitate the water-supply of towns and factories. The map of the water systems will be completely altered.

Part of these constructions have already been completed, part will be finished during the Second Five Year Plan, part later still.

The immense expenditure in the near future of water for irrigation threatens to disturb the water balance of certain river systems and even seas which has been established for

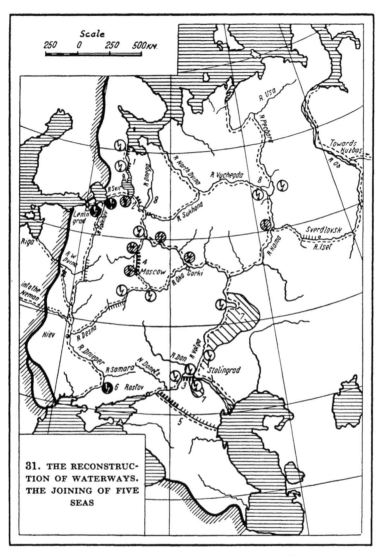

Scale
250   0   250   500 KM.

31. THE RECONSTRUC-
TION OF WATERWAYS.
THE JOINING OF FIVE
SEAS

Completed water-power stations

Water-power stations under construction
in the period of the Second Five Year Plan

The more important projected and suggested hydro-electric stations

᠁᠁ Canals completed or under construction

᠁᠁ Suggested and projected canals

〜〜 Waterways

1. The Stalin Baltic-White Sea Canal
2. The Volga-Baltic Canal
3. The Volga-Don Canal
4. The Volga-Moscow Canal
5. The Marychsk Canal
6. The Dnieper-Lenin water-power station
7. The Territories near the Volga and the
   Steppes proposed for drainage
8. Reservoirs projected with the object of
   feeding the Volga with the waters of
   northern rivers

thousands of years. The U.S.S.R. is confronted with the stupendous task of transferring the waters of rivers flowing into one sea to the rivers of other seas.

The Finnish-Scandinavian heights are attached to the continent by ridges of barren rock. Between the White and Baltic Seas there lies a hilly watershed—Karelia, cleft by glaciers and overgrown by coniferous forests.

On the one side of the watershed lie the principal agricultural regions of the U.S.S.R.; on the other side, the Khibin mountains with the richest deposits of raw material for phosphoric fertilizers in the world. On the one side of the watershed, a country of new towns and factories; on the other side, timber, granite, and marble; the Barents Sea with its wealth of fish, Pechora coal.

There was only one route through the watershed: the Murmansk railway which was burdened to its utmost limits. A waterway, which was more economical and capacious than the railway, passed all the way round Scandinavia—a distance of 5,500 kilometres. It might have been carried straight through the watershed. Its length would then have been twenty times shorter. Now it has been laid there. On Stalin's initiative the White Sea and Baltic Canal was constructed in 1933 to connect the White and Baltic Seas: it is the largest river canal in the world. The Scandinavian peninsula became an 'island'.

The canal is altering the economic structure of the region. In one year the canal can let through from north to south 3 million tons of goods. Its waterfalls will turn the turbines of five electric power stations and provide energy for the works of the vast White Sea-Baltic Combine (timber industry, wood-working enterprises, and timber-chemical works, mining industry, metallurgy, and so on).

Twenty-one million cubic metres of earth and stone have been so moved that a ribbon of water might cross the watershed at a height of 108 metres and connect the Povenetsk bay of the Onezh lake with the Sorok bay of the White Sea. The length of the waterway is 227 kilometres. It has nineteen sluices.

The canal was constructed almost without the use of

metal. The system of 128 complex hydro-technical constructions was built up out of local cheap materials. Nearly all the sluices and even locks are made of the timber which grew on the bank. The huge pressure of the water is kept back by earthen dams, which are strengthened more by this same wood than by concrete.

The canal has altered the geography of the region. Old river-beds have dried up. The River Povenchanka has ceased to exist. The lake of Vig, which was raised 6 metres, flooded 500 square kilometres and washed away dozens of islands.

Dams several kilometres long support a huge artificial reservoir—1,300 square kilometres in area and containing 5 billion five hundred million cubic metres of water. It is twice as big as the Lake of Geneva. Five fishing villages were removed from the flooded islands and transferred to the new shore. The track of the Murmansk railway was moved aside for a length of over 100 kilometres.

The Moscow River gave its name to a great city, but it is unable to give it sufficient water. The capital of one-seventh part of the world stands on the banks of a shallow river. Forests at the upper part of the river were cut down, and the naked Moscow River, which fills its banks to the brim for a short time in early spring (when in one month three-quarters of the annual flow goes past) falls, becomes shallow, and hardly moves, moving only 8 cubic metres per second. Industrial Moscow drinks up more than half its river. Within five years the growing town would drink it to the bottom.

Waterways miss Moscow. The Volga passes it from the north. The Oka from the south. Only shallow-draught ships can pass along the shallow river and reach the town, and the river port of Moscow unloads forty times less goods than the Moscow railway junction. Bulky loads—timber, oil, building stone—go from the Volga to Moscow on wheels instead of going by the cheap water route.

Soon these geographical features will be corrected. A canal track is already being dug. Part of the Volga will turn to the south at the village of Ivankovo, and then sluices will take an artificial river to Moscow which will be 127 kilometres long and 5·5 metres deep. The water of the Volga will fill the impoverished bed of the Moscow River; it will pass under the Kremlin walls and through the Oka at Gorky, and will then return to its former bed.

The amount of excavating to be done in connexion with the Volga-Moscow Canal will exceed that of the White Sea and Baltic Canal nearly six and a half times. The extent of excavations has been calculated at 134 million cubic metres; 2,900,000 cubic metres of concrete will be laid—nearly the figure of the Panama Canal, but it took twelve years to build the Panama Canal, whilst the Moscow-Volga Canal will be completed in four years.

At Ivankovo on the Volga a dam will be constructed with a sluice and hydro-electric power station. It will raise the level of the water to a mark 124 metres above sea-level.

By the aid of five pumping stations the water will rise from this mark to 162 metres. Then part of the flood will pass through the canal to the Ouchansk reservoir.

Dams will raise the canal above the level of the subsoil waters in order to keep the Volga water pure. The River Sestra will pass under the canal in a pipe, the three openings of which are 7 metres in diameter.

After standing a hundred days in the artificial lake surrounded by forests, the water will pass along a conduit to the Moscow waterworks. The rest of the water, whose volume will be equal to four Moscow rivers in summer, will flow to Moscow along the navigable course, passing on its way through the turbines of the hydro-station. Small rivers in Moscow will be replenished with water.

Volga three-deck steamers will easily pass through the Volga-Moscow Canal. The distance from Moscow to the starting-point of the Marinskaya system, which leads to the Baltic Sea, will be shortened by 1,000 kilometres.

A chain of huge newly created lakes will spring up along the canal. Villages will be transferred from place to place. The railway will be moved on one side. A deep-water port will be created in Moscow—a port of five seas.

Near Stalingrad the Don approaches the Volga. Here, during the Second Five Year Plan, Lenin's idea, expressed long ago, will be put into practice: the rivers will be connected by a canal 100 kilometres long.

A dam will traverse the Don at the town of Kalach. From here a sluiced watercourse will commence. It will cut its way through the watershed and descend into the Volga. There will be four reservoirs. Two hydro-electric power stations. Additional supplies of water to the Caspian Sea. The Kalmuck steppe will be irrigated.

The rivers of the Volga basin will find an egress into the Sea of Azov and the Black Sea. The shallow Don will be transformed into a deep waterway by means of the construction of sluices. Loads of timber will float along the canal from the Volga side, and loads of coal from the Don side.

The reconstruction of the longest river in Europe, the Volga, in whose basin there lives one-third of the population of the U.S.S.R., has been partly begun and partly prepared.

The shallowness of the Volga in summer makes navigation very difficult. The river passes through regions which have a poor power supply, but the force of the falling of its water is not utilized. In its lower part the Volga passes through a region of droughts, but it does not irrigate the land.

Several powerful hydro-electric power stations will be constructed, of which two (one on the Volga and another on its tributary—the Kama), are in process of construction. The area of the artificial reservoirs will be 20,000 square kilometres. Up to fifteen towns and a thousand villages will be covered by water.

The river will become a deep waterway, which one day will connect the Caspian Sea through the reconstructed Marinskaya system with the Baltic Sea, through the Kama-Pechora-Vichegda combination with the Arctic Ocean, through the Volga-Don Canal with the Sea of Azov and the Black Sea, through the Oka, Zhizdra, and Diesna with the Dnieper, through the Choussovaya, Isset, Tobol, and Irtish with the Ob, through the Volga-Moscow Canal, and also through the Oka and the Kliazma with Moscow. The capital of the U.S.S.R. will be connected with all the seas in the European part of the country.

The Volga Region will be irrigated over an area of 4 to 4·3 million hectares. The climate of the irrigated territories will alter.

The draining of the Volga delta, the irrigation of the Kalmuck steppe, and the reorganization of the rich fishing industries are all being planned.

A plan is at present being worked out of transferring part of the water of the rivers flowing towards the Arctic Ocean (the Onega, the Soukhona, and others) to the Volga basin. The water will be taken away from the many-rivered and excessively humid north and sent along the Volga tract to the south to the drought regions.

The reconstruction of the Dnieper has begun. The Dnieper hydro-electric power station with a full capacity of 558,000 kilowatts has been built. Its dam has covered the Dnieper rapids with water over a distance of 97 kilometres, and has thus established a direct waterway and connected the upper Dnieper with the Black Sea.

The new constructions on the Dnieper which are being considered at the present time will be able to increase the utilized power of the Dnieper to 2 million kilowatts. The reconstructed Dnieper with its tributaries will be transformed in the future into a waterway with a total length of 20,000 kilometres, which will be connected through the West Dvina, Lovat, Volkhov, and Neva with the Gulf of Finland in the Baltic Sea, through the West Dvina with the Gulf of Riga, through Samara, Volchia, and the North Donetz with the Don, through the Diesna, Zhizdra, and Oka with Moscow and the Volga, through a number of combined waterways with the Niemen and Vistula. Goods traffic between Leningrad and the Ukraine will be able to utilize cheap water routes.

The reconstruction of the Dnieper will include the irrigation of the Ukrainian steppe and north Crimea, and the draining of the marshes of White Russia and the western region.

Draining canals will be utilized for the transport of timber.

There will be an improvement in the fishing industry and the water-supply of works and inhabited areas.

The plan of construction of the Kama-Pechora-Vichegda United Waterway is being worked out.

The dams of the hydro-electric power stations will create the Kolva reservoir of 2,000 square kilometres in the north-eastern corner of the European part of the U.S.S.R. This vast artificial lake will connect the upper parts of the Rivers Kama, Pechora, and Vichegda. Waterways will connect the Volga basin with the White Sea and Sea of Barents. The backward taiga region, which is rich in timber, coal, oil, fur, and fish will find itself on the highway of rapid economic and cultural development.

The Ussa, a tributary of the Pechora, can be connected with the lower Ob. The question is being considered of the future connexion of the Pechora through the Rivers Soula and Indiga with the Bay of Indiga (on the Sea of Barents) which is frozen only for short periods.

The problem of creating a direct waterway from the Kuzbas to the Urals, a distance of over 4,000 kilometres, is being studied. At the present time bulky loads, coal in one direction and iron ores in the other, are carried by the railway which connects these two poles of the Ural-Kuznetzk Combine. The cheap water route would take part of this goods traffic upon itself. The route will be as follows: from the Kuzbas along the River Tom to its junction with the Ob, along the Ob to the mouth of the Irtish, along the Irtish to the mouth of the Tobol, along the Tobol to the mouth of the Isset, along the Isset to the Urals. A number of hydro-electric power stations will be erected.

In the west the Ural-Kuzbas waterway can be connected by the River Choussova with the Volga basin, and on the east by the River Ket with the Yenisei basin.

The dry region traversed by the East and West Manych, which lies between the Sea of Azov and the Caspian Sea, has been little investigated.

At the present time it is a dry desert area. Preparatory work for the construction of the Manych water route is being done here. It will connect the Don, and consequently the Sea of Azov, with the Caspian Sea, and will irrigate the barren lands. Its total length will be 620 kilometres—four times as long as the Suez Canal.

Oil from Baku, coal from the Donetz, meat from Kazakstan, timber from the Volga, and fruit from Central Asia will pass along this waterway.

IV. THE NORTHERN SEA PASSAGE

The U.S.S.R. is surrounded by ten seas which connect its coasts with the outside world. For the most part steamers carry export and import cargoes. During the First Five Year Plan the fleet of the Soviet Union was more than doubled and the freight turnover of its ports increased by 92 per cent. During the Second Five Year Plan the maritime freight turnover of the U.S.S.R. will increase from 18 to 51 milliard ton-kilometres.

The geographical range of maritime transport is extending. Soviet ships are more and more often calling at European and American ports.

The industrialization of new regions gives birth to new ports—Igarka in Eastern Siberia, Ochemchiri in the Transcaucasus, Kandalaksha in the Kola peninsula, and so on.

A long coast-line attaches the U.S.S.R. to the polar basin. From west to east it stretches at 158° longitude. Before the Revolution nearly the whole of this sea boundary was shut off. On the west merchant ships did not go farther than Novaya Zemlya; on the east they went no farther than the Bering Straits. The northern seas between Novaya Zemlya and the Bering Straits, which intimidated people because they were ice-covered and had never been investigated, were seen only by ships of extremely rare scientific expeditions, which were mostly foreign and not Russian. Now the Soviet fleet is successfully investigating these seas.

Every year voyages to the northern shores of Siberia

through the Arctic Kara Sea are made with the aid of ice-breakers and reconnoitring aeroplanes. In 1924 ice-breakers led the way for the first three steamers through the ice. Then four, and six, and eight, and twenty-six, and at last fifty steamers. Now the Kara Sea expedition has become an ordinary trip. At first the merchant ships went as far as the mouth of the Ob, and then to the mouth of the Yenisei. In 1933 they reached the mouth of the Lena. The great Siberian rivers, which formerly seemed hopelessly blocked up by ice, now connect Siberia with Europe. They are the export routes of timber, graphite, and fish. From the east, through the Bering Strait, Soviet ships reach the mouth of the Kolima.

There only remains now to join the eastern and western sections in order to open the Great Northern Sea Passage from the Atlantic to the Pacific Ocean round the northern point of Asia.

The expeditions of Soviet ships, headed by Professor Schmidt, in 1932 to 1934 proved the possibility of passing through the Northern Sea Passage in one voyage.

The determination to lay the passage through the polar basin is inflexible. The Central Board of the Northern Sea Passage has been created. New polar meteorological and wireless stations have been, and are still being, created on the north coasts of Asia. In order to supply the northern fleet with its own fuel, the newly discovered petroleum deposits in the extreme north of Siberia are being bored. Seaports have been built on the Siberian rivers near the mouths, e.g. the New Port on the Ob. Port Tiksi is being constructed by the mouth of the Lena. A coal base is being formed on Dickson Island. A special fleet of ice-breakers is being created. Ice-breakers, the most powerful in the world, are being built, on Stalin's initiative. Arctic aviation is being extended.

In 1934 the Central Board of the Northern Sea Passage, at whose head stands Professor O. Schmidt, was assigned the task of discovering and exploiting all the natural re-sources of the Soviet Arctic Regions. From 1935 there begins the normal exploitation of the Northern Sea Passage.

13

V. MOTOR TRANSPORT

During the Second Five Year Plan the number of motor-cars in the U.S.S.R. will increase from 75,000 to 580,000; the goods turnover of motor transport will increase from 1·1 to 16·0 milliard ton-kilometres; the lack of roads in the country will tend to become a thing of the past.

The geography of motor transport has been transformed. In former times motor-cars did not leave the streets of the towns. Now they are utilized for transport not only in towns. The largest towns are connected by motor routes, e.g. Moscow and Tiflis, Moscow and Vladivostok, Leningrad and Odessa, and so on. Motor-lorries convey grain to the railway stations from the depths of the country. In the north, tractors transport timber.

Motor transport is of particular importance in backward and mountainous regions where there are no railways.

Where formerly there were only paths trodden down by beasts of burden, there are now motor-roads.

In Siberia the new Amur-Yakut motor-road, 869 kilometres in length, runs from the railway into the depths of Yakutia, which never had any roads at all, by way of the Yablon mountain passes.

The 'road in the clouds'—the Osh-Khorogsky route, 754 kilometres long, lies right through the Pamirs. This highest motor route in the world reaches an altitude of 4,700 metres at the passes. The ancient camel path has been widened; huge boulders have been torn off and thrown down. The motor-car passes quite easily over the Roof of the World, whose inaccessibility had given rise to many legends. The ravines of the western Pamirs are crossed by the Stalinabad-Garm route. The Stalinabad-Tashkent route is being constructed over the mountain ranges. Motor-roads built over the frontier mountains, lead to the Mongolian and Tana-Touvin Republics. A road, 730 kilometres long, is being made in the Tien-Shan range, the 'Celestial Mountains'. It will connect the different parts of Kirghizia which are separated by mountains. In the Caucasus the deep ravines of Dagestan and the mountain valleys of Svanetia are connected with the outside world.   The motor-car has revolutionized the geography of mountainous patriarchal Asia.

VI. CIVIL AVIATION

Civil aviation is a new creation in the U.S.S.R.   It has many varied uses.

In the use of aviation in agriculture the U.S.S.R. occupies the first place in the world.

In order to accelerate vegetation and save the crops from drought, extra early sowing is often done in the south of the U.S.S.R.   The aeroplane flies over the muddy fields and scatters the seeds.

The sand-dunes in Central Asia, blown about by the wind, encroach on the ploughlands.   The aeroplane flies over the moving sandbanks and sows them with the seeds of plants which make the sand firm and of the saksaul, the tree of the desert.

Lightning causes forest fires.   In the unpopulated taiga there is no one to combat them, and the fire can easily spread over a vast area.   It is stopped by the aeroplane, which is specially equipped for the purpose.

The forests of the Soviet north are huge, dense, and little investigated.   The aeroplane flies over the impassable taiga, photographs it, and calculates the timber resources there.

Lands difficult of access, where no man has ever set foot, lie in the depths of Yakutia, in Choukotka, in the Arctic regions.   The aeroplane flies over them, drawing maps of them and studying them.

In 1932 Soviet aeroplane expeditions covered about 170,000 kilometres.   This is equivalent to four times the length of the Equator.

But the main role of aviation in the U.S.S.R. is its transport service.   The U.S.S.R. is a land of enormous distances. Wide expanses are overcome by speed.   A rapid aeroplane service in a country which an express train takes ten days to cross is of the highest importance.

The U.S.S.R. possesses a powerful aviation industry.   Air routes are served by aeroplanes of Soviet construction.   The largest land aeroplanes in the world are being constructed. The stratosphere is being conquered.

During the Second Five Year Plan the network of air routes in the U.S.S.R. will grow from 32,000 to 85,000 kilometres. In addition, the length of local lines will increase to 35,000 kilometres.

Aviation has connected the outlying districts with the centre and also with each other. Regular air routes cross the country—from Minsk to Vladivostok, from Leningrad to Tiflis, from Moscow to Tashkent. . . . These lines are now being equipped for all-night flights. During the Second Five Year Plan new air routes will be started—Leningrad to Odessa, Baku to Alma-Ata, Moscow to Karaganda, Odessa to Batoum, and others. The map is being covered with a dense network of air routes.

In the U.S.S.R. there are many regions where the aeroplane is almost the only means of communication.

The Khorezma oasis, which lies in the lower part of the Amu-Darya, is connected with the main railway line by a regular air route which passes over the sandy desert.

The villages of the western Pamirs, squeezed together in narrow ravines, are connected with the rest of the country not only by mountain mule-paths but by air routes as well. The aeroplane crosses the Roof of the World, sometimes rising above the eternal snow, sometimes finding its way in the mountain corridors, when it almost touches the stone walls with its wings.

Seaplane lines pass over the Siberian taiga, where the mirror-like surfaces of the rivers are the only landing-stages in those regions. When the seaplane flies from one river to another, its floats hang just over the trees and rocks.

Aviation serves as postal and passenger transport on the coast of the Far East. The frequent fogs sometimes press the aeroplane down to the sea, causing it to touch the crests of the waves, sometimes force it against the rocky cliffs of the coast.

The role of aviation in the Arctic regions is great and difficult. The aeroplane, overcoming fogs, snowstorms, frost, and bad visibility, conveys the post, searches for the beds

32. LINES OF CIVIL AVIATION

Scale

320   0   320   640 km

—————— Lines in regular service

- - - - - Lines in irregular service

▬▬▬▬ Lines of the central administration of North Sea route of sea-beasts, supplies people wintering in those regions with provisions, investigates the 'blank spaces'. It searches for clear water between the ice blocks and guides ships on their courses.

The shadow of the aeroplane passes over the sands of Kara-Kum, the rocks of the Pamirs, the taiga of Siberia, the ice-fields of the Arctic regions. The Soviet air fleet, having penetrated into the most remote and inaccessible regions where a flight is more of a feat of prowess than a transport operation, has consolidated the geographical unity of the country.

Chapter 7

THE NEW DISTRIBUTION OF THE POPULATION

THE productive forces of industry, agriculture, and transport are being distributed anew. But there has been a redistribution too of the main productive force—man—the motive force behind the changes and for whose sake the changes are taking place.

Eight per cent of the population of the world inhabit the U.S.S.R.—168 million human beings.[1] This number is increasing at the rate of 3 million a year, 8,000 a day. The rate of increase, further, is rising from year to year. Before the Revolution, the increase of the population of Russia was a third less than the increase of the population of the rest of Europe. At the present time the annual increase of the population of the U.S.S.R. is almost equal to that of Europe, although the population of Europe is two and a quarter times as great as that of the U.S.S.R. This is a proof of the increase in the well-being of the masses.

Drastic social changes have taken place in the composition of the population of the U.S.S.R. during the years 1913 to 1934.

Industrialization doubled the proportion of workers in the population, raising it to 28·1 per cent. An entirely new social group, constituting nearly half the population of the country (45·9 per cent) appeared. These are the kolkhoz members—peasants united in collective farms. The proportion of individual peasants has fallen to one-third of its former level—to 22·5 per cent. The *bourgeoisie* as a class no longer exists in the U.S.S.R.

The geographical distribution of the workers has changed. The greatest increase is to be observed in the outlying districts. The cattle-breeders and tillers of the land have overcome their professional prejudices and narrow-mindedness. They have come to new, technically perfect industrial

[1] Approximately on January 1st 1934.

199

enterprises, placed themselves before complex machines and learnt how to handle them.

SOCIAL STRUCTURE OF THE POPULATION

	1913		1934 (by 1, I)	
	Thousands	Per cent	Thousands	Per cent
I. The Proletariat (workers and employees, engineers and technical workers, etc.), including	23,300	16·7	47,118	28·1
A. Industrial workers and employees (trade, transport, building, cultural institutions and State apparatus) .	17,300	12·4	41,751	24·9
B. Rural proletariat .	6,000	4·3	5,367	3·2
II. Kolkhoz members and co-operated handicraft workers . .	None	—	77,037	45·9
III. Individual peasants (excluding kulaks) and non-co-operated handicraft workers .	90,700	65·1	37,902	22·5
IV. The *Bourgeoisie* (landowners, town *bourgeoisie*, traders and kulaks), including .	22,100	15·9	174	0·10
Kulaks . . .	17,100	12·3	149	0·09
V. The rest of the population (students, army men, pensioners, etc.)	3,200	2·3	5,769	3·4
	139,300	100·0	168,000	100·0

The movement of population in old Russia pursued its own peculiar course. The increase was smallest in the most backward national regions. The small nationalities of the north were simply dying out. Even official science recognized this fact, stating simply the 'fatal' disappearance of tribes.

In the U.S.S.R. there is not a single nationality that is in danger of becoming extinct. They are all increasing in number.

Entire nations in the U.S.S.R., consciously changing their mode of production, are changing their place of abode.

Cossacks, Kirghizians, Turkmens, Kalmucks, Gipsies, Oirots, Bouriats, and Evenks were all nomads. Nomad tribes occupied a territory which was three-quarters of the area of the country. Ten million people roaming about with their herds in the everlasting search for pastures, a miserable life in tents, constant dependence on green fodder, inevitable poverty and starvation, only because the frost would come too soon and the grass would be covered with a crust of ice.

This prehistoric mode of life was preserved right down to our times. The Tsarist Government did not try to abolish this anachronism. The nomads of Kirghizia might become settled, it said, on condition that they changed their Mohammedanism to Christianity. This was the policy of Russification.

If there were cases of nomads becoming settled in old Russia, they were only the result of the depriving of the cattle-breeders of their means of livelihood; for Russian colonizers took away the best cattle from the natives.

In the U.S.S.R. the systematic settlement of nomads is in progress: it is a process in which patriarchal and tribal survivals are abolished, in which backward cattle-breeding peoples are growing economically and developing educationally. Their settlement is organized and financed by the State.

During the First Five Year Plan more than 100,000 nomad households settled and united into collective bodies. A problem hitherto unknown to mankind is being solved: the planned distribution of collective farms over uncultivated lands.

When the nomad settles, he retains his accustomed occupation—cattle-breeding—but it is rationalized and improved.

Formerly the cattle obtained their own fodder from under the snow by means of horn and hoof. Now the collective form of economy, the work of the machine and mowing stations, organized by the State, and the help of the State agricultural enterprises—the sovkhozes—supply the cattle-breeding industry of the former nomads with a stable fodder base. Hay and silo are stored, and fodder roots are sown.

Formerly the lasso and sheep-dog were the only property of the nomad in addition to the herd. Now modern types of cattle-sheds are constructed in the regions of settlement.

Formerly the nomads were washed twice in their lives— after birth and after death; they did not know a single letter; they went to quacks for medical treatment. Now baths, schools, and medical consulting-rooms are built in the settlements. The percentage of illiteracy is decreasing rapidly.

Formerly whether it was hot or frosty, dry or rain, the nomads lived in felt tents full of holes, in birch-bark huts, or in hovels made of rags. Now real houses are being built in these new settlements.

Farms growing vegetable and grain for human consumption are developing in the regions of settlement. The geographical boundary of agriculture is extending to the extreme north, to the deserts, and to mountainous districts.

The distribution of the population is changing. Points marking new and permanent settlements are springing up on the blank map. The map tells of the change in the life of millions of people; on it is being traced the path of history.

Unevenness was the dominating feature of the territorial distribution of the population of old Russia, just as it was of the distribution of the various branches of economic life. The country combined human congestion in some regions with scantiness of population in others. The centre of the populated regions was 5,000 kilometres away from the territorial centre. The density of population fell from the south-west towards the north-east. It varied between 100 persons per square kilometre in the Vinnitsk district in the Ukraine to 0·03 in Choukotka. The population was attracted geographically to the most important and intensive agricultural regions: and here the agrarian character of Russia was revealed. The Ukraine, the Kursk Region, and the irrigated oases of Central Asia were densely populated. People flocked to the black soil and loess. A more or less dense industrial population could be observed only in a few places of the map, as the Moscow or Donbas Region, for instance.

The even distribution of production signifies a more even distribution of people. Industry is moving to the east and to the north—human beings likewise are moving to the east and to the north. During the First Five Year Plan the population of the entire U.S.S.R. increased by 12 per cent; the population of the eastern regions by 24 per cent. The population of the extreme north has doubled itself within the last six years.

This does not imply a mechanically even distribution of the population over the whole territory of the country, of course, but a move towards a more even distribution of the population. The industrialization of uncultivated uninhabited areas draws people there. Black soil has yielded up its power of attraction to minerals.

A movement of a population to the east was known in Russia even before the Revolution. The soldier in the conquered outlying districts was followed by the Russian peasant. It was not the intolerance of an established Church that drove him to the outskirts of the country, nor was it the notorious Russian passion for movement. He sought a way out of the backward and hungry village of the centre, burdened by the load of feudal survivals. He fled from the tiny plot of land he had received in 1861 in exchange for a heavy ransom when serfdom was abolished and which was now melting away; he fled from the barren soil which he neither knew how, nor was able, to improve. The emigrant from the centre colonized land to the north of Caucasus, Central Asia, Siberia. At first the Tsarist Government hindered migration in its desire to retain the people in the

central villages for tilling the landowner's soil; but after
the Revolution of 1905, when the peasants set fire to the
noblemen's country seats, it started encouraging this
migratory movement, in which it saw both a clearing of
the revolutionary atmosphere and a Russification of the
conquered colonies.

The lands of the outlying districts which were inhabited
by the enslaved nationalities were declared to be 'State
property with the right of alienation'. There followed a
mass seizure of the most fertile ploughlands, which had been
tilled by the age-long muscular labour of the natives. The
peoples of the North Caucasus, for instance, lost half
their land as a result of Russian colonization. The bayonet
dictated the new distribution of peoples. Tribes, clans,
nationalities, forced out by the Russian emigrants, went into
the desert, the taiga, or mountains. Oases and foot-hills
were covered on the map by the colour of an imperialist
nation. The native, having lost his land and his cattle,
became the drudge of the Russian colonist.

Emigration to the Soviet outlying districts has a different
meaning and purpose and presents a different geographical
picture. The abolition of ownership of the land by great
landowners, the collectivization of the peasantry and the
use of perfected methods of agricultural technique have done
away with landlessness. Migration is not a departure from
a breadless country but the planned cultivation of new
untouched lands. It is not a seizure of other people's ploughlands. People settle in uninhabited regions which they have
taken away, not from people, but from nature. It is not
isolated adventurers who come to the new lands in search
of happiness and wealth, but previously organized collective
groups. Migration is organized by the State, which allows
these collective groups to travel free or at a reduced rate,
finances housing, and supplies them with machines. It is
thus, for example, that Kamchatka is being populated: a
large and rich peninsula in the Pacific Ocean. From 1930
to 1933 15,000 immigrants settled in Kamchatka.

Before the Revolution migration was, for the most part,
agricultural. Now, in the U.S.S.R., the industrial migration

of the population is predominant.   New industrial structures, which are springing up in sparsely populated regions, are attracting people to themselves.   Migration nowadays is not the triumphal march of a chosen race, nor does it injure the interests of any nationality whatsoever.   On the contrary, the new distribution of the population is a means of raising and assisting nations that were formerly spurned and handicapped.

The Jews in Russia before the Revolution of 1917 were squeezed together by artificial laws of settlement.   It was the only nation in the country which had no right to work at agriculture or to live beyond the boundaries of the official 'pale of settlement'.   There were only a few, strictly regulated, exceptions to this rule.   A nation which composed nearly 2 per cent of the population of Russia had perforce one profession—handicraft and trade—and was compulsorily confined to the strictly limited territory of Western Ukraine and White Russia.

In the U.S.S.R. all nationalities are equal.   The 'pale of settlement' has been wiped off the face of the map: the geographical boundaries of Jewish settlement no longer exist. But this is not sufficient.   The Government and society organize and facilitate the transition of the Jews to agriculture.   Tailors and cobblers, inhabitants of poor musty little towns of the west, are becoming husbandmen.   In the U.S.S.R.—in the Ukraine and the Crimea—200,000 Jewish toilers have been drawn into agricultural production.

At the same time as they are changing their means of production, Jews are changing the location of their habitations.   Rich, but little-cultivated, regions have been assigned to Jewish agriculturists.

In the Far East, on the banks of the Bijan and Bira, tributaries of the Amur, where up till 1928 probably no Jew had ever lived, a region of Jewish colonization was created. Its area is twice that of Palestine.   By the end of the First Five Year Plan, 7,000 Jewish kolkhoz workers had moved away the taiga and settled here.   They established a highly organized mechanized form of agriculture.   But this movement has no agricultural bias.   In Birobijan an electric power station, a clothing factory, a standard house-building works, a furniture factory, a saw-mill, and a lime-works have been erected. Jewish schools and technical institutes have been opened, Jewish papers are published, and Jewish theatres perform there. In 1934 the economic and cultural development of Birobijan led to its being declared the Jewish Autonomous Area—the only territorial organization of its kind in the world.

At the populous cross-roads (Moscow), at the confluence of rivers (Gorky), at the meeting of seas and rivers (Leningrad), in the shadow of military walls (Kiev), round the outposts of colonial conquest (Alma-Ata), near the holy places of attraction to pilgrims (Sergievo), Russian history left its muddy tracks—the towns. Many of the industrial towns of Russia were not built up on the basis of raw material and power but grew out of trading and political centres. Thus the large towns of the centre have no geographical justification, receiving from afar, as they do, fuel, metal, and cotton.

The U.S.S.R. is striving to abolish the contrast between the town and the village, but this does not mean that the towns of the U.S.S.R. will be abolished. On the contrary, the industrialization of rural districts, formerly backward, neglected, and uncivilized, is giving birth to a large number of new towns. Agricultural labour is becoming a form of industrial labour, and the village is aspiring towards the level of advanced urban culture. New towns are springing up and are helping to overcome the violent opposition between the old town and the old village, which impeded productive development—new towns with a different complexion, a different significance, a different destiny, and a different national geography.

The industrial development of the U.S.S.R. has altered the structure of its population, the proportion of urban dwellers having increased. Within the years of the First Five Year Plan it increased from 18 per cent to 24 per cent. Over one-third of the dwelling-houses in the country were built after the Revolution. During the Second Five Year Plan dwelling space will increase by another third.

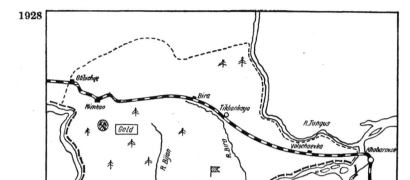

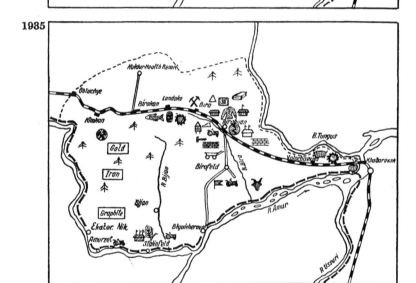

33. THE JEWISH AUTONOMOUS REGION (BIROBIJAN), 1928–35

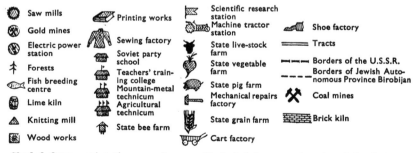

Shaded figures enterprises now in use. Unshaded figures enterprises being built during second Five Year Plan. Collective farms not drawn.

POPULATION

(millions of people by the end of each year)

					Per cent of Town Population
1913	.	.	.	. 139·3	17·7
1928	.	.	.	. 154·3	17·9
1933	.	.	.	. 166·0	24·0
1937	.	.	.	. 180·7	25·5

The towns which came into being during an extinct social order and which crossed the boundary of the Revolution have received other laws of development. It is not the lure of market stalls, nor the might of Kremlins, nor the holiness of monasteries which rally people to them. It is the industrialization of the country which distributes the population. In six years (from 1926 to 1931), the non-industrial towns of the U.S.S.R. increased the number of their inhabitants by only 12 per cent, which is equivalent to the natural increase. Co-operative and State trade deprived the market-places of their town-forming power. But the large industrial towns in the country have increased their population by 45 per cent. Those in which heavy industry predominates have grown by 50 per cent.

But it was not only in the great industrial centres that Soviet industry grew up. Towns must not go on giving birth to new factories and to millions of new inhabitants for ever. And in fact, the plan is evening out the population of the country. Middle-sized and small industrial towns increased their population by 59 per cent and those where heavy industry predominated by 77 per cent.

Although Moscow—the largest city in the U.S.S.R.— grew three times as rapidly as New York and Chicago during the years of their most vigorous development, nevertheless the rate of its growth was lower than that of a number of small towns in which large-scale industrial enterprises had sprung up. From 1926 to 1931 the population of Moscow had increased 37 per cent, whilst that of Stalingrad 104 per cent, of Chelyabinsk 106 per cent, of Makeyevka 190 per cent. Since 1932 large factories and works are no longer, as a rule, being built in Moscow and Leningrad.

Industrialization did not stop at the small towns. It went where there were no towns at all—into the taiga and the desert. It was not only that old towns were reconstructed. Nearly a hundred new towns have already been built. Over 2 million people inhabit them. Their growth cannot be reckoned in percentages because they have grown out of nothing.

The principle underlying the disposition of new towns is to be found in the transformation that is taking place in the social and economic geography of the country. The movement of the population of the U.S.S.R. is revealed most strikingly in this creation of new towns. Towns which only three or four years ago could not have been found on the map, towns which did not spring up spontaneously but were built according to plans elaborated by a special State-planning organization, 'Giprogor', towns which were erected in desert regions: this is the essence of the new geography of the country.

Territorial movements of industry lead to the rise of new towns in little-cultivated regions—principally on the basis of natural resources. Combined large-scale enterprises, requiring the labour of many thousands of workers, are built in formerly uninhabited regions. This number of workers is multiplied by the coefficient of families, and side by side with the new works, the pits, and the mines, towns are built in accordance with a planned order, designed to hold a definite number of inhabitants.

The development of agriculture—which is carried on in the U.S.S.R. on a more extensive scale than anywhere else in the world—gives birth to towns in rural regions which have become regions of large machine-tractor stations, sovkhozes, and kolkhozes.

The manifold development of nationalities leads to the construction of new towns in the former colonies of Tsarist Russia. The nomads of yesterday are building capitals.

All these facts are the various connected facets of one and the same process: the systematic abolition of the contrast

14

between the centre and the outlying districts, between the town and the village.

Although the industrial centre has declined in relation to the growth of industry in the rest of the country new gigantic enterprises have, nevertheless, been erected on its territory. Many of them sprang up outside the boundaries of the old towns—principally in regions where mineral deposits were found.

For instance, near Moscow the Stalinogorsk Chemical Power Combine was constructed on the basis of the brown coal there, and by its side the new town of *Stalinogorsk* (Bobriki) with 5,000 inhabitants.

The Ukraine has changed its appearance. Formerly it was an appendage of the centre, chiefly producing raw material, metal, and coal. Now huge enterprises of the manufacturing industry—machine-building works, chemical combines—are being constructed there and are destroying the one-sidedness of the industrial development of the Ukraine. New towns are springing up together with the new constructions. For instance, by the side of the largest metallurgical equipment works in the world, a new town, *Kramatorsk*, has been built. Side by side with the Dnieper Combine stands the new town of *Zaporozhye* which, when completed, will hold 250,000 inhabitants. There are wide, three-lined avenues in Zaporozhye, spacious many-storied houses, trams, and educational institutions.

In the sovkhoz 'Giant' which stands in the steppes of the North Caucasus, there are blocks of buildings, electricity, a theatre, a university, libraries, and schools.

In the east of the U.S.S.R. a powerful inter-regional Uralo-Kuznetsk Combine has been created. It comprises the Ural, Northern, Kazakstan, and West Siberian Regions.

The Ural Region, which possesses nearly every mineral to be met with on the globe, is known as an ancient industrial region, but, like the Ukraine, it mainly produced raw material, though it differed from the Ukraine by the fact that its works were older, smaller, and more backward.

Huge new enterprises of the extractive and manufacturing

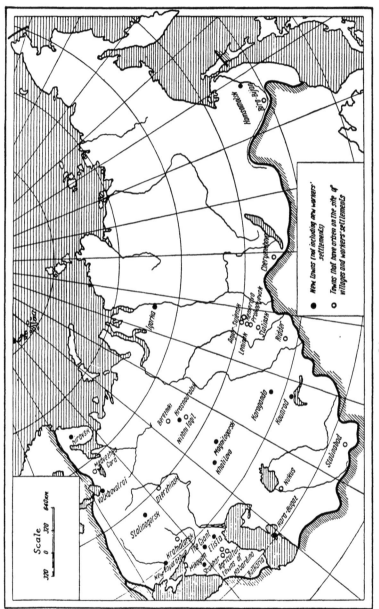

34. NEW TOWNS

Scale
370   0   370   640km

New towns (not including new workers'
settlements)

● Towns that have arisen on the site of
villages and workers' settlements

Harisomolsk
Birt-Bijan

Cheremkhovo

Ridder
Prokopyevsk
Anzhero Sudzhensk
Leninsk
Stalinsk

Igarsk

Karaganda
Naurzol

Berezniki
Krasnouralsk
Nizhni Tagil

Khibinogorsk

Magnitogorsk

Nukus
Stalinabad

Khalilovo

Medvezhya
Gora

Volkhovstroi

Kara-Bugaz

Dzerzhinsk

Stalinogorsk

Kramatorsk
The Giant
New Zaporozhye
Mikoyan
Shakhar
Elista
Agricultural
towns of
Kabardino

industry are now constructed in the Urals. In this region of petty antiquated factories hidden by the mountain forests, modern powerful combines are springing up—and new towns with them.

In the northern Urals, separated from a huge new chemical combine by a strip of pine forest, lies the newly built town of *Berezniki* (nearly 80,000 inhabitants). The town of *Krasno-Uralsk* has been built near the new non-ferrous metallurgical combine. The town extracts copper.

Together with the metallurgical and wagon-building works, a town is being built in *Novy-Tagil*.

In the southern Urals, at the foot of a brown mountain 65 per cent of which is iron, by the side of mines, an ore-concentration works, blast-furnaces, coke-furnaces, and an electric power station, the new city of *Magnitogorsk* is being built. Stone houses, factory kitchens, bread factories, theatres, medical consultation rooms, kindergartens, trams, omnibuses, educational institutions, newspapers, 170,000 inhabitants. At the foot of the mountain five years ago there was neither works nor town.

To the south of Magnitogorsk, in the Orsk Region, which is rich in iron, chromium, nickel, copper, lime, and fire-resisting clays, but which formerly had no industry at all, the following enterprises are in process of construction: a ferrous metallurgical works in Khalilov, a copper combine in Bliav, a steam and Diesel locomotive works and an oil distillery in Orsk, and a number of other large industrial enterprises. The achievements of Soviet geology have laid the foundation for the speedy transformation of backward agricultural regions into industrial regions. In accordance with the plan, new town settlements are built near the new works.

A new coal-field is developing in the semi-desert of Kazak-stan—*Karaganda*. A new town with 120,000 inhabitants is rising above the mud huts and 'yourtas'. Farther south, on the shores of the lake of Balkhash, the walls of the town of *Kounrad* designed to hold 50,000 inhabitants, are rising near the copper combine which is now being constructed.

Coal-mining in the Kuzbas, an extremely rich coal

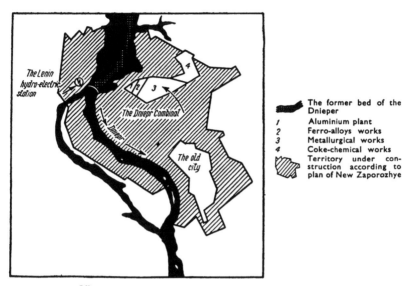

The former bed of the Dnieper
1   Aluminium plant
2   Ferro-alloys works
3   Metallurgical works
4   Coke-chemical works
Territory under construction according to plan of New Zaporozhye

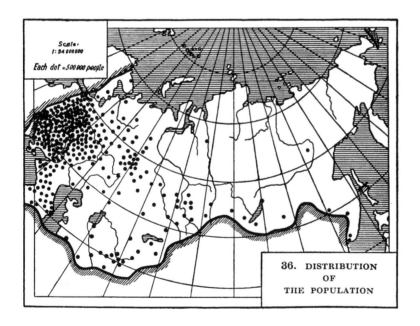

Scale:
1 : 34 000 000

Each dot = 500 000 people

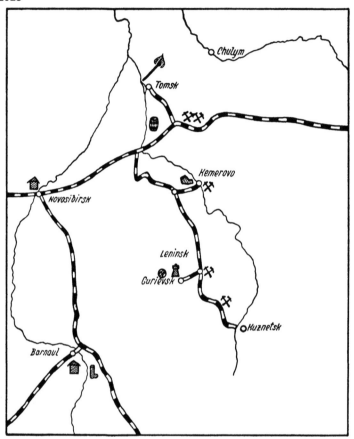

37. THE INDUSTRIALIZATION OF KUZBAS

Large enterprises indicated.   Shaded figures functioning enterprises.

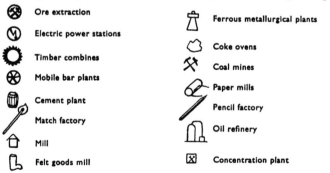

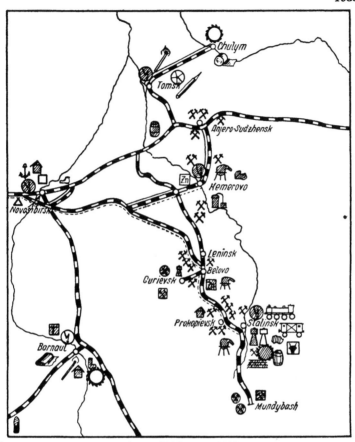

(WEST SIBERIAN REGION) IN 1928 AND 1935
Unmarked figures enterprises under construction in Second Five Year Plan.

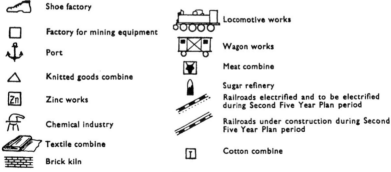

Shoe factory		Locomotive works
Factory for mining equipment		Wagon works
Port		Meat combine
Knitted goods combine		Sugar refinery
Zinc works		Railroads electrified and to be electrified during Second Five Year Plan period
Chemical industry		Railroads under construction during Second Five Year Plan period
Textile combine		Cotton combine
Brick kiln		

district, had only just begun before the Revolution. There was no metallurgy, except for the small semi-handicraft gouriev works. There was no machine-building at all. The district was a remote rural corner of Siberia.

Now the Kuzbas has become the second coal district of the land. Powerful shafts have been sunk. A modern metallurgical combine has been constructed. A second one is in process of construction. Non-ferrous metallurgy, the chemical industry, and machine-building are developing: a great and complex industrial region is coming into being. New towns are springing up. In *Stalinsk*—the town of builders and metallurgists—there are over 200,000 inhabitants. In *Prokopyevsk*—the town of miners—there are more than 100,000 inhabitants. In *Kemerovo*—over 100,000 inhabitants; in *Anjero-Soujensk*—about 100,000. This is the way in which towns grow up. The Uralo-Kuznetzk Combine is, according to Stalin, 'the pride of our country'.

In the **Far Eastern Area**, where almost the only occupations were fishing, mining, and timber producing, with the products being exported, machine-building, textile manufacturing and other industries are now being built up. The area is growing rapidly. On the site of a fishing-village on the lower Amur the large new town of *Komsomolsk* is now being built—a town which is becoming a large river port and centre of shipbuilding.

In the imperialist prison of tribes there lived 'aliens'. Not towns, but 'kishlaks' (nomad villages), 'auls' (Caucasian villages), settlements, Cossack villages, winter settlements. Not houses, but 'kibitkas' (nomad tents), 'koshes', reindeer-tents, 'vezhes', 'yourtas', 'khaloups', and huts. Not streets, but nomad tracks. Not concrete, but fibre, reeds, and turf. The few towns which did exist in the colonies were the centres of military conquest and colonization; for example, the town of Vladikavkaz in the North Caucasus, whose purpose was indicated in its name (Vladikavkaz means 'Ruler of the Caucasus'). There were also native quarters—Uzbek, Chinese, or Jewish—which were something of a cross between museums and leper ghettoes.

Central Asia was an agricultural country. Part of its peoples wandered about the sandy deserts and mountain valleys, searching their whole life for uneaten, untrodden grass. Some sowed cotton in watered oases, tilling the soil with wooden ploughs.

The nomads in Central Asia are now becoming settled and prepare artificial fodder for their beasts; farmers till the soil with the aid of tractors. Cotton-mills, chemical works, and machine-building works are being constructed; many are operating already. The workers employed at these works were almost savages not so long ago. Education is spreading rapidly; new towns are being born. The Tajiks built *Stalinabad*, the capital of the Republic, a mountain town on the edge of the desert with a branch of the Academy of Sciences, a tropical institute, and 50,000 inhabitants.

The Khirghisians built the town of *Frunze* in place of old Pishpek. The new town is the capital of the Republic, with factories, works, universities, theatres, and 100,000 inhabitants.

The Kara-Kalpaks are building their capital, *Noukouss*.

There had never been any towns in the nomad Kalmuck Region. The Kalmucks have built the town of *Elista* in the steppes—the capital of the Autonomous Region.

The peoples of the North Caucasus, thrust out of their fertile foot-hills by Russian colonization, tended their herds in the depths of the mountains, and lived on the steep slopes in huts ('saklias') which resembled birds' nests. The Karachayevs have now built the capital of the Karachayev Autonomous Area—many storied *Mikoyan-Shakhar*—in the mountain valley of the River Kuban.

The kolkhozes of the Kabardo-Balkar Autonomous Area, whose well-being is growing rapidly, have started on the reconstruction of the old villages into agrarian towns. The best architects of the centre have been invited to participate in the planning of these towns.

Precise planning: two and three-storied buildings; paved streets; green boulevards; educational and municipal institutions; clubs, a medical consulting-room, a house for the aged, and so on.

From their dark, low, stuffy huts the kolkhoz workers are moving into new, commodious, handsome houses surrounded by orchards and equipped with electricity, telephone, and wireless.

The extreme north was formerly a desert region. The natives who wandered about the meagre tundra—deer-breeders and fishermen—were few and far between. Mighty rivers crossed the tundra, but their banks were as dead as the whole land there. A new town has been constructed on the lower Yenisei, far beyond the Arctic Circle. It is five years old, it has a population of 20,000, it has saw-mills and a graphite-concentration works. In the town there is a wireless station, electricity, a dairy farm, kitchen-gardens (beyond the Arctic Circle!), crèches, schools, newspapers, a theatre, larch-paved streets. This is *Igarka*, one of the largest saw-mill centres of Siberia.

The Kola peninsula lies beyond the Arctic Circle. The frequency of occurrence of the aurora borealis at the Pole and at the Kola peninsula is identical. The distance from the Kola peninsula to the North Pole is less than from the peninsula to the Ukraine. On the old maps the Kola peninsula was traversed by a line beyond which was written 'The limits of human habitation'. A sparse chain of Russian fishing-villages lay on the sea-coast of the peninsula; within the peninsula there lived a handful of semi-nomads—Saam-Lapps—who were fast dying out. A nine-months' winter reigned over the desert mountains.

Within the last four years the Kola peninsula has become an industrial centre of importance. Apatite which gives superphosphates to the country is extracted from rich mines. The most northerly electric power stations, concentration works, and phosphorus works in the world have been built here. An aluminium combine is being constructed. The railway is being electrified, motor-roads have been built, wireless communication has been established. Arctic agriculture is developing here. The Saams have set out on the path of rapid economic and cultural development: statistics indicate a sharp increase of the birth-rate above the death-rate. Workers and engineers from the

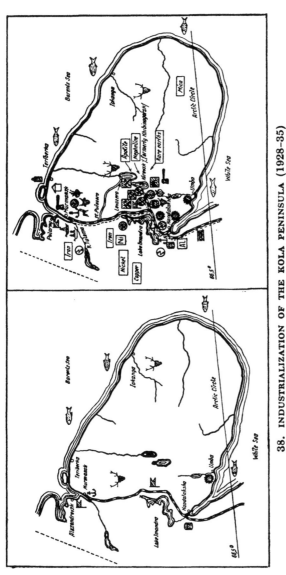

38. INDUSTRIALIZATION OF THE KOLA PENINSULA (1928–35)

Fisheries
Deer breeding
Canning factories
Cattle breeding sovkhoz
Phosphate plant

Electrical stations
Extraction of minerals
Nickel plant
Aluminium plant
Cement plant

Refrigeration plants
Ship repair factory
Ship-yards
Vegetable sovkhoz
Iodine extract plant

Furniture factory
Wood products plant
Port
Scientific station
Highway

Brick kilns
Railway line being electrified
Lumber-furnishing plants
Ore concentration plant

Large enterprises indicated.   Shaded figures existing enterprises.   Unshaded figures enterprises to be built during Second Five Year Plan period

219

most distant parts of the country are flocking here. The density of the population quickly increased from 0·1 to 0·7 persons per square kilometre. In the depths of the mountains the new town of *Kirovsk* (Khibinogorsk) has been built. For a month and a half there is night here, for a month and a half there is unbroken sunshine; the polar wind blows here; there are 40,000 inhabitants, an academy of music; the last house in the town stands on the edge of the desert.

The new towns become the transmitters of socialist industrialization. They change the lives of people and alter their outlook. Their technical education creates a higher productivity of labour. Communal kitchens and crèches liberate the creative power of women. Healthy people live in these new towns, which are spacious, sunny, and clad in foliage. New people live in a new land.

The new geography of the U.S.S.R. is not born but created. It is not a spontaneous development but the accomplishment of a plan. It is not the result of conflicting individual tendencies, but the realization by millions of a single rational will.

In the creation of this new geography one must see the creations of a new society. It will know neither wars nor pauperism, nor exploitation of man by man. Through the lines of the draft, the map is already revealing the geographical outline which will be the documentary evidence of abundance and happiness.

APPENDIX

TERRITORIES AND POPULATION

Republics, Regions, Provinces and Districts	Administrative Centre	Terri- tory, in thousand sq. Km.	Population on Jan. 1st 1933, in thousands
I. RUSSIAN Soviet Federative Socialist Republic . .	Moscow . .	*19,753*	*113,651*
1. Northern Province .	Archangel .	1,125	2,732
including: Nenetz National District . . .	Naryan-Mar .	215	17
Komi Zylyan Autonomous Province .	Syktyvkar .	375	276
2. Karelian A.S.S.R. .	Petrozavodsk .	147	372
3. Leningrad Province .	Leningrad .	331	7,016
including: Murmansk District .	Murmansk .	129	113
4. Western Province .	Smolensk . .	165	6,711
5. Moscow Province .	Moscow . .	166	12,551
6. Ivanovo Industrial Province . .	Ivanovo . .	124	4,526
7. Gorky Region . .	Gorky (formerly Nijni Novgorod) . .	130	5,032
including: Chuvash A.S.S.R. .	Cheboksary .	18	959
Mari Autonomous Province . .	Yoshkar-Ola .	23	551
8. Kirov Region . . including:	Kirov (formerly Vyatka) .	144	3,317
Udmurt A.S.S.R. .	Izhevsk . .	32	868
9. Bashkirian A.S.S.R. .	Ufa . . .	145	2,916
10. Tartar A.S.S.R . .	Kazan . .	67	2,785
11. Sverdlov Province .	Sverdlovsk .	327	4,201
including: Komi-Permyatsk National District .	Kudymkar .	23	198
12. Chelyabinsk Province .	Chelyabinsk .	171	22,630

Republics, Regions, Provinces, and Districts	Administrative Centre	Terri- tory, in thousand sq. Km.	Population on Jan. 1st 1933, in thousands
Russian Soviet F.S.R.—*cont.*			
13. Middle Volga Region (now Kuibyshev) including:	Samara .	150	6,064
Mordovian A.S.S.R.	Saransk .	26	1,415
14. Oryenburg Province .	Oryenburg .	93	1,585
15. Kursk Province .	Kursk .	77	5,268
16. Voronezh Province .	Voronezh .	117	6,918
17. Saratov Region . .	Saratov .	119	2,908
including Volga-German A.S.S.R. . .	Engels .	28	588
18. Stalingrad Region .	Stalingrad .	215	2,583
including: Kalmyk Autonom- ous Province .	Elista .	74	185
19. Azov-Black Sea Region	Rostov-on-Don .	182	5,956
including: North Don District .	Millerovo . .	31	647
Adighe Autonomous Province . .	Krasnodar .	3	137
20. North Caucasian Region	Pyatigorsk .	170	3,923
including: Dagestan A.S.S.R. .	Makhach-Kala .	57	949
Kabardino - Balkar Autonomous Pro- vince . .	Nalchik . .	12	279
Karacheyev Auton- omous Province .	Mikoyan-Shakhar	10	104
North Osetian Autonomous Pro- vince . .	Orjonididze .	6	286
Cherkess Autonom- ous Province .	Sulimov . .	3	81
Chechen-Ingush Au- tonomous Pro- vince . .	Grozny . .	16	651
21. Crimean A.S.S.R. .	Simferopol .	26	791
22. Kazak A.S.S.R. . .	Alma-Ata .	2,853	6,797
including: Aktiubinsk Province	Aktiubinsk .	596	1,061

Republics, Regions, Provinces, and Districts	Administrative Centre	Territory in thousand sq. Km.	Population on Jan. 1st 1933, in thousands
Kazak A.S.S.R.—*cont.*			
Alma-Ata Province .	Alma-Ata .	403	1,154
East Kazakstan Province . .	Semipalatinsk .	303	1,333
West Kazakstan Province . .	Uralsk . .	464	723
including:			
Guryev District .	Guryev . .	221	187
Karaganda Province	Petropavlovsk .	352	1,193
South Kazakstan Province . .	Chimkent .	489	1,243
Karkaralinsk District . . .	Karkaralinsk .	246	74
23. Karakalpakian A.S.S.R.	Turtkul . .	126	373
24. Kirghiz A.S.S.R. .	Frunze . .	197	1,302
25. Omsk Province . .	Omsk . .	1,532	2,192
including:			
Tara District . .	Tara . .	72	248
Ostyako - Vogulsk National Province	Samarovo .	755	102
Yamalsk National District . .	Salegard . .	466	30
26. West Siberian Region	Novosibirsk .	820	6,165
including:			
Narym Region .	Kolpashev .	306	129
Oirot Autonomous Province . .	Oirat-Tura .	93	122
27. Krasnoyarsk District .	Krasnoyarsk .	2,144	1,628
including:			
Taymyr National District . .	Dudinka . .	743	8
Evenkyisk National District	Turinsk Tourist Centre . .	542	5
Khakassk Autonomous District .	Abakan . .	50	173
28. East Siberian Region .	Irkutsk . .	1,791	2,221
including:			
Buryato - Mongolian A.S.S.R. . .	Ulan-Ude (formerly Verkhne-Udinsk) . .	376	605

Republics, Regions, Provinces, and Districts	Administrative Centre	Terri-tory in thousand sq. Km.	Population on Jan. 1st 1933, in thousands
East Siberian—*cont.*			
Vitimo - Alekminsk National Region .	Kalakan . .	220	10
29. Yakutsk A.S.S.R. .	Yakutsk .	3,031	328
30. Far Eastern Region .	Khabarovsk .	3,068	1,860
including:			
Amur Province .	Blagoveshchensk	205	423
Zeisk Province .	Rukhlovo .	186	122
Kamchatka Pro-vince . .	Petropavlovsk(on Kamchatka)	1,254	60
Koryaksk National District . .	Penzhinsk Tour-ist Centre .	346	13
Chukotsk National District . .	Anadyr . .	728	19
Lower-Amur Pro-vince . .	Nikolayevsk - on-Amur . .	968	85
Maritime Province	Vladivostok .	114	422
Sakhalin Province	Alexandrovsk - on-Sakhalin .	41	69
Ussuri Province .	Nikolsk-Ussuriisk	45	362
Khabarovsk Prov. .	Khabarovsk .	170	260
Jewish Autonomous Province .	Birobijan . .	73	50
II. UKRAINIAN S.S.R. .	Kiev . .	*443*	*31,901*
including:			
Vinnitsa Province	Vinnitsa . .	48	4,803
Dniepropetrovsk Province .	Dniepropetrovsk	73	3,873
Donetsk Province.	Stalino . .	52	4,074
including:			
Starobyelsk Dist.	Starobyelsk .	14	531
Kiev Province .	Kiev . .	75	6,128
Odessa Province .	Odessa . .	69	3,325
Kharkov Province	Kharkov . .	75	6,117
Chernigov Province	Chernigov .	43	2,965
Moldavian A.S.S.R.	Tiraspol . .	8	616

Republics, Regions, Provinces, and Districts	Administrative Centre	Terri- tory in thousand sq. Km.	Population on Jan. 1st 1933, in thousands
III. WHITE RUSSIAN A.S.S.R. . .	Minsk . .	*127*	*5,439*
IV. TRANSCAUCASIAN S.F.S.R. . .	Tiflis . .	*186*	*7,111*
1. Azerbaijan S.S.R. .	Baku . .	86	2,891
including: Nakhichevan A.S.S.R. . .	Nakhichevan .	5	117
Nagorny Kara- bakh Autonom- ous Province .	Stepanakert .	4	154
2. Armenian S.S.R. .	Erivan . .	30	1,109
3. Georgian S.S.R. .	Tiflis . .	70	3,111
including: Abkhazian A.S.S.R. . .	Sukhum . .	9	259
Ajar A.S.S.R. .	Batum . .	3	154
South-Osetian Au- tonomous Pro- vince . .	Stalinir . .	4	95
V. UZBEK S.S.R. . .	Tashkent . .	*172*	*5,044*
including: Khorezm District .	Urgench . .	5	354
VI. TURKMENIAN S.S.R.	Ashkhabad .	*443*	*1,269*
including: Kerki District .	Kerki . .	14	104
Tashauz District .	Tashauz . .	10	200
VII. TAJIK S.S.R. . .	Stalinabad .	*144*	*1,333*
including Gorno-Badakhshansk Autonomous Pro- vince . . .	Khorog . .	61	36
U.S.S.R. . . .	Moscow . .	*21,268*	*165,748*

NOTES

I. Administrative-territorial divisions are indicated as on January 1st, 1935. The following are the more important changes in administrative territorial division which were made in 1934:

The Jewish, Udmurtsk and Mordovian Autonomous Provinces were reorganized as autonomous republics.

15

The North-Caucasian Region was divided into the Azov-Black Sea and North-Caucasian Regions.

The Lower Volga Region was divided into the Saratov and Stalingrad Regions.

Middle Volga Region was divided into the Kuibyshev (formerly Samara) Region and the Oryenburg Province.

The Central Black Earth Province was divded into the Kursk and Voronezh Provinces.

The Ural Province was divided into the Sverdlovsk, Chelyabinsk and Obsk-Irtysh Provinces. Later the Omsk Province was formed from the Obsk-Irtysh Province and half of the West Siberian Region.

The Gorky Region was divided into Kirov and Gorky Regions.

Krasnoyarsk Region was formed from parts of the West Siberian and East Siberian Regions.

In 1935 Kalinin Province, with the centre in Kalinin, was formed from parts of the Moscow, Western, and Leningrad Provinces.

In the text, tables, and maps of this publication the above-mentioned changes have not been indicated wherever the material available has made this impossible. The Moscow, Western, and Leningrad Provinces (throughout) and West and East Siberian Regions (throughout save in this table) are given with their former boundaries.

II. Figures for population of the separate provinces of the Kazak A.S.S.R. are for 1931.

Information on areas and populations of separate provinces of the Far Eastern Territory are given approximately.

INDEX

Jarrold & Sons, Limited, The Empire Press, Norwich

For Product Safety Concerns and Information please contact our EU
representative GPSR@taylorandfrancis.com
Taylor & Francis Verlag GmbH, Kaufingerstraße 24, 80331 München, Germany

www.ingramcontent.com/pod-product-compliance
Ingram Content Group UK Ltd.
Pitfield, Milton Keynes, MK11 3LW, UK
UKHW021830240425
457818UK00006B/146